The Workers of Nations

Industrial Relations in a Global Economy

Edited by
SANFORD M. JACOBY

New York   Oxford
OXFORD UNIVERSITY PRESS
1995

Oxford University Press

Oxford   New York
Athens   Auckland   Bangkok   Bombay
Calcutta   Cape Town   Dar es Salaam   Delhi
Florence   Hong Kong   Istanbul   Karachi
Kuala Lumpur   Madras   Madrid   Melbourne
Mexico City   Nairobi   Paris   Singapore
Taipei   Tokyo   Toronto

and associated companies in
Berlin   Ibadan

Library of Congress Cataloging-in-Publication Data
Jacoby, Sanford M., 1953-
The workers of nations :
industrial relations in a global economy—
edited by Sanford M. Jacoby.
p.   cm.
Essays presented at a conference,
sponsored by the UCLA Institute
of Industrial Relations.
Includes bibliographical references.
ISBN 0-19-508904-9
1. Comparative industrial relations—Congresses.
I. University of California, Los Angeles.
Institute of Industrial Relations.
II. Title   HD6959.J33   1994   331—dc20   94-16786

1 2 3 4 5 6 7 8 9

Printed in the United States of America
on acid-free paper

The Workers of Nations

TO BENJAMIN AARON AND LLOYD ULMAN,
WHOM WE ESTEEM

Acknowledgments

The essays in this volume were first presented at a 1992 conference titled "International and Comparative Dimensions of Industrial Relations," sponsored by the UCLA Institute of Industrial Relations (IIR). Many persons contributed to the conference. Special thanks to Bruce Fallick, Paul Ong, Archie Kleingartner, and Thomas A. Kochan, who served as commentators, and to Jeannine Schummer, who administered the event.

After the conference the papers were revised and updated for publication. Thanks to Susan Hannan of Oxford University Press for guiding the volume through production, and to Margaret Zamorano of the IIR for assistance with word processing. And special thanks to Jane Wildhorn of the IIR, whose expert editorial assistance made this volume more readable.

Finally, thanks to David Lewin, director of the Institute, for suggesting the conference and for providing the resources necessary to carry it off.

Preface

The chapters in this book focus on the industrial relations aspects of economic global-ization. The volume is intended for students and scholars who seek to understand how globalization is affecting labor in the advanced industrial societies of Asia, Eu-rope, and North America. By taking a broad approach, this book should be of interest in a number of disciplines including economics, political science, and sociology. It also will be useful to private and public policy makers—in business, government, and organized labor—who want to develop a clearer understanding of the challenges and opportunities presented by globalization.

The chapters contain the latest empirical research on a wide array of issues: the fate of organized labor under regional trading pacts, the international diffusion of new forms of work organization, and the strategies that nations are pursuing to keep their work systems competitive in a global economy. One can find bits and pieces of this material in other places. But newspaper accounts tend to lack an analytical framework, while "big think" books on globalization sometimes are gaseous synthe-ses that stand or fall on their empirical precision (or lack of it).

Be forewarned, however. This volume will not take you on a country-by-country tour of industrial relations systems. Instead it compares and contrasts the experiences of different countries. The chapters in Part I chart the industrial relations *conse-quences* of economic integration; those in Part II discuss *policy issues* at the micro and macro levels.

Also, this book is not intended as a substitute for journalistic coverage of devel-opments in a fast-changing area. All of the chapters deal with medium- to long-range trends and are written with an eye to the future. Finally, though the book contains much that will interest students of developing regions, it focuses primarily on trends in the advanced industrial nations.

The title of this collection reflects a basic tension inherent in the process of economic globalization: capital—that is, money and corporations—is becoming more interna-tional, while labor remains rooted in particular places called nations. Unlike capital, labor is not highly mobile. Within nations—even relatively footloose societies such as the United States—most workers remain tied to their communities. Also, though the migration of labor between the advanced nations is increasing, it remains a trickle when compared with flows of capital.

This is not to say that labor is unaffected by globalization; quite the opposite. The most immediate effect has been on consumption, where tastes and living standards have converged rapidly. One need only invoke names such as McDonald's, Sony, or Saab to make this point obvious.

The paradox, then, is that while consumers (and product markets) are increasingly global, workers (and labor markets) are not global, even though most consumers are also workers. The literature on globalization—especially the writings of breathless visionaries—tends to disregard this paradox; it prefers to treat citizens as consumers (for whom the advantages of globalization are obvious) rather than as workers (for whom the benefits are more uncertain).

Another important difference between consumption and employment is this: whereas "tastes" are becoming similar throughout the industrialized world, employment remains enmeshed in a set of institutions peculiar to given cultures and societies. True, labor markets in all advanced nations are affected by globalization, but the impact is mediated by nationally specific structures of trade unions, government regulation, and employers' personnel policies. Even in the European Community (EC), where labor market integration has proceeded faster and farther than elsewhere in the world, vast institutional differences still distinguish the employment systems of the member nations. Thus, understanding how globalization has affected labor—the subject of this book—still requires familiarity with national employment institutions and traditions.

Nevertheless, this book is not a buzzing welter of specificity. Nations are grouped together according to similarities in their industrial relations systems. Levels of union membership are one such indicator; so are common cultural traditions such as syndicalism and Confucianism. The groupings reflect what is coming to be recognized today as the "varieties of capitalism." That such varieties exist is hardly news to students of industrial relations; indeed, much of the variance stems from institutional differences in labor markets and employment practices.

One key group comprises the corporatist countries of Northern Europe, whose high union membership and generous welfare provisions have been tested in recent years by globalization. Another group consists of countries such as the United States and the United Kingdom, where unionism is decentralized and declining, and where government plays a relatively small role in structuring employment and work systems. A third group consists of Euro-Latin countries with strong syndicalist and regional traditions, notably France and Italy. Finally, in the East Asian bloc—consisting of Japan and a group of newly industrialized countries like Taiwan and Korea—government and employers are the key actors, and unionism is relatively weak and decentralized.

This book also cuts across these national groupings by identifying trends common to all of them. One obvious trend is the fear among national labor movements that globalization is undercutting their bargaining power. Trade unions are having a difficult time throughout the advanced world; they fret constantly about the decline in their strength. A second trend is the willingness of many unions to endorse regional trading pacts such as the EC or the North American Free Trade Agreement (NAFTA) but to make their support conditional on the enforcement of strong labor standards in low-wage areas such as Mexico and Southern Europe.

The chapters in this book are concerned deeply with policy issues. In a world where most resources other than labor are mobile, a nation's competitive advantage ultimately depends on its human capital. The Japanese case has demonstrated this point convincingly. "Human capital" refers not only to skills but also to employers' policies and to labor-market institutions that promote commitment, flexibility, and cooperation. A more appropriate term would be "social capital."

Several decades ago, labor specialists in the United States predicted that industrial relations systems around the world were converging on a single model, one which closely resembled the U.S. system circa 1960. That particular hubris of modernization theory never came to pass; the United States did not serve as a model, nor did industrial relations systems converge. Now, some forty years later, we are witnessing unprecedented levels of institutional borrowing and imitation. If any one nation serves as a model today, however, it is Japan, not the United States.

Because of a belief that personnel policies play a key role in Japan's rise to industrial eminence, European and North American employers are scrutinizing Japanese companies for techniques that can be adapted for their own use. The result has been widespread adoption of lean production methods and a newfound appreciation for the virtues of cooperation at the enterprise level. This development has placed enormous pressures on European and North American unions to adapt to new systems of work organization.

The result, however, has not been straightforward replication of the Japanese model. First, that model is difficult to adopt in its entirety, even by Japanese companies operating outside Japan (a point illustrated by Ruth Milkman's chapter in this volume). Also, other national models are attracting attention, including European systems built on regional and national cooperation between labor, business, and government. Finally, the international diffusion process is characterized more accurately as experimentation and adaptation than as mindless borrowing (though some of that occurs too). In short, what is happening around the advanced world is a proliferation of organizational hybrids, as "world-class" practices are grafted onto existing national employment systems.

East Asia and continental Europe place a high value on social integration and social capital (what economists term "public goods" and "positive externalities"); these societies often blur the distinction between private and public employment practices. Conversely, the British and the Americans traditionally have emphasized the virtues of decentralization, individualism, and minimal government. Recently, however, Asia and Europe have become less group-oriented; meanwhile, in the United States, the Clinton administration is emphasizing the importance of business-government cooperation and integrative labor relations, including a role for unions. How far down this road the United States will travel remains to be seen, just as we do not know how much individualism and labor mobility can be tolerated in East Asia and continental Europe.

For the advanced nations, the major issue of the next decade will be the relationship between economic and social integration. Economic integration is a reality that cannot be avoided and which, in the long run, will bring higher aggregate incomes. On the other hand, social integration appears to be a way for advanced nations to preserve their high living standards in an increasingly open world economy. The catch, however, is that the forces unleashed by economic integration are corrosive of societal cohesion, whereas societal cohesion encourages an inward-looking, autarchic mindset that hinders economic integration. Japan, for example, is finding it difficult to sustain its large trade surpluses because its economy and society remain partially closed to the outside world. Unfortunately, we do not know yet how to reconcile economic with social integration. Nor do we know how to achieve societal cohesion in a large decentralized nation such as the United States, where business remains suspicious of government and where organized labor is weak. The chapters in this volume, however, contain exciting ideas and suggestions. As the Chinese curse has it, we "live in interesting times."

Los Angeles   S. M. J.
August 1994

II   POLICY ISSUES, 151

Contents

Contributors

Christopher L. Erickson is an assistant professor at the Anderson Graduate School of Management, UCLA.

Jeffry A. Frieden is an associate professor of political science at UCLA.

Miriam Golden is an associate professor of political science at UCLA.

Sanford M. Jacoby is a professor of history and management at UCLA and is associate director of the UCLA Institute of Industrial Relations.

Sarosh C. Kuruvilla is an assistant professor at the School of Industrial & Labor Relations, Cornell University.

Peter Lange is a professor of political science at Duke University.

Ruth Milkman is an associate professor of sociology and women's studies at UCLA.

Daniel J. B. Mitchell is a professor at the Anderson Graduate School of Management, UCLA.

Kenneth L. Sokoloff is a professor of economics at UCLA.

Michael Storper is a professor of geography and urban planning at UCLA.

George Tsebelis is an associate professor of political science at UCLA.

Michael Wallerstein is a professor of political science at Northwestern University.

The Workers of Nations

1

Social Dimensions of Global Economic Integration

SANFORD M. JACOBY

We live and work in a global economy; world trade is growing faster than world incomes. Trade can dissipate international tensions, but it is equally capable of intensifying them. Nations feel compelled to change their economic and social policies to conform to global patterns. This pressure is felt particularly by labor market institutions—wage structures, workplace practices, social insurance, and labor relations— all of which have been undergoing major changes in the developed nations. The changes have been accelerated by regional trading pacts such as the European Community (EC) and the North American Free Trade Agreement (NAFTA).

Greater trade has been accompanied by greater mobility of capital. Every day billions of dollars, yen, and other currencies shuttle instantaneously across the planet. To attract and retain fickle investors, nations must rely on their physical infrastructure and their human talents. In the United States and the United Kingdom, both formerly world leaders, there is a painful awareness that neither talent nor infrastructure is globally competitive. Nations that organize work differently—Germany, Italy, Japan, Sweden, and others—have tricks to teach the old leaders about deploying human talents more effectively to promote cooperation and competitiveness.

This introductory chapter provides a framework for understanding the issues and evidence discussed in later chapters. It reviews major trends currently under way in the advanced nations, beginning with the impact of economic globalization on labor and trade unions. It proceeds to analyze how nations have responded to globalization, differentiating between external strategies (to affect labor markets in other countries) and internal strategies (to make their own institutions more competitive). Finally, this chapter discusses cross-cutting international trends including the substitution of economic regionalism for economic globalism, a growing recognition that societal cooperation is a key factor for ensuring national competitiveness, and the widespread decentralization of labor relations and employee involvement.

ECONOMIC CHANGES

World economic growth and productivity rose rapidly during the 1960s but began to slow in the 1970s. The deceleration continued for much of the 1980s and early 1990s; some regions (such as Europe) were affected more severely than others (such as East Asia). Despite the slowing in growth, markets became increasingly internationalized in the 1980s. Trade in goods and services grew rapidly. Meanwhile capital markets transcended national boundaries, a remarkable but not fully intended result of computer technology, "petrodollar" recycling, and the shift from fixed to floating exchange rates.

Growth of world trade and finance has hastened the spread of multinational corporations (MNCs) that operate in, and depend on, the economies of many world regions. Conversely, MNCs have contributed directly to market globalization via their foreign direct investments. Foreign investment exploded in recent years; between 1983 and 1989 it grew more rapidly than world trade itself.[1]

MNCs are primarily investing in North America, Europe, and East Asia, although investments in Latin America and other parts of Asia are steadily increasing. How the receiving nation should regard such investment is a matter of controversy. That MNCs create jobs is not disputed; the issue is whether they create "good" jobs and whether governments should consider a company's national origins when giving tax and trade preferences. Japanese MNCs tend to maintain ties to the home country. Their foreign factories rely on intermediate goods manufactured in Japan, thus creating a link between foreign investment and the home economy. European and North American MNCs tend to rely less heavily on home-country suppliers. For example, U.S.-based Japanese MNCs import to the United States nearly three times more components (as a percentage of sales) than U.S-based European MNCs.[2]

Once the hub of the world trading system, the United States no longer is the dominant figure. Economic power has been redistributed toward Europe and Japan. Europe now holds the same share of world gross domestic product (GDP) as North America (roughly 25%) while Japan and the rest of East Asia account for almost 20 percent. The content of U.S. trade is also changing. During the postwar years, the core of the U.S. economy was composed of mass-production manufacturing firms that produced a high volume of standardized goods at low cost. Now the United States is finding that it cannot compete on cost against industrializing countries such as Brazil, Mexico, Spain, and Taiwan. Exports from the United States increasingly are "niche products" that command a high price because of their quality, technological sophistication, and responsiveness to consumers' tastes. In this segment of the market the United States encounters intense competition from the Japanese, who have perfected the art of high-quality manufacturing, and from the Europeans, who have had long experience with the subtleties of niche production.[3]

Economic globalization never could have occurred without a number of international institutions for facilitating foreign trade and investment. The oldest of these is the Bretton Woods system of fixed exchange rates, which was in effect from the end of World War II until 1973, shortly after the United States devalued the dollar and pushed the world towards the present regime of floating rates. Another catalytic institution is the General Agreement on Tariffs and Trade (GATT), which—through a series of multilateral negotiations that have been under way since the 1950s—

has been responsible for the reduction of tariffs and other barriers to international trade.

These institutions, both created after World War II, were intended to support a multilateral trading system in which trade and capital flowed freely around the globe. Little appreciated at that time was the importance of a powerful nation to serve as institutional guarantor and of a strong currency to meet the liquidity needs of the trading partners. The United States and the U.S. dollar played those hegemonic roles; Bretton Woods was essentially a fixed-rate dollar standard. Since 1973, however, the centrality of the United States and of the dollar standard has declined gradually but steadily.[4]

Because the United States increasingly is absorbed in its own problems, it devotes less energy to efforts to expand the multilateral trading system. For example, the most recent cycle of GATT negotiations (the Uruguay round) dragged on since the early 1980s, unable to reach agreement on a variety of tariff issues. As for the dollar, ever since the United States abandoned convertibility in 1971, other nations have been seeking a substitute currency system to provide the stability and predictablity that the dollar offered under Bretton Woods. This goal was part of the logic behind the European Monetary System (EMS), devised by French President Valéry Giscard D'Estaing and West German Chancellor Helmut Schmidt in 1978. The EMS narrowed the range of exchange rate fluctuations among member currencies in Europe, thus setting in motion the chain of events that culminated in the 1992 creation of a "single European market." The EMS also resulted from a perception that the nations of Europe—now rebuilt and heavily dependent on exports—individually were too small to realize the economies of scale necessary to compete with the United States and Japan.

All of these events—the end of Bretton Woods, the decrease in returns on GATT, the rise of Japanese capitalism, and the reinvigoration of the European community—have combined to create a new international regionalism. Instead of multilateral trade supported by the United States, the world presently is moving toward trilateral trading blocs in Europe, North America, and East Asia. Although world trade continues to expand, the First World is spending much of its energy on creating regional institutions and trade relationships that are partial substitutes for more internationalized trade. Substitution already is occurring in foreign investment. For example, the proportion of total Japanese foreign investment going to East Asia is rising, while the shares going to Europe and North America are declining. Ultimately, regionalization will slow the pace of interregional trade even as it strengthens the blocs' ability to compete with each other.

Most advanced in this process is the European Community, which presently consists of twelve member nations. Like other international bodies, the EC originated in the postwar years, specifically 1950, which is when Jean Monnet initiated the United Europe project. This step led to the 1957 Treaty of Rome, which created the Community. During the 1960s and 1970s, the EC steadily reduced intra-EC tariffs, quotas, and other duties. Significant barriers remained, however, to the movement of capital, labor, and services. Starting in the late 1970s, the EC accelerated the process of market integration, initially with the creation of the EMS. Then, in 1987, the EC passed the Single European Act, which called for a full integration of the internal market by 1992. To debate the complicated issues related to integration—many of them labor and social questions—the EC created a European Parliament, based in Strasbourg. Power, however, resides with the Council of Ministers, which is made up of the member nations' prime ministers. The final step came late in 1991; at that time the members negotiated the Maastricht Treaty on European Unity, which proposes a single currency and an independent central bank before the end of the century.

The Maastricht Treaty has met with less than complete enthusiasm. Initially, Denmark rejected the treaty and fewer than half of the French voters supported it. Much of the difficulty is due to the recession gripping the Western European nations. Recession drove Britain and Italy from the EMS in 1992, though this allowed them to reflate their economies at lower exchange rates. That sort of monetary autonomy would not be permitted under Maastricht. In other words, if the member nations cannot adhere to the EMS, it is unlikely that they will accept the monetary discipline proposed by Maastricht. Even so, the long-term prognosis for Maastricht is positive.[5]

Another sign that Europe is not yet a superstate is the unwillingness of the EC's members to cede authority to pan-European institutions. Under the principle of "subsidiarity," the EC is not permitted to legislate in areas where a solution can be achieved by individual member states. Also, the 518 directly elected members of the European Parliament have quite limited legislative powers. Action originates with the European Commission and the Council of Ministers, both of which are dominated by the larger member nations. The commission has seventeen members (two each from France, Germany, Italy, Spain, and the United Kingdom, and one each from the other seven smaller nations); its decisions are made by a majority vote. The Council of Ministers, composed of the ministers of the member governments, acts on proposals emanating from the commission. Inside the council, nations are represented semi-proportionately: larger nations receive more votes than smaller ones, although the former must seek alliances with the latter in order to receive a "qualified majority." Thus the EC—despite the rhetoric—remains a collection of sovereign nations.

These nations, however, are increasingly interdependent and have made large strides toward economic integration. Agricultural, trade, environmental, and transportation policies are being "harmonized" throughout Western Europe; the EMS still exists, though in a somewhat weakened form; and product and financial markets are integrated more closely now than a decade ago.

North America is another region experimenting with formal integration. In 1989 Canada and the United States began operating a Free Trade Agreement (FTA), which eliminates most tariffs on goods produced in either country. Some new bilateral codes were established for specific industries such as agriculture and automotive products, but neither economic nor social policies are being harmonized in the European sense. The agreement has had a greater impact on Canada than on the United States: about 80 percent of Canada's exports go to the United States, while the United States sends roughly 20 percent of its exports to Canada. Of particular concern to the Canadians are provisions of the FTA that liberalize restrictions on U.S. investment in Canada; the Canadians dread losing control over their natural resources to foreign investors. They also fear that U.S. branch plants will close and return to the United States because companies no longer enjoy tariff advantages by producing in Canada. Indeed, these fears—some of which already have been realized—were an important reason for the Conservatives' defeat in Canada's 1993 elections.[6] The next step in the process is NAFTA, which duplicates with Mexico the conditions that the United States and Canada have negotiated with each other. Like the FTA, NAFTA contains no provisions for monetary or social integration. Instead it is intended primarily to encourage exports and to make it easier for U.S. and Canadian firms to invest in Mexico. Unlike the FTA, which was ratified virtually without comment in the United States, NAFTA proved very controversial, became an issue in the 1992 presidential campaign, and was approved only by a very narrow majority in the U.S. House of Representatives. Mexico is at an intermediate stage of economic development, with lower wages and labor standards than are in the United States or Canada. Hence, organized labor and many public officials fear that NAFTA will accelerate the loss of jobs to Mexico.[7]

These tensions—between a high-wage north and a lower-wage south—are not unique to the relationship between Mexico and the United States. Canadians perceive the United States as having inferior standards regarding social insurance and workplace protection; Denmark and Germany have the same view of southern EC members such as Portugal and Spain. Fear that these differences will lead to "social dumping" (capital flight to avoid high labor standards) has been central to the negotiations over NAFTA and the European single market. To reduce the possibility of capital flight, the EC has long supported infrastructural investments in its poorer member nations—for roads, communications, and the like—much as Germany is presently spending millions on the development of its eastern portion. Also, the EC has adopted a Social Charter calling for harmonization of labor standards throughout the community—something we will discuss below.

To date, North America has not gone far in the direction taken by Europe. NAFTA contains only fairly weak provisions for raising labor and environmental standards in Mexico. Although the labor standards are comprehensive, the mechanism for enforcing them—a trinational commission—is weak. The commission does not have the power to issue subpoenas or conduct on-site investigations, nor does it require Mexico to enforce the rights of workers to organize and bargain without government interference. The only areas subject to formal dispute resolution are safety and health, minimum wage, and child labor. Moreover, the agreement offers little direct economic aid or debt relief that would speed Mexico's economic development. On the other hand, NAFTA ultimately may be less significant than the EC. After all, American firms are free to invest in Mexico even without NAFTA, and have been doing so. Even so, the bulk of foreign direct investment by the United States is flowing to Asia and Europe, not to Mexico and Latin America.[8]

In East Asia, little formal institution building has occurred to support economic integration, even though (or perhaps because) the region's economic development has been so astoundingly rapid. Along with Japan, the Little Tigers—Hong Kong, Korea, Taiwan, and Singapore—were extremely successful in the 1980s. Meanwhile China—potentially the world's largest consumer market—is experiencing swift growth. Trade among the East Asian countries is not especially large; they are export-oriented economies that ship most of their products to higher-income markets in the United States and Europe. Japan, however, is playing a key role in the region. As noted, its East Asian investments are large and are growing rapidly.

To the Japanese, East Asia represents a base in which to manufacture exports that no longer can be made profitably in Japan. Yet the Japanese continue to make high-value-added components at home and then ship these to their Asian branch plants for final assembly. This is one reason why Japan's exports to East Asia now count for nearly one-third of its total exports, double the level of five years ago. At this point, however, Japan remains a supplier of capital but not of consumer markets. It imports relatively little from East Asia, while its Asian branch plants export primarily to Europe and North America. It remains to be seen whether Japan will become a net importer and will create the institutions necessary for a multilateral regional trading bloc, a pattern known as the "flying goose formation."[9]

The Impact on Labor

In the advanced nations, globalization has had mostly a negative effect on organized labor's bargaining power and political influence. Competition from lower-cost producers is exerting downward pressure on wages and employment in many unionized industries, from steel to textiles to apparel. To secure a competitive advantage farther up the value chain, employers are shifting toward the production of more technology-intensive goods and services. This step, however, has harmful consequences for unions, at least in the short term. It reduces the demand for manual workers—who form a large portion of most labor movements—while boosting employment of non-manual employees, a group in which rates of unionization tend to be lower.

Historically, employers were willing to agree to collective bargaining when unions could promise to "take wages out of competition." The promise made sense when markets were fixed within national boundaries and employers themselves were immobile. Today, however, markets are international and unions find themselves unable to standardize wages across borders. This situation diminishes their usefulness to employers. Also, modern employers now find it far easier to relocate. Even aircraft can be repaired or paperwork processed almost anywhere in the world. The mere threat of relocation saps labor's bargaining power even further. Government employees are virtually the only group free of this threat. Thus it is hardly surprising that throughout the advanced countries, unionization rates in the public sector are holding up better than in other industries.[10]

Another historical justification for unionism was based on labor's putative link to mass economic prosperity. According to underconsumptionist theories, particularly Keynesianism, unions—by raising mass purchasing power—were supposed to maintain aggregate demand and to prevent major depressions from occurring. This macroeconomic rationale for collective bargaining was embodied in the 1935 National Labor Relations Act, the legislation that ushered in the era of mass unionism in the United States. Similar justifications for unionism were offered in Europe and in Japan.[11] The identification of unions with societal prosperity promoted public attitudes favorable toward unions during the long postwar upswing. Labor and its political allies reinforced this perception by placing a high priority on anti-unemployment policies—everything from public-sector employment to deficit spending and currency devaluations.

Today, however, as nations orient themselves increasingly toward trade, the Keynesian rationale for unionism is wanting. In an open economy there is no guarantee that organized workers will spend their earnings on domestically produced items; union wage premiums may well go toward the purchase of imports. (In the United

States, so-called "buy American" and "union label" campaigns have been notably unsuccessful.) Also, the availability of cheaper imports causes the public to believe—in countries as different as Germany and the United States—that unionized workers have priced themselves out of world markets. Whereas traditional wage bargaining and generous social welfare benefits once were regarded as public goods, they are viewed now as a drag on national efficiency, and not only by conservative economists. The alternative supposedly is to make welfare benefits more "realistic" and to tie compensation more closely to enterprise conditions; these trends are ongoing throughout the OECD (Organization for Economic Cooperation and Development) nations.[12]

Even countries that traditionally have depended on exports—such as Austria and Denmark—are facing new constraints on their ability to maintain low unemployment rates. The coordination required by the European Monetary System makes it difficult, if not impossible, for member nations to pursue countercyclical deficits and devaluations unless they are prepared to suffer the consequences of leaving the EMS. And under the Maastricht Treaty, the constraints are even tighter. Maastricht's Economic and Monetary Union (EMU) requires that total public debt and budget deficits (as percentages of GDP) be reduced respectively to 60 percent and 3 percent by the end of the 1990s. The labor movement—once the champion of full employment—therefore is left without a viable macroeconomic program in the EC countries. This is an important reason why trade unionists in Norway, Sweden, and some other EC applicants are wary of EC membership.[13]

Even if EMU never is implemented, international currency speculation already is inhibiting nations from pursuing laborist economic strategies. A huge amount of speculative capital is washing around the world, another legacy of the Bretton Woods breakup. Speculative capital is easily swayed by short-term considerations of its best interests; anything that threatens to cheapen a currency, such as laborist economic policies, may trigger an anticipatory run. Among other things, this situation jeopardizes the strategy of using deficit financing to take up slack in the labor market. Thus the one bright spot for organized labor—high membership rates in government—is dimmed by declining public-sector employment.[14]

Yet the international situation is not entirely hopeless for unions. True, globalization has impaired labor's bargaining power and weakened its Keynesian strategies, but the impact on union membership has been much more varied. During the 1970s and 1980s, some countries—notably Denmark, Finland, Sweden, and Belgium—showed substantial gains in union density (the proportion of the labor force belonging to unions). In other nations, however, union density declined sharply: Japan and the United States in both decades; Italy, the Netherlands, and the United Kingdom in the 1980s. In most of the other OECD nations, density rose in the 1970s and remained stable in the 1980s (see Table 1.1).

The recent variation in density trends is nothing new. Disparities in union growth rates have existed since the beginning of the century.[15] The immediate postwar decades were the only exception; in those periods, unionization was stable or increasing everywhere in the advanced world. Nor are disparities in union density levels a new phenomenon. In 1950, for example, density differed sharply among nations, ranging from 28 percent in the United States to 68 percent in Sweden. Significantly, those nations with the highest density levels in the 1950s tended to have

Table 1.1. Union Density Trends, 1950–1987[a]

	1950	1970	1987
High density			
Belgium	37	66	—
Denmark	53	66	95
Finland	33	56	85
Sweden	68	79	96
Moderate density			
Australia	56	52	56
Austria	62	64	61
Canada	33	32	36
Germany	36	37	43
Ireland	39	44	51
Italy	44	39	45
Netherlands	36	39	35
Norway	46	59	61
United Kingdom	44	51	50
Low density			
France	31	22	15
Japan	46	35	28
United States	28	31	17

Source: Bruce Western, "Unionization Trends in Postwar Capitalism: A Comparative Study of Working Class Organization," Ph.D. dissertation, UCLA, 1993; David Blanchflower and Richard Freeman, "Going Different Ways: Unionism in the U.S. and Other Advanced OECD Countries," *Industrial Relations* 31 (Winter 1992): 56–79.
[a]Union membership of nonagricultural members as a proportion of nonagricultural employees.

the largest density gains in the 1980s; countries with the lowest levels tended to have the largest losses (see Table 1.1). Thus labor movements differ in their ability to weather economic globalization; this ability is related to factors that predate the present period.

Recent studies have identified some of the features of countries whose density levels remained robust in the 1980s. A common factor is a corporatist industrial relations system, in which bargaining is highly centralized (unions negotiate at the national level, either for one industry or for all industries); government consults labor unions regarding national economic policies; and one or a few national organizations speak for all of organized labor. Prime examples include Austria, Germany, and the Scandinavian countries, though significant variations exist even in this group.[16] On the other hand, countries with the largest density losses since 1970 typically have decentralized bargaining systems (unions negotiate at the company or plant level, with little coordination across firms); their political systems do not include organized labor as a stakeholder; and national labor federations are weak. Examples include Japan, the United States, and possibly Great Britain.

It is not fully understood how corporatism bolsters density levels. Blanchflower and Freeman argue that centralized bargaining reduces wage dispersion, which in turn reduces employer resistance to collective bargaining. That is, corporatism is more effective at taking wages out of competition than is a decentralized industrial relations system. Conversely, decentralized systems permit a widening of the union/ nonunion wage gap, especially during inflationary periods such as the 1970s. This situation strengthens the determination of employers to shed existing unions and/or fight the creation of new ones. Union wage premiums increased in the United States during the 1970s to an extent unmatched elsewhere in the world, whereas wage dispersion was stable or declined in the corporatist nations.

Yet an explanation of union density trends based on wage dispersion tells only part of the story. First, the union wage premium in the United States is far less today than in the 1970s; yet density rates are continuing to fall. Second, the focus on wage dispersion begs a more fundamental question: what causes unions to have centralized or decentralized bargaining systems in the first place? Union density is one possible answer. After all, high rates of union membership make centralized bargaining feasible. Also, the historical evidence suggests that countries with relatively high density were those which adopted centralized bargaining. Thus the process may be a feedback loop in which high density stimulates centralized bargaining, which in turn maintains high density.

What accounts for long-term national variations in union density? *Size* is one factor. Wallerstein notes that countries with historically high density levels have small populations (e.g., Austria, Belgium, and the Scandinavian countries); small size reduces the cost of union organizing. Sisson, Stephen, and Swenson, however, link size to employers' organizing costs. That is, density is high in small countries because industry is concentrated; thus employers find it easier to band together to take wages out of competition. Another explanation turns on *politics*. Ulman and Jacoby observe that employers in Germany and Scandinavia recognized unions in order to nudge socialist labor movements away from radical goals such as nationalization. Elsewhere, however, labor's politics were less threatening. In the United States, unions were conservative and craft-oriented; French and Italian unions were syndicalist or confessional, posing to employers little threat of expropriation. Finally, Rothstein and Western emphasize a third factor: the existence of union-controlled national *unemployment insurance schemes* (the Ghent system). In Ghent nations, workers become union members to ensure coverage if and when they become unemployed. The absence of a Ghent system explains why density is much lower in Norway than in Sweden; its presence accounts for high density levels in Belgium.[17]

Putting these explanations together, we can draw the following conclusion: Over the past ninety years or more, union membership rates have been highest where labor is socialist and bargaining is centralized. Often, but not always, these are small countries with concentrated economies, in which labor has control of social resources such as the unemployment system. Conversely, density has been lowest in large countries, especially those with factionalized or conservative labor movements and decentralized bargaining.

Since the early 1970s, high-density labor movements have been better able than low-density movements to maintain or even raise membership despite the shocks associated with economic globalization. Centralized bargaining surely is one reason for this. It makes unionism more palatable to employers, both by reducing wage dispersion and (as we shall see) by making labor markets less prone to wage inflation. The other reasons pertain to the factors that created high density in the first instance, such as socialist traditions that support collective action and union-controlled welfare institutions that keep workers in unions. Where density was relatively low in the early 1970s, however, and where neither centralized bargaining nor strong collective traditions were present, unions have been unable to maintain membership in the face of globalization. This certainly is true of the United States, where the present travails of organized labor recall previous periods of economic restructuring such as the 1870s and the 1920s.

Attitudes of Labor

Throughout the advanced industrial world, unions are debating how to adjust to the changes wrought by globalization. The concerns are universal. In the United States, where union membership has fallen sharply over the past fifteen years, the same issues are being discussed as in Denmark and Sweden, where membership today is larger than ever before. Even if the debates do not lead to international labor solidarity, they provide a common ground that brings national labor movements closer together.

Where labor comes down in the debate over globalization depends largely, though not exclusively, on economic considerations. The unions most threatened by economic integration are those on the edge. Within countries, these are the unions representing low-wage workers; across countries, they are the labor movements that rank near the bottom of the high-wage group. Low-wage industries in advanced countries—for example in textiles, shoes, and apparel—have neither skills nor technology sophisticated enough to keep unit labor costs below those found in less developed nations. (It is debatable whether this is the case because, say, clothing workers in Germany are "overpaid" or because those in Greece are "underpaid.") These often are labor-intensive industries in which small changes in labor costs can have a large effect on profitability. In the presence of transferrable technology, such industries are vulnerable to shrinkage.

Among nations, those near the bottom of the high-wage group, such as Britain and the United States (Table 1.2), tend to have proportionately more labor-intensive jobs than other high-wage nations. The United States, for example, still contains large pockets of "low-tech" manufacturing jobs rarely found in countries such as Switzerland or Sweden. With Mexican wages currently less than one-fifth of those in the United States, the threat of job loss is obvious. Recent economic research suggests that workers in these "low-tech" industries will suffer substantial job losses under NAFTA. Hence the AFL-CIO remains deeply displeased with the NAFTA agreement and is seeking a social charter for North America. British trade unionists, like their American colleagues, tend to be more pessimistic about the formation of regional trading blocs than their counterparts in other high-wage nations. Only recently, after the emergence of the European Social Charter, did the British labor federation (the Trades Union Congress) reverse its long-standing opposition to the EC.[18]

Of course, threats of job-loss can be exaggerated easily. Countries such as Brit-

Table 1.2. International Labor Costs and Productivity, 1991–1992 (for manufacturing)

	Hourly compensation (dollars)	Output index (1982 = 100)	Hourly compensation index (1982 = 100)	Unit labor costs index (own currency 1982 = 100)
Belgium	22.01	126	155	113
Canada	17.02	125	156	128
Denmark	20.02	115	163	149
France	16.88	110	166	129
Germany	25.94	123	158	126
Italy	19.41	131	232	160
Japan	16.16	165	147	100
Netherlands	20.72	128	128	99
Norway	23.20	104	202	152
Sweden	24.23	116	207	169
United Kingdom	14.69	123	197	132
United States	16.17	132	141	110

Sources: U.S. Bureau of Labor Statistics, *International Comparison of Hourly Compensation Costs for Production Workers in Manufacturing, 1992*, Report No. 844 (Washington, D.C., 1993); *Monthly Labor Review* 116 (April 1993): 100.

ain and the United States—precisely because of their comparatively low labor costs—remain attractive investment destinations for foreign capital. In recent years both nations have acquired several dozen Japanese "transplant" automotive parts and assembly plants, whereas France and Germany have virtually none. For British labor, these plants have provided a boost; American unions regard them as a mixed blessing because most of the U.S. plants remain unorganized.[19]

Also, it is possible to overstate the importance of labor costs in an employer's siting calculus. Surveys in Europe and the United States have shown repeatedly that production costs are only one of several factors that companies consider when deciding where to open facilities. One recent European study found that direct production costs had a weight of only 26 percent in corporate decisions about site. The other factors included workforce skills (14%), physical infrastructure (25%), and the institutional framework (35%). The latter is based on perceptions of the "stability" of political and industrial relations; Germany rates high on this factor.[20]

Labor also is affected by noneconomic considerations. Many social democratic unions in Northern Europe have long supported European integration as a way of achieving political stability and labor solidarity in the region. Some unions, however, are wary of European integration if it leads to cuts in social welfare provisions. German and Scandinavian unionists view their nations' generous welfare programs as the greatest achievement of social democracy and as the source of its political appeal. Similarly, one reason why Canadian unions were so strongly opposed to the FTA was their belief that it would undercut Canada's social programs, which are more generous than those of its southern neighbor. Finally, the old Communist-affiliated unions opposed the EC when it was established initially in the 1950s, interpreting it as an anti-Soviet move. (The USSR also regarded it in this way and conse-quently created COMECON.) Today several Communist federations, including the French CGT, remain opposed to the EC or deeply skeptical about it.[21]

SOCIETAL STRATEGIES

Despite the concerns of labor (and of other groups, such as farmers), the issue is not whether to participate in regional trading blocs. Economic integration will occur whether or not nations adopt formal institutions to control it. Institutional design, however, can shape the *kind* of integration that occurs. This is especially true of labor-market integration because labor markets differ so much from other markets affected by trade. Labor is relatively immobile and heterogeneous; labor markets remain separated by large economic and legal disparities. Removing the legal dispari-ties without reducing wages is the primary external problem facing the advanced na-tions.

Regional economic integration, however, is not the only global strategy that nations are pursuing. No country wants to fully trust its economic fate to integration because such a course is risky and would weaken national sovereignty and cultural identity. The alternative is to simultaneously pursue integration as well as internal strategies that bolster a nation's competitiveness. Even in Europe, where integration has proceeded farther than anywhere else in the world, nations retain their economic relevance. Not only workers but also many companies remain dependent on domestic markets; not all of capital is dispersed geographically. And one need not be a libertar-ian to recognize that governments have interests of their own which depend ulti-mately on the level of economic activity within their borders. Thus the nation is an arena of interdependence between employers, labor, and government, though these groups do not always acknowledge that fact. Nations, then, must devise institutions that promote the cooperative social relations which lead to optimal economic out-comes.

External Policies

The following discussion focuses first on external policies for facilitating labor-market integration. Then the analysis shifts to the internal socioeconomic strategies that advanced nations are pursuing.

Europe. To date, the world's most ambitious attempt at transnational labor-market coordination is the Charter of Fundamental Social Rights of Workers (the "Social Charter"). Proposed by Jacques Delors, head of the European Commission, the So-cial Charter is a sweeping document that aims to achieve convergent working condi-tions throughout the EC. It does so by proposing uniform, EC-wide minimum stan-dards of employment; these are pegged to current standards in the advanced nations. Although the charter was (and is) opposed by Britain, which views it as contradicting the EC's principle of subsidiarity, the Council of Ministers approved the charter late in 1989. Currently it is being implemented through specific proposals that flesh out its many details. Areas covered by the Social Charter include:

Freedom of labor mobility

Employment and remuneration, including part-time jobs

Social benefits

Freedom of association and collective bargaining

Vocational training

Equal treatment for women and for men

Worker participation and consultation

Workplace health and safety

Protection of children, the elderly, and the disabled

Although the Social Charter is a major proposal, it is not unprecedented. In the 1970s and 1980s, the EC proposed a number of resolutions seeking to establish Communitywide labor standards. Several of these were enacted; others, including the so-called Vredeling initiative on employee participation and consultation in multinational enterprises, roused strong opposition from employers (notably U.S.-based multinationals) and were amended beyond recognition.[22]

The purpose of the charter is to regulate the social effects of economic integration in Europe. Proponents claim that without explicit EC-wide standards, there is the risk that integration will harm countries with above-average labor standards, especially if integration proceeds along the low road of removing labor-market "barriers" to integration. The resulting social tensions could erode support for the integration process and paralyze the EC. To avoid this outcome, the charter takes the alternative approach of creating common labor rights throughout the EC. European union leaders compare the approach to an elevator: instead of bringing (say) German standards down to Portuguese levels, the charter will try to raise Portuguese standards to German levels. In fact this is really the old trade-union tactic of making standardization coextensive with the labor market, one whose boundaries now extend far beyond Germany.[23]

Whatever the theoretical justification for the Social Charter, it will not be easy to implement. For example, the charter calls on the EC nations to harmonize their social security systems, seemingly a straightforward proposal. Yet each nation's social security system is complex and unique. Each has a distinctive set of insurance policies and a distinctive apportioning of responsibilities between governments, employers, and individuals.

The goal of the charter is to "support emerging practices" rather than to achieve "monolithic harmonization." But the former can be accomplished only by enacting additional, more explicit legislation. As the Vredeling experience shows, this next stage of legislative specification may result in watered-down standards. Indeed, recent draft legislation on European works councils, which attempts to implement charter provisions on employee representation, is encountering some of the same problems that sapped the Vredeling initiative in the early 1980s.[24]

The Social Charter represents the interests of labor in nations with high standards and, to a lesser extent, in those with lower standards. It also offers protection to governments that fear loss of jobs and taxes to lower-standard nations. Also, many high-wage employers, especially the least mobile ones, will benefit from the charter, since it imposes higher costs on their competitors.[25] Least likely to gain from the Social Charter are employers from the EC's less developed nations. These employers, however, stand to reap huge gains by gaining access to the EC's richest markets. The tradeoff—social standards for market access—is critical to the logic of the charter.

Another way of achieving labor-market integration is to pursue trans-European collective bargaining with multinational employers. Already several large European companies—including Thomson, BSN, and Bull—participate in such bargaining. The number can be expected to increase if the EC enacts the proposal on European works councils because the latter will provide a structure for transnational comparison and negotiations.[26]

Transnational bargaining offers obvious advantages to labor. It provides a defense against "whipsawing," in which a company pits its employees in one nation against those in another. In addition, transnational bargaining makes it easier to enforce EC labor standards. The modern approach to transnational bargaining has existed since the 1960s, when multinational corporations first became widespread. Now there is a fair chance of seeing it become prevalent in Europe.[27]

Whether this happens will depend on European employers, who presently are debating the issue. Zygmunt Tyszkiewicz, secretary general of UNICE, the European employers' federation, says that his membership is divided about evenly on the appropriateness of transnational negotiations. Those in favor view it as a way to preempt EC-wide labor legislation because presumably the EC would not legislate where a negotiated solution exists or is possible. The opposing employers fear that EC legislation will make it difficult to achieve realistic transnational agreements because labor would know "they could get what they wanted from legislation, if they didn't get it at the negotiating table."[28]

Employers' attitudes will solidify as it becomes clear whether or not the charter will trigger an avalanche of EC labor legislation. Attitudes also will depend on how companies organize themselves spatially to serve the EC's markets. In either case, large differences in wages and productivity within Europe will remain a barrier to transnational bargaining; so will differences in welfare systems and labor laws. These are not insuperable barriers, however. Managers and professionals already show rising rates of geographic mobility across Europe. Within multinational corporations, managers and professionals are covered by companywide (i.e., transnational) human resource policies. As in other realms of employment, the norms initially established for these high-status employees eventually may become standard practice for other workers as well.[29]

North America. Organized labor in the United States views the Social Charter as a model for labor-market integration in North America. The AFL-CIO, which opposed NAFTA when it was first proposed by President Bush, later promised to support the treaty if it would include side agreements forcing Mexico to raise and enforce its labor and environmental standards. Thomas Donahue, secretary-treasurer of the AFL-CIO, sounded like any Northern European labor leader when he said that "Further integration among the nations of North America and the entire hemisphere is probably inevitable. If it is organized properly, it can be advantageous. But it is neither inevitable nor desirable for us to have a framework of integration that pits workers against each other and bases competition on the lowering of wages and standards."

With this promise, the Clinton administration set to work negotiating side agreements on labor and the environment. But when the agreements were announced in August 1993, Lane Kirkland and other top union leaders rejected them as "political window dressing on a bad agreement." Kirkland's main objection was the lack of practical means of safeguarding worker rights; the agreement, he said, "has no teeth." In a major setback for the Clinton administration, AFL-CIO leaders vigorously opposed NAFTA when it came before Congress, although the proposal ultimately passed.[30]

Even if NAFTA leads to stronger enforcement of Mexican labor laws, it will be more difficult to standardize labor conditions across North America than in Europe. Wage differentials between Mexico and its northern neighbors are much larger than those existing in Europe. Also, as noted, the United States has a larger "low-tech" manufacturing sector than do the advanced European nations. Already a downward pressure on wages and working conditions is present in a number of U.S. industries; even without NAFTA, capital is steadily flowing south. The "Big Three" U.S. auto companies currently have a total of sixty-four plants in Mexico, making General Motors the largest private employer in that country. The fact that capital already is moving originally convinced the AFL-CIO that the most pragmatic approach to regulating economic relations with Mexico would be to endorse NAFTA with side agreements on labor and environmental standards. U.S. unions, however, are far weaker, both numerically and politically, than their European counterparts. Therefore U.S. (and Canadian) unions will need to pursue other strategies than a revised NAFTA or a "Social North America" if they are to maintain their members' jobs and living standards.[31]

Internal Strategies

As global competition intensifies—former French prime minister Edith Cresson called it "a world economic war"—the advanced nations are being forced to consider the factors that give their economies an advantage. Natural resource endowments matter less now than in the past, as demonstrated by Japan. Certainly competitiveness still depends, as it did thirty years ago, on having successful macroeconomic policies that generate price stability and high employment. But such policies matter less now than in previous decades. Monetary options are constrained by currency pacts such as the EMU, while the nature of competition is changing in ways that make macroeconomic policy less important.[32]

Competitiveness in the advanced nations formerly turned on capital and production costs; low inflation and steady growth helped to control these costs. Mass production firms could hire unskilled laborers and make them extremely productive by putting them to work in capital-intensive factories. Minimizing cost in these settings was a matter of producing as much in as little time as possible. Today, however, mass-production technology is available for export to industrializing countries such as Brazil, China, and Korea. To maintain living standards, the advanced countries are forced to compete on factors other than cost: product quality, time to market, stylishness, and speed of innovation. These factors require knowledge- and skill-intensive production methods unlike Taylorized mass production.

Left to their own devices, individual firms never will generate socially adequate supplies of knowledge and skill because of the high positive externalities attached to these goods. Firms could form coalitions to supply knowledge and skill; in the United States and elsewhere, industrial research coalitions are becoming increasingly prevalent. The task would be made much easier, however, if government and other bodies (e.g., the unions, through apprenticeships) played coordinating roles. Then, too, governments are necessary to provide the institutions that generate a skilled and knowledgeable workforce, from the educational system to the industrial relations system. Although these points today may seem obvious, informed opinion in the United States only recently has come to see that "social" factors such as education and industrial relations are as important as capital spending and fiscal policy in determining national economic performance.

We turn now to a discussion of the major types of industrial relations systems in the advanced countries and their implications for economic performance. (The term "industrial relations" is construed broadly to connote the social institutions structuring the relationship between employment and the economy.) Recent studies reveal strong links between industrial relations practices and the economic performance of nations (inflation, growth, unemployment) and of firms (productivity, profitability, labor turnover). Although a nation's industrial relations system is not entirely a matter of choice, it is not entirely fixed. Borrowing and imitation are possible; in fact, they have become quite common. Now, more than at any time in the postwar period, industrial relations policy has become part of the search for competitive advantage. Providing a stable and highly skilled workforce is a prerequisite to attracting and retaining global capital.[33]

To categorize various systems, ideal types have been constructed on the basis of two dimensions: whether wage bargaining is centralized or decentralized, and

Figure 1.1. Industrial relations systems.

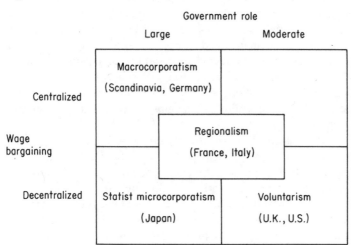

Government role

whether government plays a large or a small role in the economy and in industrial relations. This classification yields three types of systems: "macrocorporatism," "statist microcorporatism," and "voluntarism." A fourth type, "regionalism," combines elements of the other three. (Regional systems bring together key social actors at the urban or provincial level to cooperate on training, technological innovation, and other activities.) The categories shown in Figure 1.1 are not meant to sanction one approach over another; there is no such thing as one best way. Centralized systems tend to produce better macroeconomic than microeconomic results; the reverse is true under decentralization.

Different industrial relations systems increasingly share the premise that cooperation between workers, employers, and government produces social integration—overlapping goals between key social actors—and that social integration fosters economic flexibility and high-wage growth. Yet the systems are moving along different paths to achieve such integration. One important point of division is the level at which cooperation is sought. Tracing out a diagonal path in Figure 1.1, one moves from the macrocorporatist countries, which seek nationwide ("peak-level") consensus, to the regionalists, for whom cooperation is a local or provincial matter, to the voluntarists, who regard enterprise-level cooperation as the basis for social integration. Japan lies off this diagonal because its system is a hybrid of peak-level corporatism without labor and enterprise-level cooperation with labor. The other divide concerns the state; in this case the voluntarist countries' rejection of a major coordinative role for government places them off to one side.

Macrocorporatism. The Northern European nations attracted a lot of attention in the 1970s and 1980s because their corporatist industrial relations systems were associated with favorable macroeconomic outcomes. These countries (Austria, Denmark, Finland, Germany, Norway, and Sweden) recovered rapidly from the oil price increases of the 1970s, maintaining steady growth with relatively low unemployment and inflation rates. The key to success was their centralized bargaining systems, which helped to restrain inflation despite periodic price shocks.

Corporatist countries have other virtues in addition to their economic success. Though their labor movements are powerful, they have stable industrial relations systems and comparatively low strike rates. They also offer some of the world's most comprehensive welfare benefits, a reflection of their social democratic heritage and their centralized bargaining systems.[34]

Corporatist wage setting combines centralized bargaining, wage synchronization, and government coordination of wage norms. Under centralized bargaining, national unions and employers' associations set wages for most of the economy. Cross-sectoral synchronization is facilitated by several factors: high union density, national unions able to impose bargains at the plant level, and a powerful peak-level labor federation that can coordinate its member unions. Employers have their own associations, which parallel the centralized union structure. The final ingredient is government, which often is a party to wage negotiations. Such involvement ranges from passive suggestions of appropriate wage targets to more active offering of employment policies and welfare benefits in return for wage restraint.

Corporatist arrangements encourage wage restraint by making it easier to achieve a macroeconomic consensus between unions, employers, and government; expectations are synchronized and are made more "rational" when leaders meet and confer regularly. Also, corporatism allows governments to trade social programs for labor's cooperation. In addition, when union power resides at the peak level, local unions at prosperous companies cannot easily exceed the national wage pattern and engage in the beggar-thy-neighbor leapfrogging that raises wage dispersion.[35]

Yet corporatism is not essential to macroeconomic virtue. The relationship between centralization and economic performance is not linear; actually it has a "two-hump" form. Countries that are the mirror image of the corporatist economies, such as Japan and the United States, have high wage dispersion and decentralized wage setting. Yet their economic performance was good to excellent during the 1970s and 1980s, with positive employment growth, moderate increases in real wages, and low strike rates. In decentralized countries, labor markets are sensitive to market forces: shocks are followed by reequilibration, while employers, facing moderate real wages, expand employment by moving down their demand curves.[36]

The worst possible situation is found in countries that are neither corporatist nor decentralized but something between the two: Belgium, the Netherlands, and France are examples. Here, central unions are divided into multiple federations along political and confessional lines. Governments do not include them as social partners, nor do the unions have much power over their local affiliates. Unemployment is difficult to remedy because unionized "insiders" at the enterprise level have little incentive to consider the plight of the unemployed when conducting local wage negotiations. Each local union maximizes its bargaining power; the result is a series of uncoordinated bargains that can be accommodated only by an increase in unemployment. As long-term unemployment rises and the jobless move outside the labor force, wages become more sensitive to changes in demand. This situation kindles inflation that can be reduced only at the cost of permanently higher unemployment, a trap called "Eurosclerosis."[37]

Despite its merits, corporatism has faced many difficulties in the last five years. There is growing evidence that the generous welfare programs found in the corporatist countries are incompatible with economic efficiency; welfare expenditures are proving more difficult to restrain than real wages. The social democratic parties are faring poorly in Germany and much of Scandinavia; their conservative opponents are less willing than in the past to grease the wheels of consensus. Employers, who were always a key element in originating and sustaining corporatism, have begun to reassess its benefits, notably in Sweden. There the SAF (the private employers' federation) is pushing to decentralize wage negotiations. This effort is partly a response to the differential impacts of globalization on various Swedish companies; it is also a reaction to the costs of the welfare state and to the wage competition touched off by interunion rivalry.[38]

As formerly corporatist bargaining becomes more decentralized, strikes are likely to increase. This outcome may seem counterintuitive; one usually associates strikes with labor strength. Yet it fits with the two-humped model, in whose middle region (where corporatist countries will be situated as they decentralize) labor is too disorganized to trade on its militancy but still is strong enough to strike against individual firms. Such strikes remind us that the corporatist countries never achieved a utopia free of opposing interests. Instead, corporatist institutions were structured so as to draw unions and employers towards a cooperative, rather than conflictual, resolution of their differences.[39]

Finally, the EC poses numerous problems for the corporatist countries. Loss of economic sovereignty will hinder governments from increasing debt or devaluing the currency to secure labor's cooperation. Also, centralized bargaining is not an appropriate forum for securing promises that individual firms will reinvest in the homeland. Although unions hope the Social Charter will solve this problem, the charter will not affect labor standards outside the EC, where employers have begun to move. BMW and Bosch are opening plants in nonunion South Carolina; Audi is investing in Hungary; and Volkswagen is building plants in the Czech Republic. German unions expect to do well under the EC, using the charter and their skill-based productivity to offset high wages. Eastern European countries, however, have plenty of skilled labor and at much lower cost, from one-sixth to one-half of German levels.[40]

Statist Microcorporatism. In a memorable phrase, T.J. Pempel once referred to the Japanese political economy as "corporatism without labor." At the macro level, this term describes accurately how the Japanese economy operates. Consensus is achieved through overlapping organized groups. Government works closely with industry to secure export markets, to rationalize markets, and to control the value of the yen. Firms are organized politically into numerous peak-level industry associations. They also belong to *keiretsu* groups, which revolve around large trading companies. These groups include everything from banks to the smallest subcontracting firms. As Pempel reminds us, however, labor is the one element missing from Japan's highly coordinated system. Most of the organized workforce belongs to company unions, whose national federations are weak and politically insignificant.[41]

At the micro level, however—inside the workplace—the Japanese have an elaborate system for involving employees in decision making, one that sociologist Ronald Dore calls "private welfare corporatism." Small teams of multiskilled workers receive responsibility for making many production decisions. As a result, supervision is lean and investments in employee training are high. To facilitate training, companies give core Japanese workers (prime-age males) assurances of employment security, reinforced with an array of corporate welfare services. Company unions provide channels of communication that increase employee identification with the firm and dampen labor mobility. Private welfare corporatism is a way of representing labor's interests and achieving consensus, which mirrors the macro forms of cooperation found in Northern Europe. Such microcorporatism also compensates partially for the lack of labor representation in the Japanese political economy. Thus Japan is a two-tier system combining statist "corporatism without labor" with enterprise "welfare corporatism."[42]

This two-tier approach also exists elsewhere in East Asia, notably in Singapore, Taiwan, and South Korea. Like Japan, the Little Tigers have shown impressively high growth rates in recent years. Their success is due in part to "an undogmatic recognition that markets must be managed in order to provide support for entrepreneurial activities." In the early 1960s, for example, when Korea began its industrialization, the government nationalized the banks and decided which industries to promote. Imports competing with Korean goods were subject to high tariffs or were banned entirely. Korean companies were organized into *chaebol,* which negotiated economic policy with the government and with one another. As in Japan, labor was absent from this system of interest representation, though elements of welfare corporatism were present at the enterprise level.[43]

Not everyone would agree that statist industrial policy is responsible for East Asia's rapid, export-led growth. Some economists point to other nations in East Asia—Hong Kong, for example—which have experienced equally rapid growth but without macro-level concertation of interests. Others insist that MITI (Ministry of International Trade and Industry) and similar planning agencies are less powerful and less omniscient than alleged. Yet neither side in this debate challenges the competitive advantage that Japan and other Asian countries derive from corporatism at the enterprise level via company unions, corporate welfare systems, and team production. Indeed, this feature of the Japanese system has been imitated most widely in countries with laissez-faire traditions.[44]

Voluntarism. Britain and the United States share a long history of ideological antipathy to economically activist government, whether in the form of industrial policy or of peak-level concertation of interests. Exceptional sectors can be found, such as railroads and oil; so can exceptional periods, such as the world wars and the postwar Labor governments. Since the 1970s, however, both countries have reverted to tradition. "Industrial policy" again is a dirty term in the lexicon of Anglo-American political economy. Tripartite consensus is derogated as privileging "special interests" or as the first step down a slippery slope leading to a fascistic "state capitalism."

As for labor, the Trades Union Congress and the AFL-CIO remain frozen out of national decision making, a situation that weakens them further in other realms. Internally the TUC and the AFL-CIO are comparatively decentralized bodies in which power resides with their constituent national unions. Within the national unions, the local (branch) level is more important than in continental Europe. Even when industrywide bargaining occurs, it often takes place on two levels, through the negotiation of local supplements to national agreements. In recent years, the upper level has declined or has disappeared entirely; thus bargaining is more decentralized than ever. As a result, British and American unions are ill equipped to arrest the decline in their membership; this decline is aggravated by widening union-nonunion wage differentials. Institutions that might bolster union membership in other ways, such as the Ghent system or macrocorporatist social welfare bargaining, are absent. As a result, union membership declined sharply in the 1980s; Britain's percentage loss was second only to that of the United States.[45]

Declining unionism has helped to keep wages down in Britain and America (Table 1.1); consequently those countries are attractive locales for foreign investors. But, with the exception of the automobile industry, many of the jobs being created by foreign multinationals are inferior, in wages and working conditions, to those found in the investors' home countries. This is true not only of Japanese multinationals but also of those from Germany, Belgium, and other countries.[46]

It is somewhat ironic, then, that British and American employers are looking to Japanese microcorporatism as a model for developing the skill, flexibility, and cooperation they need to compete in world markets. The result has been a rapid diffusion of practices such as employee involvement in decision making, production teams, cross-training, and total quality management (TQM). According to one recent survey, about 40 percent of U.S. firms now use team systems and TQM. As in Japan, however, large American companies are segmenting their workforces between core employees, who increasingly are made to feel part of the enterprise, and peripheral employees, who are hired part time or by subcontractors.[47]

In those British and American companies where unionism has deep roots, employers increasingly are asking unions to help them operate the new production systems. Yet organized labor remains divided on how much cooperation to extend. In Britain, where the term "Japanization" has an ugly ring, the TUC is unsympathetic to microcorporatism. The EETPU (Electrical, Electronic, Telecommunications, and Plumbing Union) became a pariah in the British labor movement when it signed a single-union, no-strike agreement with Hitachi; ultimately it was expelled from the TUC for moving too far toward microcorporatism. The AFL-CIO has been less hostile to microcorporatism, in part because the United Automobile Workers (UAW), the federation's bellwether union, has embraced many aspects of microcorporatism, notably at General Motors' Saturn plant in Tennessee, at the NUMMI (GM-Toyota) plant, and elsewhere. The UAW is discarding old work rules, adopting team production, and participating in training and welfare programs that promote "jointness" with the auto companies. Former UAW vice president Irv Bluestone envisions unions signing "Enterprise Compacts" with employers to make companies globally competitive in quality and innovation.[48]

The UAW has drawn severe criticism from its members and from other unions for cooperating too closely with management and for dispersing too much authority to the plant level. Critics contend that this situation will intensify competition between plants and thus will drive down average industry wages.[49] The criticism, however, will not deter most American unions from pursuing microcorporatism, simply because doing so is a defensive necessity. Far more than British labor, American unions face a huge nonunion sector that is rapidly adopting Japanese-style policies and achieving higher productivity as a result. One might term the trend in the progressive parts of the nonunion sector "microcorporatism without labor." Unless American unions can prove that their kind of employee representation is essential to microcorporatism, they are destined to dwindle away.[50]

Regionalism. Another trend under way in several countries is the search for flexible coordination at the municipal and regional levels—that is, outside the firm *and* outside national government. Such coordination lends itself to industries that are concentrated geographically, depend on high levels of skill, and consist of small to medium-sized firms with fewer internal resources than the industrial giants following the micro- and macrocorporatist routes. To minimize risk and to promote positive externalities ("social capital"), firms and trade unions in these regional districts support common institutions for supplying skilled labor, such as vocational training institutes. As a result, the cost of interfirm labor mobility is reduced and successful firms can expand without damaging others in the region. Other forms of cooperation include mutual credit institutions serving the local industry. Not all participating firms need be small. For example, the Toulouse aircraft manufacturing district is centered around large firms. The paradigmatic industrial districts, however, such as those of Emilia-Romagna, are not controlled by any single firm.[51]

Industrial districts predominate in France and Italy, where one finds agglomerations of fairly small firms, often family-owned, producing high-quality "niche" items that do not lend themselves to mass production. This is the case for two reasons: first, the manufacture of these items requires craft skills that are not amenable to economies of scale; and second, production runs are small because the items are sensitive to shifting styles or are customized for particular users. Such industries include luxury items, leather goods, footwear, apparel, and machine tools. In both France and Italy, the prosperity of these districts is accelerating the decline of national unions and is shifting bargaining to regional and local levels.[52]

One can find industrial districts around the world, from Baden-Wurtemburg to Scotland to San Jose. The German districts are supported more strongly by national than by purely regional institutions, such as the apprenticeship system, and by firm-specific structures that inhibit labor mobility, such as works councils. In the United States, on the other hand, many industrial districts are associated with high-technology industries such as biotechnology (Seattle, Minneapolis) or computers (Boston, San Jose), which have little or no need for skilled manual labor. Several older industrial districts, however, now are attempting to revitalize themselves through cooperative credit and training institutions in places as diverse as Cincinnati (machine tools), Erie (metalworking), and New York (garments). Cooperation at the municipal level, with the participation of employers, unions, and local government, may well turn out to be an appropriate approach for a nation as large as the United States. In the United States, macrocorporatist strategies are infeasible in view of labor's weakness at the national level and the country's great ethnic and industrial diversity. Microcorporatism may make sense for large companies, but it is illogical or unaffordable for smaller, less capital-intensive employers.[53]

CONCLUSIONS

Increasing global trade is a fact of economic life; it is creating a more integrated world economy. But can nations construct durable institutions to channel global trade in desirable directions? The GATT negotiations remain deadlocked, unable to resolve numerous tariff issues. Meanwhile the fallback strategy—the creation of regional trading blocs—is hampered by the recession which has plagued the advanced nations since 1990. Prospects for the European Economic and Monetary Union remain uncertain, as does the fate of the North American Free Trade Agreement.

Even in good times, regional economic integration is not an easy task. As we have seen, nations differ widely in the institutional structures that guide their economies. These differences are greatest in the labor market, where one finds idiosyncratic wage structures, welfare programs, and industrial relations systems. Labor-market institutions are intrinsically difficult to harmonize because of their complexity. They also represent enormous sunk costs in a given way of doing things.

On a more positive note, the reluctance to tamper with these institutions stems from a growing recognition that they can expedite growth and contribute to a nation's comparative advantage. Only now are we beginning to understand how the fine details of labor markets and industrial relations systems are related to positive economic outcomes. Seemingly noneconomic phenomena such as cooperation, trust, and loyalty have profound implications for economic performance, and some institutions are better than others at generating these phenomena. For this reason, institutional designs such as macro- and microcorporatism yield better results than less coordinated systems. Also, because some systems are outperforming others, institutional imitation and diffusion across national borders exists and will continue to exist.

Nevertheless, present realities make it unlikely that huge trading blocs soon will stretch across East Asia, North America, and Europe. Instead, in the next ten years we may see the breaking off of smaller blocs composed of countries with comparatively homogeneous socioeconomic institutions. The Scandinavian countries currently are seeking to expand their mutual economic and political ties; while Canada and the United States have moved much closer to North American integration than has Mexico. Meanwhile, Britain still finds itself unable to fit easily into a bloc dominated by statist conceptions of economic organization. If fracturing were to occur, the greatest losers would be low-wage countries bordering richer neighbors, such as Mexico and Portugal.

However the total situation turns out, two things are clear: First, the nation state is unlikely to disappear any time soon. Second, global trade and currency flows will continue to increase regardless of the specific institutions that regulate them. Thus the stress points identified in this volume—those between national labor and global capital—will continue to generate controversy and concern well into the next century.

NOTES

1. Michael Borrus and John Zysman, "Industrial Competitiveness and American National Security," in Wayne Sandholtz et al., eds., *The Highest Stakes: The Economic Foundations of the Next Security System* (New York, 1992), 37.

2. On the debate over the national identities of multinational corporations, see Robert Reich, *The Work of Nations: Preparing Ourselves for 21st Century Capitalism* (New York, 1991), and Laura D. Tyson, *Who's Bashing Whom? Trade Conflict in High-Technology Industries* (Washington, 1993). On MNC imports, see Paul Magnusson, "Why Corporate Nationality Matters," *Business Week,* July 12, 1993.

3. Michael Piore and Charles Sabel, *The Second Industrial Divide: Possibilities for Prosperity* (New York, 1984).

4. Charles Kindleberger, *The International Economic Order: Essays on Financial Crisis and International Public Goods* (Cambridge, 1988); Ronald I. McKinnon, "The Rules of the Game: International Money in Historical Perspective," *Journal of Economic Literature* 31 (March 1993); Fred Block, *The Origins of International Economic Disorder: A Study of the U.S. International Monetary Policy from World War II to the Present* (Berkeley, 1977).

5. George Ross, "After Maastricht: Hard Choices for Europe," *World Policy Journal* 9 (Summer 1992): 487–513; Stanley Hoffman, "Goodbye to a United Europe?" *New York Review of Books,* May 27, 1993; Daniel Gros and Niels Thygesen, *European Monetary Integration* (New York, 1992).

6. Roy J. Adams and Jerry P. White, "Labor and the Canada-U.S. Free Trade Agreement," *ILR Report* 27 (Fall 1989), 15–21; William C. Symonds, "Whoever Succeeds Mulroney is in Trouble on Trade," *Business Week,* March 8, 1993, 57; S.E. Reynolds and J.E. Seidelman, "Structural Impacts of the U.S.-Canadian Free Trade Agreement," *Canadian Public Policy-Analyse de Politiques* (March 1993): 86–92.

7. Sidney Weintraub, "The Case for Free Trade with Mexico: Why Progressives Should Support a North American Free Trade Area," Progressive Policy Institute, report no. 9 (Washington, D.C., 1991); Richard Rothstein, "Continental Drift: NAFTA and Its Aftershocks," *The American Prospect,* no. 12 (Winter 1993): 68–84.

8. Thomas Karier, "Trade Deficits and Labor Unions," in Lawrence Mishel and Paula Voos, eds., *Unions and Economic Competitiveness* (Armonk, 1992), 27; "NAFTA Labor Accord Draws

Criticism," *Daily Labor Report*, no. 179, September 17, 1993, A-10.

9. Lester Thurow, *Head to Head: The Coming Economic Battle Among Japan, Europe, and America* (New York, 1993), 213–14; "Special Report: Japan," *Business Week*, July 5, 1993, 74.

10. David Blanchflower and Richard B. Freeman, "Going Different Ways: Unionism in the U.S. and Other Advanced OECD Countries," *Industrial Relations* 31 (Winter 1992): 56–79.

11. Daniel J.B. Mitchell, "Inflation, Unemployment, and the Wagner Act," *Stanford Law Review* 38 (April 1986): 1065–95; Theodore Cohen, *Remaking Japan: The American Occupation as New Deal* (New York, 1987); Peter A. Hall, ed., *The Political Power of Economic Ideas: Keynesianism Across Nations* (Princeton, 1989); Egon Matzner and Wolfgang Streeck, eds., *Beyond Keynesianism: The Socioeconomics of Production and Full Employment* (Brookfield, 1991).

12. See, for example, P.D. Linneman, M.L. Wachter, and W.H. Carter, "Evaluating the Evidence on Union Employment and Wages," *Industrial & Labor Relations Review* 44 (October 1990): 34–53.

13. Jeffry Frieden, "Labor and the Politics of Exchange Rates: The Case of the European Monetary System," in this volume; Loukas Tsoukalis, *The New European Economy: The Politics and Economics of Integration,* 2nd ed. (Oxford, 1993).

14. T. R. Cusack, T. Notermans, and M. Rein, "Political-Economic Aspects of Public Employment," *European Journal of Political Research* 17 (July 1989), 471–500; Richard Freeman, "Contraction and Expansion: The Divergence of Public and Private Sector Unionism in the U.S.," *Journal of Economic Perspectives* 2 (September 1988).

15. Gerald C. Friedman, "Politics and Unions: Government, Ideology, and the Labor Movement in France and the U.S., 1880–1914," Ph.D. dissertation, Harvard University, 1985, 30–31.

16. For example, German negotiations are less centralized than those in Scandinavia; in contrast, Scandinavian labor is represented by multiple peak organizations. Separate federations exist for manual, nonmanual, and government employees, whereas the DGB represents most of German labor. See Colin Crouch, "Conditions for Trade Union Wage Restraint," in Leon Lindberg and Charles Maier, eds., *The Politics of Inflation and Economic Stagnation* (Washington, 1985); C. Blyth, "Level of National Bargaining," in OECD, *Collective Bargaining and Government Policies in Ten OECD Countries* (Paris, 1979).

17. Michael Wallerstein, "Union Organization in Advanced Industrial Democracies," *American Political Science Review* 83 (June 1989): 481–501; John D. Stephen, "Industrial Concentration, Country Size, and Trade Union Membership," *American Political Science Review* 85 (September, 1991): 941–49; Keith Sisson, *The Management of Collective Bargaining: An International Comparison* (Oxford, 1987); Peter Swenson, *Fair Shares: Unions, Pay, and Politics in Sweden and West Germany* (Ithaca, 1989); Lloyd Ulman, "Who Wanted Collective Bargaining in the First Place?," *39th Annual Proceedings of the Industrial Relations Research Association,* New Orleans, December 1986; Sanford Jacoby, "American Exceptionalism Revisited: The Importance of Management," in Jacoby, ed., *Masters to Managers: Historical and Comparative Perspectives on American Employers* (New York, 1991); Bruce Western, "Unionization Trends in Postwar Capitalism: A Comparative Study of Working Class Organization," Ph.D. dissertation, UCLA, Los Angeles, 1993; Bo Rothstein, "Labor Market Institutions and Working-Class Strength," in Sven Steinmo, Kathleen Thelen, and Frank Longstreth, eds., *Structuring Politics: Historical Institutionalism in Comparative Analysis* (New York, 1992).

18. Edward Leamer, "Wage Effects of a U.S.-Mexican Free Trade Agreement," Mexico-U.S. Free Trade Agreement Conference, Brown University, October 1991.

19. Harry C. Katz, *Shifting Gears: Changing Labor Relations in the U.S. Automobile Industry* (Cambridge, 1985).

20. Juergen Kuehl, "Lessons from EC Labor Markets," in Richard S. Belous, Rebecca S. Hartley, and Kelly McClenahan, eds., *European and American Labor Markets: Different Models and Different Results* (Washington, D.C., 1992), 38.

21. Adams and White, "Labor and the Canada-U.S. Free Trade Agreement"; Gosta Esping-Andersen, *The Three Worlds of Welfare Capitalism* (Princeton, 1990).

22. For an overview of the Social Charter, see John T. Addison and W. Stanley Siebert, "The Social Charter of the European Community: Evolution and Controversies," *Industrial & Labor Relations Review* 44 (July 1991): 597–625. Also see Hugh G. Mosley, "The Social Dimension of European Integration," *International Labour Review* 129 (1990); and Ton de Vos, *Multinational Corporations in Democratic Host Countries: U.S. Multinationals and the Vredeling Proposal* (Brookfield, Vt., 1989).

23. Friedrich-Ebert Stiftung, "The European Labor Market," in Belous et al., eds., *European and American Labor Markets,* 124; Christopher Erickson and Sarosh Kuruvilla, "Labor Cost Incentives for Capital Mobility in the European Community," in this volume.

24. See Daniel J. B. Mitchell, "Employee Benefits in Europe and the U.S." in this volume; John Grahl and Paul Teague, "Integration Theory and European Labour Markets," *British Journal of Industrial Relations* 30 (December 1992): 524. Also see John T. Addison and W. Stanley Siebert, "The Social Charter: Whatever Next?" and Mark Hall, "Behind the European Works Councils Directives: The European Commission's Legislative Strategy," both in *British Journal of Industrial Relations* 30 (December 1992).

25. The same motive once impelled high-wage, high-benefit U.S. employers to endorse the 1935 Social Security Act as a way of narrowing labor costs in relation to less generous firms. See Sanford Jacoby, "Employers and the Welfare State: The Role of Marion B. Folsom," *Journal of American History* 80 (Fall 1993).

26. Duncan Campbell, "Multinational Labor Relations in the European Community," *ILR Report* 27 (Fall 1989); Paul Marginson, "European Integration and Transnational Management-Union Relations in the Enterprise," *British Journal of Industrial Relations* 30 (December 1992).

27. Robert Flanagan and Arnold Weber, eds., *Bargaining Without Boundaries: The Multinational Corporation and International Labor Relations* (Chicago, 1974); John P. Windmuller, *International Trade Secretariats: The Industrial Trade Union Secretariats* (Washington, D.C., 1991).

28. "European Employers Group Considering TransEuropean Collective Bargaining," *Daily Labor Report*, April 18, 1991, A-5.

29. Paul Evan, Yves Doz, and Andre Laurent, eds., *Human Resource Management in International Firms* (New York, 1990); Malcolm Borg, *International Transfers of Managers in Multinational Corporations* (Uppsala, 1988).

30. James Parks, "Strong Labor Standards Vital to Inter-American Economic Equity," *AFL-CIO News,* May 17, 1993, 12; John Oravec, "Side Deals Fail; AFL-CIO Fights NAFTA," *AFL-CIO News,* August 23, 1993, 1; "Peterson Threatens to Subpoena Administration Officials on NAFTA," *Daily Labor Report,* September 10, 1993, AA-1. Also see Ray Marshall, "Work Organization, Unions, and Economic Performance," in Mishel and Voos, eds., *Unions and Economic Competitiveness.*

31. Rothstein, "Continental Drift"; John Judis, "Free Trade: Gut Check," *In These Times,* June 28, 1993.

32. Cresson quoted in Thurow, *Head to Head,* 31.

33. Michael H. Best, *The New Competition: Institutions of Industrial Restructuring* (Cambridge, 1990); Industrial Relations Research Association, *Human Resources and the Performance of the Firm* (Madison, 1987). Also see Sanford M. Jacoby, "The New Institutionalism: What Can It Learn from the Old?," *Industrial Relations* 29 (Spring 1990).

34. The literature on European corporatism is vast. A sample includes Michael Bruno and Jeffrey Sachs, *Economics of Worldwide Stagflation* (Cambridge, 1985); Lars Calmfors and E.J. Driffil, "Centralization of Wage Bargaining and Macroeconomic Performance," *Economic Policy* (April 1988): 13–60; Fritz Scharpf, *Crisis and Choice in European Social Democracy* (Ithaca, 1991); David Soskice, "Wage Determination: The Changing Role of Institutions in Advanced Industrial Economies," *Oxford Review of Economic Policy* 6 (Winter 1990), 36–61; Philippe Schmitter and Wolfgang Streeck, "Interest Group Intermediation in the European Community," *Politics and Society* 19 (June 1991); Peter J. Katzenstein, *Corporatism and Change: Austria, Switzerland, and the Politics of Industry* (Ithaca, 1984).

35. Robert Flanagan, David Soskice, and Lloyd Ulman, *Unionism, Economic Stabilization, and Incomes Policies: European Experience* (Washington, D.C., 1983); Ezio Tarantelli, "Monetary Policy and the Regulation of Inflation and Unemployment," in Morley Gunderson, Noah Meltz, and Sylvia Ostry, eds., *Unemployment: International Perspectives* (Toronto, 1987).

Golden argues that union monopoly (the number of union federations) is a better explanation than centralization of wage restraint and other salutary outcomes. Germany, which has a powerful DGB but a two-tiered wage system, is an example of this finding. See Miriam Golden, "The Dynamics of Trade Unionism and National Economic Performance," *American Political Science Review* 87 (1993): 439–54.

36. Richard Freeman, "Labor Markets, Institutions, Constraints, and Performance, National Bureau of Economic Research, Working Paper no. 2560 (Cambridge, 1988).

37. Assar Lindbeck and Dennis J. Snower, *The Insider-Outsider Theory of Employment and Unemployment* (Cambridge, 1988).

38. Peter Lange, Michael Wallerstein, and Miriam Golden, "The End of Corporatism? Wage Setting in the Nordic and Germanic Countries," in this volume. Also see Alfred Pfaller, Ian Gough, and Goran Therborn, eds., *Can the Welfare State Compete? A Comparative Study of Five Advanced Capitalist Countries* (London, 1990); Hans-Goran Myrdal, "The Hard Way from a Centralized to a Decentralized Industrial Relations System: The Case of Sweden and the SAF," in Otto Jacobi and Dieter Sadowski, eds., *Employers' Associations in Europe: Policy and Organization* (Baden-Baden, 1991).

39. George Tsebelis and Peter Lange, "Strikes Around the World: A Game Theoretic Approach," in this volume; Robert M. Axelrod, *The Evolution of Cooperation* (New York, 1984).

40. Wolfgang Streeck, "More Uncertainties: German Unions Facing 1992," *Industrial Relations* 30 (Fall 1991): 317–49; Andrei Markovits and Alexander Otto, "German Labor and Europe '92," *Comparative Politics* (January 1992), 163–80; "The European Community: Back to the Drawing Board," *The Economist* 3 July 1993, 5–20.

41. T.J. Pempel and Keiichi Taunekawa, "Corporatism Without Labor? The Japanese Anomaly," in Philippe Schmitter and Gerhard Lembruch, eds., *Trends Toward Corporatist Intermediation* (Beverly Hills, 1979), 231–70; Ronald Dore, *Flexible Rigidities: Industrial Policy and Structural Adjustment in the Japanese Economy, 1970–80* (Stanford, 1986); Chalmers Johnson, *MITI and the*

Japanese Miracle: The Growth of Industrial Policy, 1925–1975 (Stanford, 1982); Michael Gerlach, *Alliance Capitalism: The Social Organization of Japanese Business* (Berkeley, 1992).

42. Ronald Dore, *British Factory-Japanese Factory: The Origins of National Diversity in Industrial Relations* (Berkeley, 1973); Robert E. Cole, *Strategies for Learning: Small-Group Activities in American, Japanese, and Swedish Industry* (Berkeley, 1989); Sanford Jacoby, "Pacific Ties: Industrial Relations and Employment Systems in Japan and the U.S. since 1900," in Howell John Harris and Nelson Lichtenstein, eds., *Industrial Democracy in America: The Ambiguous Promise* (New York, 1993).

German works councils serve many of the same enterprise-oriented functions as Japanese unions, though the existence of strong national unions forces the German councils to pursue what one might term "adversarial cooperation." See Norbert Altmann and Klaus Dull, "Rationalization and Participation: Implementation of New Technologies and Problems of the Works Councils in the FRG," *Economic and Industrial Democracy* 11 (1990): 111–27; Lowell Turner, *Democracy at Work: Changing World Markets and the Future of Labor Unions* (Ithaca, 1991).

43. J.A. Kregel and Egon Matzner, "Agenda for the Reconstruction of Central and Eastern Europe," *Challenge* 35 (September 1992): 34; Alice Amsden, *Asia's Next Giant: South Korea and Late Industrialization* (New York, 1989); Walter Galenson, *Labor and Economic Growth in Five Asian Countries: South Korea, Malaysia, Taiwan, Thailand, and the Philippines* (New York, 1992); Archie Kleingartner and Hsueh-yu Peng, "Taiwan: A Study of Labor Relations in Transition," UCLA Institute of Industrial Relations, Working Paper no. 184 (Los Angeles, 1990).

44. Kenneth Sokoloff, "Some Thoughts and Evidence on Industrial Policy: Industrialization in South Korea and Mexico," in this volume; Gary R. Saxonhouse, "Industrial Policy and Factor Markets: Biotechnology in Japan and the U.S.," Australia-Japan Research Centre, Research Paper no. 36 (Canberra, 1986).

45. Good overviews of British industrial relations can be found in P.B. Beaumont, *Change in Industrial Relations: The Organization and Environment* (London, 1990); Howard Gospel, *Markets, Firms, and the Management of Labour in Modern Britain* (Cambridge, 1992). On the United States, see Richard B. Freeman and James Medoff, *What Do Unions Do?* (New York, 1984); Thomas Kochan, Harry Katz, and Robert McKersie, *The Transformation of American Industrial Relations* (New York, 1986).

46. See Ruth Milkman, "The Impact of Foreign Investment on U.S. Industrial Relations: The Case of California's Japanese-Owned Factories," in this volume. Also see Michael Cimini, "BASF Lockout Ends," *Monthly Labor Review* 113 (March

1990): 65; Harris Collingwood, "Uncle Sam Doesn't Understand: Labor Department Investigates Violations of Child-Labor and Overtime Laws at Food Lion," *Business Week* (January 11, 1993): 40.

47. Paul Osterman, "How Common is Workplace Transformation and How Can We Explain Who Adopts It? Results from a National Survey," Working paper, Sloan School of Management, MIT, December 1992; Stephen Hill, "Why Quality Circles Failed But Total Quality Management Might Succeed," *British Journal of Industrial Relations* 29 (December 1991), 541–68; Paul Adler, "Time-and-Motion Regained," *Harvard Business Review* 71 (January-February 1993): 97–108.

48. Leonard Rico, "The New Industrial Relations: British Electricians' New-Style Agreements," *Industrial & Labor Relations Review* 41 (October 1987): 63–78; Barry Bluestone and Irving Bluestone, *Negotiating the Future: A Labor Perspective on American Business* (New York, 1992).

49. Mike Parker and Jane Slaughter, *Choosing Sides: Unions and the Team Concept* (Boston, 1988); Charles Heckscher, *The New Unionism: Employee Involvement in the Changing Corporation* (New York, 1989).

50. Several authors have tried to do precisely this—prove that formal representation is critical to generating high productivity in microcorporatist systems. The problem, however, is that productivity is as likely to rise through a company union (as in Japan) as through a union affiliated with the AFL-CIO. This fact, more than unpleasant memories, explains why U.S labor remains opposed to legal reforms that might legitimize company unions. See Maryellen Kelley and Bennett Harrison, "Unions, Technology, and Labor-Management Cooperation," in Mishel and Voos, eds., *Unions and Economic Competitiveness*; Sanford Jacoby and Anil Verma, "Enterprise Unions in the United States," *Industrial Relations* 31 (Winter 1992): 137–58.

51. Michael Storper, "Boundaries, Compartments, and Markets: Paradoxes of Industrial Relations in Growth Pole Regions of France, Italy, and the United States," in this volume. Also see Paul Hirst and Jonathan Zeitlin, eds., *Reversing Industrial Decline? Industrial Structure and Policy in Britain and Her Competitors* (New York, 1989); Edward Goodman and Julia Bamford, eds., *Small Firms and Industrial Districts in Italy* (London, 1989); Robert D. Putnam, *Making Democracy Work: Civic Traditions in Modern Italy* (Princeton, 1993); Michael Storper and Robert Salais, *Worlds of Production: Collective Action and the Economic Identities of Nations and Regions* (forthcoming, 1994); Allen Scott, "The Role of Large Producers in Industrial Districts: A Case Study of High Technology Systems Houses in Southern California," *Regional Studies* 26, no. 3 (1992): 265–73.

52. Richard M. Locke, "The Demise of the National Union in Italy: Lessons for Comparative

Industrial Relations Theory," *Industrial & Labor Relations Review* 45 (January 1992): 229–49; Miriam Golden and Jonas Pontusson, eds., *Bargaining for Change: Union Politics in North America and Europe* (Ithaca, 1992).

53. E.M. Bergman, G. Maier, and F. Toedtling, eds., *Regions Reconsidered: Economic Networks, Innovation, and Local Development in In-* *dustrialized Countries* (London, 1991); Charles Sabel and Gary Herrigel, "Regional Prosperities Compared: Massachusetts and Baden-Wurtemburg in the 1980s," *Economy and Society* (November 1989): 374–404; Martin Kenney and Richard Florida, *Beyond Mass Production: The Japanese System and Its Transfer to the U.S.* (New York, 1993).

I

INDUSTRIAL RELATIONS CONSEQUENCES

The first part of this volume examines the industrial relations consequences of globalization. What role do labor markets play in the globalization process? How is labor affecting—and responding to—the process of economic integration? These questions are considered in Part I, which focuses on labor markets, labor movements, and the multinational dimensions of work organization.

LABOR MARKETS

Labor market issues lie at the heart of many concerns surrounding economic integration in Europe and North America. Unions in higher-wage countries fear that integration may lead to what the Europeans term "social dumping": the movement of jobs and capital from north to south, followed by a leveling down of wages and social welfare provisions. To prevent this, the Northern European unions have been champions of the Social Charter, which proposes to standardize labor regulations across the European Community (EC); the AFL-CIO is pursuing a similar strategy in North America.

In Chapter 2, Christopher L. Erickson and Sarosh C. Kuruvilla analyze the prospects for social dumping in Europe. Their findings are not happy news for Northern European workers. Unit labor costs are lower in Southern Europe, either because (as in Spain) productivity levels are as high as in the northern countries while wages are lower, or because (as in Portugal and Greece) the compensation gap with the north is greater than the productivity gap. In addition, they find that foreign direct investment grew rapidly in Southern Europe in the 1980s.

Yet *levels* of foreign investment remain low. It may be that employers loathe uncertainty and are delaying investments until the issues raised by the Social Charter and by the Maastricht Agreement have been settled. Alternatively, it may be that labor costs are not a critical determinant of investment decisions; rather, employers may be more sensitive to factors such as physical infrastructure and stability of industrial relations.

Along with social dumping, another key issue is labor market flexibility. Flexible labor markets are those in which workers can move easily from declining to expanding areas and industries. Inflexible labor markets hamper the gains in efficiency to be achieved from economic integration; cross-national "harmonization" of labor markets has the opposite effect. In Chapter 3, Daniel J. B. Mitchell provides comparative data on labor markets in Europe and in the United States, and shows that European labor markets tend to be less "flexible" when judged by measures such as labor turnover and layoffs.

Mitchell focuses on employee benefits as a factor determining flexibility. He thinks it will be necessary but difficult to achieve harmonization across the EC in the provision of benefits such as old-age pensions and health insurance. Difficulties stem from the disparate ways in which benefits are structured in each nation; these range from purely public programs to programs mixing public with private (employer-provided) benefits. Because the United States is viewed as having relatively flexible labor markets, some European countries would like to shift toward an American-style privatized benefits system. Yet this may be a mistake, says Mitchell, because private programs retard labor mobility; in a public system, workers need not be concerned that they will lose their benefits if they change employers. Europeans would be better off staying with their current welfare systems unless or until they can ensure the portability of benefits.

LABOR MOVEMENTS

Europe's most generous welfare programs are found in the corporatist countries of Northern Europe, where tripartite "consensus" decision making influences labor market outcomes. Whether corporatism can withstand the pressures of globalization is a major question for the powerful labor movements of Austria, Germany, and Scandinavia (Denmark, Finland, Norway, Sweden). During the 1970s and early 1980s, these nations exhibited low inflation and steady growth, which were attributed to the social integration and cooperation fostered by macrocorporatism. Today, however, it is widely believed that the bloom has faded from the corporatist rose. In Sweden the economy is faltering, social democracy is weakening, and centralized negotiations have disintegrated.

Yet much of the speculation about the fate of corporatism is just that—speculation. In Chapter 4, Peter Lange, Michael Wallerstein, and Miriam Golden provide detailed facts about trends in Scandinavia and Germany since 1970. The data presented are unique; they are not available from any other source. They include figures on union strength and centralization, as well as on measures of government-union-employer interaction in setting wages.

Lange, Wallerstein, and Golden observe that corporatism underwent some significant changes in the 1980s. Union membership shifted from the private to the public sector, while wage negotiations became less centralized in Denmark and Sweden. Overall, however, they find claims of corporatism's demise to be premature. They report "no general trend towards decay or collapse of corporatist institutions." Macrocorporatism, with its strong and centralized unions, continues to exist as a viable alternative to less statist and less laborist systems. Nevertheless, over the next decade we must reappraise the relative performance of these varieties of capitalism.

Although the corporatist countries have powerful labor movements, historically their strike rates have not been high. This paradox is discussed in Chapter 5, where George Tsebelis and Peter Lange examine strike trends in the advanced industrial countries. During the 1980s, globalization and rising unemployment caused a weakening of organized labor in the OECD (Organization for Economic Cooperation and Development) nations. Conventional theory predicts that strikes should have declined in the 1980s, and in some countries they did so. Yet elsewhere, strike rates remained the same or even increased. To account for these divergent trends, Tsebelis and Lange develop an ingenious explanation based on game-theoretic concepts.

Tsebelis and Lange's model predicts a curvilinear relation between strike rates and labor strength, whereby few strikes occur in countries with high and with low labor strength and many more strikes take place in countries with intermediate labor strength. Macrocorporatist countries have low strike rates both because the strength of labor inhibits employers from provoking strikes and because the political influence of labor allows it to trade strikes for beneficial social legislation and other goods.

But what about the 1980s? When a strong labor movement weakens, say Tsebelis and Lange, it slides to the middle of the curve (a higher rate of strikes); when a labor movement of intermediate strength weakens, it changes from a high- to a low-strike region. This is precisely what happened in the 1980s, when "strong-labor" countries such as Norway and Sweden experienced an increase in strikes, while strike rates declined in other countries.

Tsebelis and Lange's research suggests that we need to rethink macrocorporatism. Although observers once regarded it as the archetype of social integration and cooperation, it also might be conceptualized as a fragile truce between two heavily armed groups—employers and workers. When one side weakens, the truce fails. National wage negotiations, however, are zero-sum distributive games. Even though wage disputes may proliferate as labor weakens, social integration still can persist in other areas such as the formulation of macroeconomic policy or the improvement of plant-level productivity. Whether this is true in the Northern European countries requires additional research. Lange, Wallerstein, and Golden's finding—that most features of Nordic corporatism remained stable in the 1980s, with the exception of wage bargaining—is consistent with both an increase in strikes and the continuation of cooperation in other realms.

THE WORKPLACE

In addition to macrocorporatism, the Northern European countries are known for their innovative employment practices, including works councils and sociotechnical work systems. The Japanese have developed even more productive work methods. Japanese "enterprise corporatism" combines employee involvement in production decisions with company unions and corporate training, welfare, and job security programs. As world labor markets become more highly integrated, diffusion theory would predict the spread of the Japanese approach throughout Europe and North America—indirectly through imitation and directly through the expansion of Japanese multinational firms.

Yet as Ruth Milkman shows in Chapter 6, theory does not accord with reality, at least not in California. Nearly one-fifth of the Japanese-owned factories in the United States are located in California, but few have adopted innovative Japanese work practices. Skills are low, training is minimal, and pay is based on job classifications—much as in American-owned factories. Few of the Japanese-owned plants use production teams or regular job rotation. Milkman's interviews found that plant managers were strongly opposed to unions and were working hard to keep unions out of their facilities. These plants are almost entirely nonunion and rely heavily on recent immigrants from Asia and Latin America.

The one exception is the motor vehicle industry, where Japanese-owned assembly firms rely on the same innovative practices as they use at home. The assembly plants, however, are not the norm; they are larger and more capital-intensive than most Japanese-owned plants in California. Yet the automobile industry has received the most publicity from the media and has shaped our perceptions of Japanese transplants. Milkman's research rectifies the imbalance.

Although California is a long way from Southern Europe or from Britain, it offers many of the same attractions. Land and energy are cheaper than in Japan, and relatively cheap workers are abundant. Like most of the United States, California has been slow to adopt a high-wage/high-skill strategy. Although the state contains some technologically advanced sectors, particularly those employing university graduates, its manufacturing industries are languishing. Large portions of California have a labor force that resembles Southern Europe's. Indeed, Milkman finds that the major reasons why Japanese firms opened plants in California were proximity to the Pacific Rim, low labor costs, and the availability of a tractable workforce.

In short, California may be a harbinger of what lies ahead for other regions, though Milkman is careful not to blame Japanese companies for the situation. Rather, she says, the Japanese simply are taking advantage of America's failure to create an environment that encourages high-wage, high-skill manufacturing systems. How can nations create such environments? That question will be taken up in the second part of this book.

2

Labor Cost Incentives for Capital Mobility in the European Community

CHRISTOPHER L. ERICKSON
SAROSH C. KURUVILLA

On December 31, 1992, the twelve economies making up the European Community (EC) took a major step toward becoming a single market with the initiation of the internal market program allowing for the free movement of goods, people, and money across borders. One major hypothesized effect is that capital will flee from high-labor-cost countries to those with low labor costs, or that "social dumping" will occur: a lowering of labor standards and social protection in the wealthier countries in response to competition from countries with substantially lower labor standards and costs.[1] One aspect of this issue involves labor protection and social policies, which are expected to be addressed to a greater or lesser extent by the Social Charter and its supporters' goal of long-term upward harmonization of social policies. However, even if standards are equalized, there remains the issue of labor costs. Labor costs can be a key component of competitive strategy, and it seems doubtful that harmonization policies will be able to equalize the currently large differences in manufacturing labor costs across the EC countries. Despite the considerable attention given to harmonization of labor standards, relatively little attention has been paid to the question of the levels of labor costs within the EC.

This chapter attempts to assess the importance of labor costs in the social dumping debate by bringing empirical evidence to bear on a series of questions involving the manufacturing labor cost structures in the EC countries: How far apart are compensation costs across these countries? Are they converging? Do the differences in compensation costs across the countries reflect differences in labor productivity; that is, are unit labor costs in fact equalized across these countries? How do the industry compensation cost structures compare, and how is this measure relevant to the social dumping debate? We also look at the state of foreign direct investment in the EC now. Measuring 1980 unit labor costs at expenditure weighted purchasing power parity (PPP) exchange rates, and analyzing growth rates and dispersion patterns of compensation costs and growth rates of productivity since then, we find the following: While labor productivity, as measured by output per employee hour, is in fact lower in the less developed EC countries (in particular, Portugal, Greece, and Ireland), compensation differentials between Portugal and Greece compared to Northern Europe are much larger than productivity differentials; and while Spanish productivity is close to Northern European productivity, its compensation costs are much lower. We find no evidence of significant convergence of compensation levels or structures or, most importantly for the question at hand, of unit labor costs since 1980; in fact, the evidence indicates that the "compensation gap" has been widening while the "productivity gap" has been narrowing. This analysis thus suggests that social dumping may well be a serious concern, in that at least the economic incentive to do it seems to be present for investors from wealthier countries such as Germany, as well as for investors outside the EC.

THE ISSUE OF SOCIAL DUMPING

The capital mobility aspect of social dumping has become a matter of concern for workers, unions, and governments with the elimination of controls on foreign direct investment. While the term "social dumping" may seem normative and ideological, it has in fact gained wide usage in the debate over the single market; for example, the *Economist* (July 3–9, 1993) reports that "There was an uproar in France earlier this year over Hoover's decision to close a factory in Dijon and concentrate its vacuum-cleaner production at a plant near Glasgow where the workforce was prepared to accept new working practices. This was decried as 'social dumping' by Britain, which with its opt-out from Maastricht's social charter would increasingly poach jobs from its neighbors." We now examine the issue of (and the policy response to) social dumping.

As Mosley (1990: 160) notes, "social dumping could take place in at least three different ways: (1) through the displacement of high-cost producers by low-cost producers from countries in which wages, social benefits, and direct and indirect costs entailed by protective legislation are markedly lower; (2) firms in high-labor-cost countries would be increasingly free to relocate their operations, thereby strengthening their bargaining power vis-à-vis their current workforce to exert downward pressure on wages and working conditions; and (3) individual states might be tempted to pursue a low-wage and perhaps anti-union labor market strategy as part of their efforts to catch up economically."[2] The general expectation is that the first two types of mechanisms (i.e., displacement or movement from high-cost to low-cost countries, or the use of the threat of such movement as a means of lowering costs in high-cost countries) are the most probable means by which social dumping will occur in the EC.

Such fears have led to support for the introduction of a Social Charter, which has been the subject of intense debate.[3] The final and substantially diluted version of the charter was accepted in principle by eleven of the twelve EC countries in December 1989, with Britain dissenting.

Briefly, the charter covers a range of issues designed to harmonize labor protection and social policies across member states. This is attempted via proposals regarding freedom of movement; employment and (minimum) remuneration; improvements of living and working conditions; social protection; freedom of association and collective bargaining; vocational training; equal treatment for men and women; information, consultation, and participation of employees in management; health, protection, and safety at the workplace; and protection of children, adolescents, the elderly, and disabled persons. The draft action program that was intended to be used to actually develop realistic objectives in respect to the matters in the charter contains forty-seven different proposals.

Progress on the social dimension has been mixed. Notable successes include the directive on harmonization of national regulations on collective redundancies (providing for information and consultation with workers' representatives in cases of mass layoffs), the directive covering the rights of workers in cases of mergers and firm insolvency, various directives on gender equality, and a series of directives on health and safety issues. However, there have also been a number of areas in which the EC countries have failed to reach agreement. These include worker rights to information, consultation, and participation; parental leave; equality between part-time and full-time workers; collective bargaining rights; and social protection benefits, including health care.

The various EC actors (governments, employers [UNICE], and unions [ETUC]) have different positions on these issues, and many of the arguments underlying the different positions reflect competitive interests of the actors. We now briefly examine the interests and positions of the various parties to get a sense both of how they regard the role of labor policies in determining their competitiveness, as well as the extent to which these interests are overlapping—and therefore the extent to which standards are likely in fact to be equalized.

All the trade union bodies that make up the ETUC are in general agreement with the Social Charter (although some feel it does not go far enough). Streeck (1991) discusses the uneasy alliance between Northern European unions and Southern European interests that has led to support by the former for the Community's regional aid program, which will transfer funds for development to the poorer countries, and support by the latter for the Social Dimension, which aims to equalize labor costs across the EC. He notes, however, that "whether or not regional assistance and social policies can be properly balanced and finetuned, so that infrastructural investment in the South does not result in job loss in the North, and declining wage differentials under the Social Dimension do not enhance agglomeration [of industrial activities in the North] in spite of improvements in Southern infrastructure, remains an entirely open question" (Streeck 1991: 328). Thus, we want to emphasize that although the unions are united behind the Social Charter, this unity is based on a potential unstable balancing of competing interests.

Employers and governments are less united. Employers in high-wage countries, notably Germany, Belgium, and the Netherlands, are broadly supportive of the Social Charter because it seeks to prevent capital flight from high-wage to low-wage countries; the governments of those countries fear an erosion of their tax bases as a result of enhanced capital mobility, and they do not want other countries to have the competitive advantage of fewer regulations. In particular, Germany and Denmark are supportive of matters relating to increased worker consultation, information sharing, and participation at the strategic level, because their systems currently include such participative arrangements. Most of the other European countries have some reduced form of participation[4] and are in general support of consultation rights (Turner, 1991). Britain and Ireland, the two countries without any significant form of worker participation, see the introduction of these measures as likely to render the community, and their positions within it, less competitive.

The differential interests of the parties are also manifested in debates over other issues in the charter. For example, Britain argues that proposals to equalize the wage and service conditions of part-time workers with full-time workers would significantly increase British labor costs. Britain also opposes the proposals for employer financed health care and parental leave, as well as the proposal to equalize collective bargaining laws, all on the grounds that its competitive position will be weakened.

As a result of this variance in interests regarding the issues in the charter, the mechanisms by which decisions are taken are likely to vary. One indication of this variance in mechanisms came at the Maastricht summit on December 10–11, 1991, when the countries decided that laws on working conditions, information, and worker consultation would be taken by qualified majority voting (the larger countries have more votes than the smaller countries, and a majority is defined as fifty-six out of seventy-six votes), while laws on rights of workers who are terminated, social protection, and third-country nationals will have to be decided by unanimous vote. Issues of collective bargaining, strikes, and union recognition will be decided based on either subsidiarity (left to individual countries to devise ways to meet EC objectives), or will be left entirely within the purview of individual countries. Moreover, Britain has been given the freedom to "opt out" of the charter for the time being, with the option of "opting in" if they are willing to do so at a later date.

Thus, given that subsidiarity is the principle that is likely to be used for matters on which the parties do not reach agreement, and given the possibility that the idea of "opting out" could gain wider acceptance, it is likely that there will be persistent differences in labor standards across the EC countries that could impact their competitive positions. Furthermore, mandating the equalization of certain high-cost benefits (e.g., parental leave and employer funded health care), even if it were politically possible, would almost certainly still not equalize total compensation costs in the community, given the wide variance in wages and other employer payments in the EC today: in 1989, total hourly compensation costs in all of manufacturing ranged from $17.51 in Germany to $2.80 in Portugal, in US$ at current exchange rates.

However, if compensation costs alone determined international competitiveness, there would be very little industry in high-wage countries. As Mosley (1990) and Lange (1992) point out, high-wage countries are likely to have compensating advantages, such as a skilled workforce, better infrastructure, modern plant and equipment, and, perhaps, labor productivity that is high enough to offset the disadvantages of higher compensation costs. It is this issue this chapter seeks to address: What is the relationship between compensation costs and labor productivity and what does this relationship imply for the likelihood of social dumping? We proceed by calculating unit labor costs (or compensation costs per unit of output) in manufacturing in the twelve EC countries.

DATA

Compensation cost data were obtained from an unpublished source from the U.S. Department of Labor, Bureau of Labor Statistics (BLS), "Hourly Compensation Costs for Production Workers in Manufacturing, 33 Countries." The BLS defines hourly compensation as "(1) all payments made directly to the worker—pay for time worked (basic time and piece rates plus overtime premiums, shift differentials, other bonuses and premiums paid regularly each pay period, and cost-of-living adjustments), pay for time not worked (vacations, holidays, and other leave), all bonuses and other special payments, and the cost of payments in kind—before payroll deductions of any kind and (2) employer contributions to legally required insurance programs and contractual and private benefit plans. Hourly compensation costs do not include all items of labor costs: the costs of recruitment, employee training, and plant facilities and services—such as cafeterias and medical clinics—are not covered because data are not available for most countries. The labor costs not covered account for no more than 4 percent of total labor costs in any country for which the data are available."[5]

These data thus seem to be appropriate to the social dumping question, since they measure labor costs to the employer, not just hourly wages. And this distinction does matter: Table 2.1 gives the percentage differential in 1977 and 1985 between this measure of manufacturing hourly compensation and earnings per hour in manufacturing defined by the International Labour Office (ILO) as "cash payments received from employers, including remuneration for normal working hours; overtime pay; remuneration for time not worked; bonuses and gratuities; cost of living allow-

Table 2.1. Percentage Differential of Manufacturing Compensation Costs over Wages, 1977 and 1985

Country	1977	1985
Belgium	70.1	80.2
Denmark	6.9	13.7
France	64.0	78.9
Germany	63.8	73.6
Greece	56.3	60.9
Ireland	20.1	29.5
Italy	68.4	47.9
Luxembourg	39.3	43.1
Netherlands	66.4	78.3
Portugal	26.3	31.9
Spain	58.3	44.4
U.K.	15.5	20.2

Source: U.S. Bureau of Labor Statistics and International Labour Office, *Yearbook of Labor Statistics.*

ances and special premiums."[6] In 1985, this differential between earnings and total cost to the employer ranged from 13.7 percent in Denmark to 80.2 percent in Belgium; note as well that it rose in every country except Italy and Spain between 1977 and 1985.

Our output (or value added) data, used to calculate productivity and unit labor costs, are gross domestic product (GDP) at market prices from the national accounts of the various countries, as reported in the OECD (Organization for Economic Cooperation and Development) publication, *National Accounts 1977–1989, Detailed Tables Volume II*. We also use an alternative BLS measure of GDP for individual manufacturing industries in Germany and France.

Our data on number of employees are taken from the *National Accounts*, and in a few cases (noted in the tables) from the International Labour Office, *Yearbook of Labour Statistics*. The hours worked per week are from the International Labour Office *Yearbook*, and the weeks of vacation and holidays per year are from the European Trade Union Institute's *Collective Bargaining in Western Europe in 1989*.

The purchasing power parity exchange rates are from the publication *World Comparisons of Purchasing Power and Real Product for 1980*, from Phase IV of the United Nations World Comparisons Project. PPP exchange rates for all of GDP are also available from the *National Accounts*, and exchange rates were obtained from the *National Accounts* and the BLS.

Finally, we get some of our statistics, such as the index of real output per employee for all of the countries, and GDP in manufacturing for Spain, from the World Bank, *World Tables*; again, these cases are reported in the footnotes to the tables.

METHODS

Our primary goal here is to address the policy question of whether the economic incentive for social dumping within the EC was strong as the Community approached the single market; we do not propose any new methodologies for addressing the thorny and long-debated problem of how to measure productivity across countries. We choose to follow the basic methodology of one of the most recent attempts to tackle this issue—Hooper and Larin (1989), who calculate productivity and unit labor costs for ten countries including six of the wealthier EC countries—and we refer the reader to that paper for a full accounting of the methods.[7]

However, we would like to lay out the basic conceptual issue. "Labor Productivity," defined in this instance as GDP in manufacturing divided by total hours in manufacturing, must be converted to some kind of common currency to allow comparisons across countries. Market exchange rates, however, tend to introduce distortions. The United Nations has been working on this problem over the last few decades with its "International Comparison Project"; the result of this project has been the calculation of PPP exchange rates, which come closer to allowing a comparison of the "true value" of output across countries. PPP exchange rates are available through the late 1980s for total GDP, but, as Hooper and Larin point out, this total GDP PPP may not be appropriate for manufacturing alone: it is better to weight individual output category PPPs used in manufacturing by their expenditure weights.[8] Following Hooper and Larin, we use the expenditure weights in the following sectors to calculate our expenditure-weighted PPPs: Food, Beverages, and Tobacco; Clothing and Footwear; Fuel and Power; House Furnishings; Pharmaceutical-Therapeutical Health Care; Transport/Communications; Recreation Equipment; and Consumer Durables. The measure thus derived is still far from perfect, but gets us closer to a "true" PPP for manufacturing alone.

Table 2.2 presents labor productivity estimates for 1980 using the three types of conversion factors (market exchange rates, GDP PPPs, and expenditure-weighted PPPs). The table shows that there are reasonably large differences, particularly between the measures based on market exchange rates and PPPs. The expenditure weighting also seems to make a difference, particularly in Portugal, Italy, Greece, and Ireland, perhaps reflecting differential balances of manufacturing in total GDP. We choose this expenditure-weighted PPP as our conversion factor of choice, although it imposes one major data limitation: the expenditure weights are only available for 1980. We will calculate unit labor costs for 1980 and then examine growth rates of hourly compensation and productivity over the period of the 1980s.[9]

The other component which goes into the measurement of unit labor costs, hourly compensation, can be more precisely measured and can, in contrast, be meaningfully converted using market exchange rates, because this is a cost concept rather than an output concept. In sum, we calculate unit labor costs (ULC) by converting compensation costs into common currency at market exchange rates (the labor cost to foreign investors of investing in the country) and dividing by manufacturing value added converted at expenditure-weighted purchasing power exchange rates (the value of the output that the labor will produce). ULC can then be interpreted as the labor cost per unit of output, or labor costs controlling for labor productivity.

RESULTS

The first column of Table 2.3 reports average manufacturing hourly compensation levels *in dollars* at market exchange rates in the twelve countries in 1980 and the ranking of those countries in terms of this measure. In 1980, the five countries with the least expensive compensation costs, in ascending order of cost, were Portugal, Greece, Ireland, Spain, and the United Kingdom; Germany, Denmark, and the BeNeLux countries had the highest compensation costs.

But, obviously, hourly compensation alone is not the whole story; ideally, one wants to control for productivity as well: if the lower hourly compensation costs in the poorer countries reflect productivities which are lower in equal proportion, then the economic incentive for social dumping is not present. To address this issue, we calculate rough measures of unit labor costs, as described in our methods section.

The second column of Table 2.3 presents our measures of manufacturing labor productivity (output per hour in dollars at expenditure-weighted PPP exchange rates: the final column of Table 2.2), while the final column of Table 2.3 presents our estimates of ULCs and the ranking of the countries according to this measure.[10]

Note that the ranking of the countries in terms of hourly compensation does not precisely coincide with the ranking in terms of unit labor costs: for example, Belgium has the highest hourly compensation but only the sixth highest ULC due to high labor productivity, whereas the United Kingdom has the eighth highest hourly compen-

Table 2.2. Output per Hour in Manufacturing, 1980

Country	Output/hour US$, market exchange rates	Output/hour US$, PPP exchange rates	Output/hour US$, expenditure–weighted PPP
Belgium	22.94	15.49	15.94
Denmark	16.65	10.80	9.96
France	17.36	12.23	11.46
Germany	16.65	11.13	11.00
Greece	7.88	8.57	6.33
Ireland[a]	8.35	7.35	6.07
Italy	14.23	14.14	11.85
Luxembourg	17.30	12.49	12.20
Netherlands	17.05	12.28	12.19
Portugal	4.78	7.58	5.05
Spain	11.59	11.66	11.12
U.K.	9.64	7.94	6.65

Sources: GDP in manufacturing and number of employees from OECD, *National Accounts, Main Aggregates* (except for Spain: GDP from World Bank, *World Tables*); hours per week in manufacturing from International Labour Office, *Yearbook of Labour Statistics*; vacation and holiday weeks per year from European Trade Union Institute.
[a]Ireland 1979.

Table 2.3. Hourly Compensation and Unit Labor Costs in Manufacturing, 1980

Country	Mfg compensation level 1980, current US$ $US	Rank	Output/hour US$, exp.–weighted PPP	Unit labor costs US$, expenditure—weighted PPP $US	Rank
Belgium	13.11	1	15.94	82.25	6
Denmark	10.95	5	9.96	109.94	3
France	8.94	6	11.46	78.01	8
Germany	12.33	2	11.00	112.09	1
Greece	3.73	11	6.33	58.93	10
Ireland[a]	4.81	10	6.07	79.24	7
Italy	8.00	7	11.85	67.51	9
Luxembourg	11.98	4	12.20	98.20	5
Netherlands	12.06	3	12.19	98.93	4
Portugal	2.06	12	5.05	40.79	12
Spain	5.96	9	11.12	53.60	11
UK	7.43	8	6.65	111.73	2

Sources: GDP in manufacturing and number of employees from OECD, *National Accounts, Main Aggregates* (except for Spain: GDP from World Bank, *World Tables*); hours per week in manufacturing from International Labour Office, *Yearbook of Labour Statistics*; vacation and holiday weeks per year from European Trade Union Institute; hourly compensation from U.S. Bureau of Labor Statistics.
[a]Ireland 1979. The estimates of unit labor costs by Hooper and Larin (1989) for the countries that overlap are: Belgium, 97; France, 76.4; Germany, 101.1; Italy, 59; Netherlands, 87; and U.K., 107.4.

sation but the second highest ULC due to low labor productivity, as measured here. It is clear, then, that average labor productivity is not directly proportional to compensation.

In terms of the comparative magnitudes of the ULCs, the main finding from this table is that labor productivity was slightly more than twice as high in Germany as in Portugal in 1980, while hourly compensation costs were closer to six times higher, yielding unit labor costs 2.5 times higher in Germany than in Portugal. The Greek and Spanish ULCs are also low (about one-half of the German ULC).[11]

We do not want to take these exact figures as something written in stone, but lacking a systematic bias leading to gross overestimation of labor productivity in Portugal, Greece, and Spain compared to Germany, it does look as though unit labor costs are much lower in those countries than in Germany. In fact, if anything we would expect the bias to go in the opposite direction: marginal labor productivity (or perhaps even "potential productivity") should be underestimated by average productivity in less-developed countries compared to more-developed countries, given the larger and more advanced capital stocks in the wealthier countries.

It is possible that the differences in overall manufacturing ULCs reflect differential industrial mixes across these countries: perhaps an advantage in overall manufacturing ULC does not hold in all industries. We do not have detailed industrial output for the twelve countries, but we do have it for France and Germany. Table 2.4 presents hourly compensation costs, labor productivity, and unit labor costs in total manufacturing and fourteen manufacturing sub-industries in 1980 for these two countries. The third and fourth columns indicate that labor productivity is generally higher

Table 2.4. Hourly Compensation, Productivity, and Unit Labor Costs in Manufacturing Industries, France(FR) and Germany(GE), 1980

Industry	Compensation		Productivity		Unit labor costs	
	FR	GE	FR	GE	FR	GE
All manufacturing	8.94	12.33	12.57	11.85	71.10	104.07
Food, beverages, tobacco	8.98	10.62	16.42	13.69	54.70	77.60
Textiles and apparel	6.84	9.96	8.17	7.75	83.71	116.88
Paper	9.91	11.41	12.03	10.50	82.37	108.62
Printing and publishing	10.32	13.17	12.86	10.50	80.25	125.47
Chemicals	10.63	13.56	15.89	14.60	66.91	92.89
Rubber and plastics	8.64	11.29	9.96	10.72	86.78	105.35
Leather and leather products	7.16	8.83	8.12	8.16	88.14	108.19
Stone, clay and glass	9.72	11.73	13.57	11.65	71.62	100.66
Primary metals	10.24	13.68	13.09	10.84	78.21	126.21
Fabricated metal products	8.76	11.81	10.69	10.48	81.94	112.73
Machinery and instruments	8.88	11.93	11.79	11.05	75.29	108.00
Electrical machinery	8.82	11.73	12.14	11.30	72.67	103.83
Transportation equipment	10.16	15.27	10.17	12.22	99.88	124.99
Lumber, wood and furniture	7.67	11.52	9.88	8.94	77.61	128.90

Source: U.S. Bureau of Labor Statistics.

in France than in Germany, though this is not true in three of the industries: Rubber and Plastics, Leather and Leather Products, and Transportation Equipment. However, columns one and two and five and six indicate that hourly compensation and unit labor costs are higher in Germany in all of the industries. We do not want to push this too far: France and Germany are probably a lot more similar as economies than, say, Germany and Portugal. On the other hand, if the ULC ranking for total manufacturing is the same for all industries in these two countries where hourly compensation costs are relatively close together, we would be surprised if ULCs were higher in Portugal, Greece, or Spain than in Germany in many industries.[12]

In sum, our analysis of levels of manufacturing unit labor costs in 1980 indicates that the dramatic compensation differential across the countries is *not* entirely offset by labor productivity differentials.

ARE MANUFACTURING COMPENSATION COSTS CONVERGING?

Now that we have some sense of where ULCs were in 1980, our goal in this section and the next is to examine movements of hourly compensation and productivities over the 1980s to get a sense of whether the components of ULC have been converging.

First, we examine the question of whether hourly compensation costs in manufacturing across the twelve countries are converging, which tells us about movements in the numerator of the ULC formula, but is also interesting in itself.[13] Table 2.5 shows annual growth rates of real manufacturing compensation costs over the 1980s in the twelve countries at common currency and prices in German deutsche marks (DM). Note that from the perspective of the German investor, the growth rate of compensation costs at German prices and market exchange rates is relevant to the question of whether he should invest; for the social dumping question, we must focus on the perspective of the German investor (or, from the perspective of any outside investor; we choose Germany for obvious reasons).

At first blush, the table does seem to indicate some degree of convergence: if we divide the twelve countries into quartiles based on their hourly compensation costs in 1980 (see the ranking in Table 2.3), we find that the average growth rate of hourly compensation in the top quartile was 0.45, in the second quartile 0.54, in the third quartile 2.67, and in the fourth quartile 2.18.[14] Yet, when the overall level of dispersion of compensation in the community is considered, there is no evidence of convergence. Specifically, Figures 2.1 and 2.2 show the variance of log manufacturing compensation costs across the twelve countries, at current exchange rates, over the period 1975–1988.[15] Figure 2.1 indicates that this measure of the dispersion of compensation costs within the community rose from 1977–1979, fell precipitously until 1982, and has risen overall since then to a level in 1988 above the level in 1975. In 1988, the value of this measure was essentially the same as in 1980 (.56 in 1980, .55 in 1988). Figure 2.2 excludes Portugal, which is somewhat of an "outlier," from the analysis. Again, there is a big drop in the early 1980s but an overall rise since 1982, so that the dispersion of compensation levels across these eleven community countries was around the 1980–1981 level in 1988. These figures do *not* strongly

Table 2.5. Growth Rate of Real
Manufacturing Hourly Compensation in EC,
1980–1989

Country	Annualized real comp growth 1980–89, real DM, current exchange rates
Belgium	−0.66
Denmark	1.34
France	1.56
Germany	1.65
Greece	2.13
Ireland	3.30
Italy	3.79
Luxembourg[a]	−1.27
Netherlands	0.36
Portugal	1.11
Spain	2.72
U.K.	1.50

Sources: Hourly compensation from U.S. Bureau of Labor
Statistics; price indexes and exchange rates from OECD, *National Accounts, Main Aggregates Vol.1 1960–1989.*
[a]Luxembourg 1988.

indicate convergence; if anything, they seem to indicate divergence in the later 1980s.[16]

TRENDS IN PRODUCTIVITY AND UNIT LABOR COSTS

Now consider Table 2.6, which shows the growth rate of manufacturing productivity in terms of output per employee over the 1980s in the twelve countries; in conjunction with the estimates of levels of unit labor costs in Table 2.3 and the analysis of growth rates of compensation costs in Figures 2.1 and 2.2 and Table 2.5, this should give us some sense as to whether unit labor costs converged during the 1980s.

Table 2.6 indicates that productivity growth (measured in terms of real output per employee) from 1980 to 1987 was three times higher in Portugal and Spain than in Germany, and also somewhat higher in Greece. This seems to indicate (in conjunction with the compensation growth rates reported in Table 2.5) that from the perspective of a German investor, unit labor costs *are not* significantly converging. Note in particular from Table 2.5 that the growth rate of hourly compensation in German currency over the period 1980–1989 was actually less for Portugal than Germany and higher, but not dramatically higher, than the output-per-employee growth rate differential, in Greece and Spain than in Germany. As for the other high-cost coun-

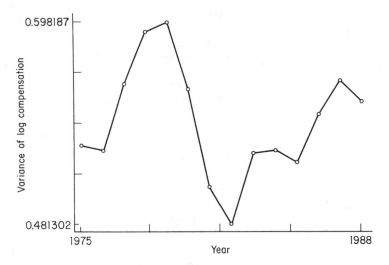

Figure 2.1. Compensation variance across EC countries.

tries, convergence of ULCs looks most credible in the BeNeLux countries (because of low compensation cost growth) and in the United Kingdom (because of high productivity growth), but not in Denmark. In sum, it does not look as though the wealthy and poor countries (or at least Germany and Denmark compared to Spain and Portugal) are significantly converging in terms of ULCs.

Even if our measures of productivity growth are suspect (given that, due to data limitations, we are measuring the growth of output per employee rather than output per hour), keep in mind that the hourly compensation growth rate numbers are more consistent, and that we may be able to draw inferences about the growth of ULCs

Figure 2.2. Compensation variance excluding Portugal.

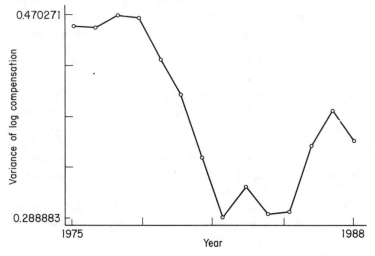

Table 2.6. Growth Rate of Manufacturing
Productivity in EC in 1980s

Country	Annualized growth of real output/ employee 1980–1987
Belgium	4.01
Denmark	0.22
France	2.57
Germany	1.07
Greece	1.21
Ireland	——
Italy	4.96
Luxembourg	2.96
Netherlands	4.60
Portugal	4.09
Spain	3.36
U.K.	5.54

Source: Output/employee index from World Bank, *World Tables.*

from those numbers alone. That is, if one expects that convergence of productivity is occurring in the classical sense (less developed countries catching up with more developed),[17] then the fact that hourly compensation is not growing much faster in the less developed countries (particularly Portugal and Greece) would indicate that ULCs may be growing farther apart.

INDUSTRY COMPENSATION STRUCTURES

We now address the question of the degree of variation in manufacturing compensation costs within the twelve countries in recent years. This issue is important because it gives us a further sense of whether the economies are moving in the same direction (and so might smoothly integrate into one economy), and also because it provides clues about whether social dumping is likely to occur evenly across manufacturing sub-sectors.

Table 2.7 presents indexes for 1980 and 1989 (1975 = 100) and levels for 1989 of the dispersion of compensation costs, as measured by the standard deviation of log hourly compensation multiplied by 100, across sixteen manufacturing industries in eleven of the countries, excluding Luxembourg. This measure has been computed previously for different mixes of countries and industries by Krueger and Summers (1987), who interpreted it as an indicator of development,[18] and Freeman (1988), who interpreted it as an indicator of labor market structure.

We do not directly address these interpretations, but instead ask how these structures have evolved over the period 1975–1989 and what effect this may have for cross-country investment and adjustment to the single market. In all of the countries except France, Italy, the Netherlands, and the United Kingdom, this measure increased be-

Table 2.7. Dispersion of Manufacturing Industry Hourly Compensation within EC Countries, 1980 and 1989[a]

Country[b]	1980 (index 1975 = 100)	1989 (index 1975 = 100)	1989 level
Belgium	106.6	106.1	16.85
Denmark	115.6	97.0	10.51
France	94.0	91.3	13.72
Germany	101.9	112.2	16.05
Greece	123.1	92.2	16.52
Ireland	102.5	111.5	21.07
Italy	73.6	77.0	12.47
Luxembourg	—	—	—
Netherlands	92.2	106.8	13.62
Portugal	102.8	116.2	26.96
Spain	111.6	102.8	17.18
U.K.	94.7	115.0	18.61

Source: U.S. Bureau of Labor Statistics.
[a]Dispersion = the standard deviation of logarithm of hourly compensation, 16 manufacturing industries, multiplied by 100.
[b]Netherlands 1975–87, Portugal 1975–87, Spain 1977–88; 14 industries in Greece, Netherlands, and Spain.

tween 1975 and 1980, but it increased between 1980 and 1989 in only six of the countries: Germany, Ireland, Italy, the Netherlands, Portugal, and the United Kingdom, while falling in the other five.[19] The industry dispersion was higher in 1989 than in 1975 in seven of the eleven countries. As for levels of dispersion in 1989, Portugal, Ireland, the United Kingdom, and Spain had the highest levels of industry compensation inequality, while Denmark, Italy, the Netherlands, and France had the lowest.

This all suggests that these countries were not "moving in the same direction," nor were they converging along this dimension of intra-country manufacturing compensation cost structure as they approached 1992 and the single market; for example, the industry compensation dispersion was "high and rising" in Portugal but "low and falling" in Denmark. This raises doubts about how smooth the transition is likely to be. The lessons for the question of social dumping? First, these results suggest that the labor-cost incentive for investment is uneven across industries: for example, Portuguese hourly compensation in 1987 in lumber, wood products, and furniture was 11.7 percent of German costs, while the ratio in electric and electronic equipment was 22.2 percent. Second, the fact that the degree of dispersion is growing at unequal rates and in different directions across the countries suggests that these differential incentives (at the industry level), masked in the analysis of overall manufacturing ULCs, may be shifting over time.

Taken together, this analysis of the compensation and productivity structures of the EC countries suggests a few basic conclusions. First, productivity differences do not appear to account for all of the big compensation differentials between the richer and poorer EC countries; the economic incentive for moving production to lower-cost countries does seem to be present at this aggregate level of analysis. Second, in terms of ULCs and dispersion of compensation costs, the countries are not "converging." Finally, compensation dispersion tends to be higher in some of the less developed countries, suggesting that the incentive for social dumping may well exist differentially across industries.

EVIDENCE ON FOREIGN DIRECT INVESTMENT IN THE EC

The question at hand is whether, with the removal of most barriers to trade within the EC, producers in high-cost countries will move their operations to low-cost regions. Of course, we do not have any direct evidence on what will happen once the barriers are removed, but we do have evidence on foreign direct investment in the EC countries in the 1980s. While these figures are revealing, it is important to keep in mind at least three caveats: (1) investment before 1992 reflects whatever was happening because of (or in spite of) existing barriers that were removed for intra-EC transactions after 1992, (2) considerable uncertainty exists over the state of the Social Charter and so the cost of investing in the poorer countries, and (3) non-European countries may have been investing heavily in certain EC countries in order to gain a foothold before 1992.

Table 2.8 shows the share of average annual foreign direct investment inflows in gross domestic capital formation for the twelve EC countries in 1980–82 and

Table 2.8. Foreign Direct Investment in the EC

Country	Share of annual foreign-direct-investment inflows in gross domestic capital formation (percentage)		Overall growth rate of U.S. direct investment from
	1980–82	1985–87	1984 to 1989
Belgium[a]	7.6	6.6	50.3
Denmark	1.1	0.8	52.4
France	1.8	2.7	119.5
Germany	0.3	0.6	58.8
Greece	6.3	7.4	65.2
Ireland	4.4	1.8	108.9
Italy	0.8	1.3	154.0
Luxembourg	7.6	6.6	125.3
Netherlands	5.8	8.4	116.4
Portugal	2.1	4.1	150.6
Spain	4.1	7.3	106.9
U.K.	8.2	8.8	90.1

Sources: Share of inflows in capital formation from United Nations, *World Investment Report 1991: The Triad in Foreign Direct Investment,* Table 2, p. 7; growth of U.S. direct investment from U.S. Dept. of Commerce, *Survey of Current Business,* various issues.
[a]Belgium and Luxembourg are combined in the first two columns.

1985–87 (columns one and two), as well as the growth rate of U.S. foreign direct investment in each of the twelve countries over the period 1984–89 (column 3). Note from the first two columns that foreign direct investment as a percentage of gross domestic capital formation rose from the earlier period to the later period in all the countries but Belgium-Luxembourg, Denmark, and Ireland. This share was highest in 1985–87 in the United Kingdom, the Netherlands, Greece, and Spain, and nearly doubled from 1980–82 to 1985–87 in Portugal, Spain, and Italy, three of the countries to which "social dumping" might be expected to occur (it also doubled in Germany, but starting from a much lower level). U.S. direct investment grew by more than 150 percent in Italy and Portugal, but also more than doubled in Luxembourg, France, the Netherlands, Ireland, and Spain. As for the comparative magnitude of U.S. investments in these countries, by 1989 U.S. companies had 28 percent of their EC foreign direct investment in the United Kingdom, 21 percent in Germany, 13 percent in France, and 10 percent in Italy, but only 4 percent in Spain, 0.3 percent in Portugal, and 0.2 percent in Greece.

These numbers probably raise as many questions as they answer, most of them beyond the scope of this chapter. For example, a thorough analysis of these growth rates of foreign direct investment over the course of the 1980s would require a model of the initial levels and why the shares are shifting. However, for our purposes, we note that foreign direct investment has been growing fastest in some of the poorer countries; this is consistent with fears regarding social dumping and with the proposition that ULCs are not converging: if they were converging, we would not expect to see such growth in investment in the poorer countries, but probably the opposite. On the other hand, we also note that these investment flows to the poorer countries are not massively larger than the flows to the wealthier countries.

CONCLUSIONS

We have analyzed data on ULC levels in 1980 and growth rates of compensation costs and productivity since then, concluding that there is a gap in unit labor costs within the EC that is not narrowing significantly. Analysis of the manufacturing industry compensation structures indicates that the countries are not all moving in the same direction in terms of this measure of internal equality, and also suggests that social dumping may occur unevenly across sectors within manufacturing. Existing patterns of investment in the EC are consistent with the view that ULCs are not converging and that the incentive for social dumping is present.

One major question this analysis raises is why we have not yet seen massive foreign investment in the poorer countries, given the dramatic differences in labor costs. One possibility, discussed in the previous section, is that the level of uncertainty regarding the final terms of the Social Charter is sufficiently high to induce investors to wait until the issues are settled. Another possibility is that the producers in the high-cost countries prefer to use the threat of social dumping as a bargaining chip with the unions in their home countries, rather than actually moving production. A third possibility is suggested by Streeck (1991), who discusses the transformation of the German economy toward a high-wage, high-skill, and high-value-added production system where employers abandon the low-wage, low-quality model; under this type of system, employers in the high-wage countries might not consider labor costs as an important component of their competitiveness. A fourth possibility is that investors interested in pursuing the low-wage, low-skill approach may choose to locate production facilities in low-cost areas outside the EC such as Eastern Europe and Southeast Asia.

Finally, even if employers in the wealthier countries are interested in pursuing low-wage, low-skill mass production in the poorer countries, we do not claim to have adequately addressed the question of whether the level of development in the poorer countries, ranging from infrastructure and communications to education, is high enough to allow for any significant amount of foreign direct investment— whether these countries have the capacity to increase their productivity dramatically. For example, in 1981 the illiteracy rate among those fifteen years and older was 7.1 percent in Spain, 9.5 percent in Greece, and 20.6 percent in Portugal.[20] We conclude by acknowledging that, although our analysis suggests that the unit labor cost incentive for social dumping is present, these illiteracy levels suggest that the level of development in the poorer countries may be low enough so as to dictate the nature of the foreign direct investment which actually occurs, at least until the Community's regional aid program begins to have a substantial effect. Future research may wish to examine these issues in more detail.

NOTES

We thank the U.S. Bureau of Labor Statistics for providing unpublished compensation data. Financial support was provided by the UCLA Institute of Industrial Relations. We thank Paul Ong, who served as discussant for this paper at the original UCLA conference. In addition, we benefited from advice and comments on earlier drafts of this paper by C. Keith Head, Daniel J. B. Mitchell, Deborah Swenson, and Lowell Turner.

1. For a recent journalistic discussion of the issues, see Balls (1991).

2. The term "social dumping" is also sometimes used to refer to the movement of workers from low-wage countries to high-wage countries. For example, Streeck (1991) discusses the possibility of immigration of unskilled workers to Germany with the elimination of barriers to the free movement of people within the EC. Flanagan (1992) finds that EC migration has failed to respond to specific instances of reduction of legal barriers to migration since the 1957 Treaty of Rome, but also finds that the wage incentive for out-migration from the poorer countries is higher now than at any point since the Treaty.

3. See Addison and Siebert (1991), Silvia (1991), and Turner (1991) for a detailed account of this debate.

4. Ten out of the twelve countries have some form of works councils, for example.

5. U.S. Bureau of Labor Statistics, Appendix.

6. International Labour Office, *Yearbook of Labour Statistics*.

7. We also refer the reader to that paper's technical references. Two more recent technical contributions are Turvey (1990), which discusses the measurement of labor productivity, and Summers and Heston (1988), which discusses recent developments in the World Comparisons Project.

8. Of course, output weights would be even better than expenditure weights, but they are not available.

9. Even for this year, we want to emphasize that this is a crude approach to measuring levels of labor productivity and unit labor costs. It is important to keep in mind that we are measuring average, rather than marginal, labor productivity here; ideally, given the right data, we would want to take into account the size and quality of the capital stock as well.

10. Hooper and Larin (1989) used BLS GDP data which are not available for the other six EC countries; we use *National Accounts* estimates for all twelve, which differ somewhat from the BLS estimates. This explains the deviations from the Hooper and Larin estimates reported in the note to the table. Note, however, that deviations of our estimates from the Hooper and Larin estimates are all within 18 percent.

11. These differences are less dramatic when GDP is converted at market exchange rates rather than expenditure-weighted PPPs: the German ULC is 1.7 times the Portuguese ULC, 1.6 times the Greek ULC, and 1.4 times the Spanish ULC. Yet, note that there is still a substantial gap—for example, using this measure and conversion factor, labor's share of value added is about 74 percent in Germany, but only 43 percent in Portugal.

12. We acknowledge the potential importance of market exchange rate fluctuations in determining the compensation differences, however.

13. Leamer (1991) uses a different data set to examine convergence of industrial wages in the EC, among other groups of world countries. He concludes that "A considerable amount of wage equalization occurred between 1978 and 1989 (within the EC)" (p. 9). In contrast, Flanagan (1992), who examines some of the same data we do in his study of wage convergence among the original EC-6 and EC-9, finds that "the dispersion of labor costs and wages eventually falls dramatically in the late 1970s, only to rise again in the last half of the 1980s. By the end of the period (1989), the dispersion of hourly labor costs in manufacturing among the original EC-6 is only slightly below dispersion in 1960. The same is true of data for the EC-9" (p. 12).

14. Note, however, that if the BeNeLux countries are excluded, the average growth rate of the other three countries in the top two quartiles, Germany, Denmark, and France, is 1.52.

15. Flanagan (1992) presents similar graphs for the original EC-6 and EC-9 countries. Keep in mind that Greece entered the community in 1981 and Spain and Portugal in 1986.

16. In a related study, Mitchell (1983) found convergence of European wages with American wages through 1980, but not over the first few years of the 1980s. He attributed this finding to dollar appreciation.

17. For a recent test of this convergence hypothesis, which finds convergence among the world's most industrialized countries as well as countries with above-average literacy rates, see Zagardo (1991).

18. Krueger and Summers (1987: 27) note that "in general, developed capitalist countries tend to have greater dispersion in wages across industries than underdeveloped, socialist or communist countries. This may reflect the greater level of human capital attainment in the more developed capitalist countries."

19. The fact that within-country inequality, as measured by industry compensation dispersion, increased in only six of the eleven countries between 1980 and 1989 is interesting in itself, given the consensus in the literature that wage inequality is increasing, or labor market structure is decreasing, throughout the advanced capitalist world.

20. United Nations, *Statistical Yearbook;* 1981 is the last year for which this measure is available.

REFERENCES

Addison, John, and W. Stanley Siebert. 1991. "The Social Charter of the European Community: Evolution and Controversies." *Industrial and Labor Relations Review* 44 (July): 597–625.

Balls, Edward. 1991. "A More Level European Playing Field for Labour Costs." *Financial Times,* November 11, p. 6.

European Trade Union Institute. 1989. *Collective Bargaining in Western Europe in 1989.*

Flanagan, Robert J. 1992. "European Wage Equalization since the Treaty of Rome." March revision of paper presented at the conference "Labor Responses to European Unification in Western Europe," University of California, Berkeley, April 26–27, 1991.

Freeman, Richard. 1988. "Labour Markets." *Economic Policy* (April): 63–80.

Hooper, Peter, and Kathryn A. Larin. 1989. "International Comparisons of Labor Costs in Manufacturing." *Review of Income and Wealth,* Series 35, no. 4 (December): 335–55.

International Labour Office. Various years. *Yearbook of Labour Statistics* (Geneva: International Labour Office).

Krueger, Alan B., and Lawrence H. Summers. 1987. "Reflections on the Inter-Industry Wage Structure." In Kevin Lang and Jonathan Leonard, eds., *Unemployment and the Structure of Labor Markets* (New York: Basil Blackwell).

Lange, Peter. Forthcoming. "The Politics of the

Social Dimension: Interests, Rules, States and Redistribution in the 1992 Process." In Alberta Sbragia, ed., *Europolitics* (Washington, D.C.: Brookings Institution).

Leamer, Edward. 1991. "Wage Effects of a U.S.-Mexican Free Trade Agreement." UCLA Anderson Graduate School of Management, mimeo, p. October.

Mitchell, Daniel J. B. 1983. "International Convergence with U.S. Wage Levels." *Proceedings of the 36th Annual IRRA Meeting.*

Mosley, Hugh. 1990. "The Social Dimension of European Integration." *International Labour Review* 129 (2).

Organization for Economic Cooperation and Development, *National Accounts 1977–1989,* Volumes I and II.

Silvia, Stephen. 1991. "The Social Charter of the European Community: A Defeat for European Labor." *Industrial and Labor Relations Review* 44 (July): 626–43.

Streeck, Wolfgang. 1991. "More Uncertainties: German Unions Facing 1992." *Industrial Relations* 30 (Fall): 317–49.

Summers, Robert, and Alan Heston. 1988. "A New Set of International Comparisons of Real Product and Price Levels Estimates for 130 Countries, 1950–1985." *Review of Income and Wealth,* Series 34, No. 1 (March): 335–55.

Turner, Lowell. 1991. "The Single Market and the

Social Europe Debate." Paper presented at the conference "Labor Responses to European Unification in Western Europe," University of California, Berkeley, April 26–27.

Turvey, Ralph. 1990. "Labour Productivity." In Ralph Turvey, ed. *Developments in International Labour Statistics* (London: Pinter Publishers for ILO).

United Nations. 1991 *World Investment Report 1991: The Triad in Foreign Direct Investment* (New York: United Nations).

United Nations. 1987. *World Comparisons of Pur-* *chasing Power and Real Product for 1980* (New York: United Nations).

U.S. Department of Commerce. 1986, 1990. *Survey of Current Business* (June).

U.S. Bureau of Labor Statistics. "International Comparisons of Hourly Compensation Costs for Workers in Manufacturing."

World Bank. Various years. *World Tables*.

Zagardo, Janice Turtora. 1991. "Worldwide Convergence of Productivity Levels: Recent Empirical Evidence." *Business Economics* (October): 19–25.

3

Employee Benefits in Europe and the United States

DANIEL J. B. MITCHELL

Countries face choices in establishing national systems of employee social insurance and employee benefits. They may rely heavily on private employers to provide for such needs as retirement income and health insurance. They may rely almost entirely on government to meet these needs. Or they may utilize a mix of both approaches. The choice that countries make about these matters ideally should reflect labor-market pressures and the employment relationship.

Industrialized countries generally have made basic decisions about social insurance and benefits a long time ago. They are, in a sense, stuck with approaches designed in the past which may or may not accord with modern labor-market conditions. But sometimes events occur which allow reexamination of social insurance and benefit approaches. In particular, the countries which form the European Community (EC) are now wrestling with social issues including the role of social insurance and private employee benefit plans.

BACKGROUND ON THE EUROPEAN COMMUNITY

The EC had its roots in post-World War II notions of forming a "United States of Europe" whose members would behave more cooperatively and peacefully than had been the norm through the two World Wars. Initially, limited institutions of economic cooperation were created. These arrangements led to the Treaty of Rome in the late 1950s, which established the European Economic Community, a common market originally composed of France, West Germany, Italy, the Netherlands, Belgium, and Luxembourg.

In the 1980s, the EC moved to develop its political and economic institutions. It now has a legislative branch (Parliament), a judicial branch (Court), and an executive branch (Council, Council of Ministers, and Commission). Under the Single European Act of 1986, the EC has moved toward tighter economic integration with uniform regulations and goals under the heading "Europe 1992." Further ahead is a monetary union, perhaps with a single currency, or at least more tightly fixed exchange rates among the member nations.

A PORTRAIT OF EUROPE 1992

At present, the EC consists of twelve countries. In the future others may join or affiliate including some of the former communist-bloc nations. The gains from greater economic integration under Europe 1992 have been estimated at about 5 percent of the combined gross domestic product (GDP) of the EC countries. Even now, the EC has a population about 30 percent larger than the United States. The size of the EC and its possible long-term destiny as a United States of Europe make comparisons with the United States in regard to social insurance and employee benefits logical.

Within the EC are countries with a wide range of living standards. Measured by pay levels, for example, the lowest wage state (Portugal) has manufacturing wage rates only about one fifth as high as the highest wage state (Germany) (Figure 3.1a). This range is not out of line, it might be noted, with that found among the developing and developed countries of the Pacific Basin (Figure 3.1b) Thus, the issues in the benefits and social insurance area being faced in Europe may well apply to many countries outside the EC.

SOCIAL EUROPE

Various influences have played a role in developing a model for "Social Europe." First, as part of the 1992 integration process, there will inevitably be more economic competition among the EC member states. Fears have been expressed that such competition could lead to "social dumping," a phrase which suggests that the standards of the least developed countries within the EC would be forced upon the highly developed. To head off such a possibility, the various EC political institutions have been formulating common standards—including standards affecting social insurance and employee benefits—which would apply to all states.

Second, European countries—unlike the United States—have traditions of corporatism, i.e., formal participation of interest groups in the making of economic and social policy. Generally, for policies relating to the labor market, the social partners are identified as organized labor (unions) and organized management. As Social Europe develops, these interests are playing a role in formulating new EC-wide labor market standards.

Third, again in comparison with the United States, European countries have long traditions of substantial government regulation and intervention in the marketplace (including government-owned commercial enterprises). The result is that private employee benefits are seen as extensions of social policy. A clear line is not necessarily drawn with the EC between private policy and social policy.

Fourth, the EC Commission has developed a major bureaucracy in Brussels which formulates and researches policy options. With regard to social insurance and

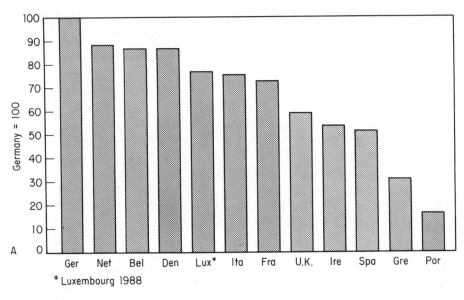

A

*Luxembourg 1988

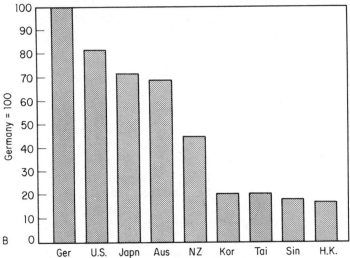

B

Figure 3.1. Hourly compensation in manufacturing, 1989, in EC countries (A) and Pacific Basin countries (B). *Source:* U.S. Bureau of Labor Statistics, *Supplementary Tables for BLS Report 794,* October 1990, Table 2.

employee benefits, Directorate-General V plays the key role in proposing labor standards. However, private employee benefit plans, especially pension funds, have the potential of being major financial institutions. Thus, the financial Directorate-General (XV) has begun to take a role.

EUROPE 1992 AND EMPLOYEE BENEFITS

What will the economic integration of Europe 1992 mean for employee benefits? To answer that question, it is important to look at the economy as a whole. Generally, Europe 1992 will mean more product market competition and restructuring of industry. The key symptom of these developing pressures is the continued call in Europe for labor market "flexibility." On the pay side, this could mean less rigid pay determination, perhaps with arrangements such as profit sharing to adjust pay levels up or down as product market trends dictate. On the employment side, there could well be more pressures for labor mobility, both voluntary and involuntary (i.e., layoffs). How well do existing social insurance and employee benefit arrangements fit in with this more fluid (and more risky) labor market?

There are parallels between these projected developments in Europe and pressures on the employment relationship which occurred in the United States during the 1980s (and which are still continuing). Due to deregulation, exchange rate shifts and international competition, corporate restructuring (mergers, spinoffs, acquisitions), and changing technology, the American employment relationship was destabilized. In particular, existing American benefit systems came under pressure because they were designed with a stable and secure workforce in mind. Thus, the question just posed can be expanded: How do EC and U.S. benefits and social insurance stack up in relative terms when placed under common labor market pressures?

Of course, there are substantial variations in social insurance and employee benefit practices between EC countries. One feature of Europe 1992 could be more immigration within the member countries. Were immigration to increase, there could be pressure to "harmonize" social security and employee benefit systems so that workers who move across international frontiers do not forfeit benefit entitlements.

A FOUR-COUNTRY COMPARISON

"Harmonization" is a loose concept. But once one examines the diversity among EC member countries, it becomes apparent that uniformity of social insurance and benefits will not be possible in the foreseeable future. In France, for example, retirement is covered almost entirely by "national" arrangements (public social security combined with quasi-private funds which cover all employers). Health insurance is also provided on a national basis. That is, in France, retirement and health insurance are not really an enterprise-level concern.

In Germany, retirement benefits are provided by a combination of a national program and enterprise-level pension plans. But health insurance is mainly provided under a nationally coordinated system. That is, retirement is often an enterprise-level concern, but health care is not.

Britain relies for retirement income provision on a basic national social security system and a second tier national system from which individual employers can contract out and set up their own private pensions, and personal pensions. The latter are arrangements whereby individual workers can contract out of either the national second tier plan or their employer's substitute plan and set up a private personal saving arrangement of their own. But on the health side, Britain relies largely on its national system of socialized medicine.

These three European systems can be compared, in turn, with the American approach, which is heavily linked to enterprise-level systems of pensions and health insurance. Like Britain, the United States has a mix of social security, private pensions, and personal pensions (individual retirement accounts). But on the health side, the United States has no national system for persons under age 65. Health insurance is largely private and is mainly provided through employers except for the elderly.

In all four countries, a significant portion of pay is not for direct hours worked but is diverted to benefits, payroll taxes to pay for social insurance, and miscellaneous programs such as vacations. And in all four, the direct component of pay has tended to fall over time. However, France and Germany divert more compensation than does the United Kingdom, which looks roughly like the United States in that regard (Figure 3.2).

Of the three European states, France diverts the largest share of compensation to legally required programs and Britain the least (Figure 3.3). Germany takes an intermediate position. The French share of compensation diverted to legally required programs is in fact understated since the quasi-private (but mandatory) national pension systems are treated as if they were voluntary in the official statistics.

Figure 3.2. Direct pay for hours worked in manufacturing as percentage of total compensation. *Source:* U.S. Bureau of Labor Statistics, *Supplementary Tables for BLS Report 794,* October 1990, Tables 10–13.

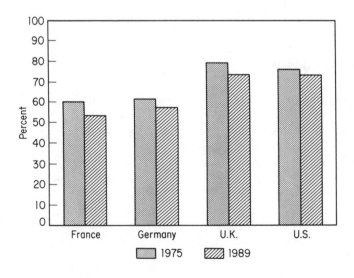

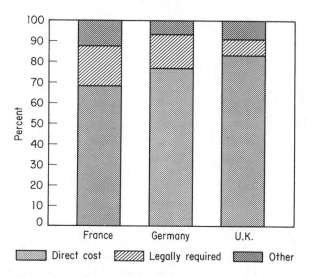

Figure 3.3. Composition of pay: 1984, manufacturing, mining, construction, utilities. *Source:* Office for Publications of the European Communities, *Labour Costs 1984: Principal Results* (Luxembourg: EC, 1986), 184–85.

INTERNAL AND EXTERNAL LABOR MARKET FLEXIBILITY

Various measures can be examined concerning the existing flexibility of European labor markets as compared with the United States. Employee turnover is lower in Europe; workers with less than two years' tenure on their current job are much more common in the American labor market. By that measure, France and Germany show substantially lower mobility than Britain, which is still lower than the United States (Figure 3.4). One might expect that employee benefit arrangements would reflect these differences, but—surprisingly—that does not seem to be the case. As will be noted later, the U.S. benefit system is predicated on immobility even though American workers are comparatively mobile.

European countries have fretted about their inability to create jobs as fast as the United States during the 1970s and 1980s. Employment-to-population ratios have fallen in France, Germany, and the United Kingdom, but have risen in the United States (Figure 3.5). There is concern that when jobs are lost in Europe, workers do not move to new employment but instead remain where they are. Indeed, the proportion of European job losers and leavers who remain unemployed for six months or more is substantially higher than in the United States (Figure 3.6).

Because it is more cumbersome in Europe to lay off workers, and because "regular" employment is more heavily regulated than contingent employment, European employers have been shifting toward the latter where possible. Unfortunately, official data do not isolate most contingent workers such as temporaries and those with short-term fixed contracts. Britain seems to have gone farther with part-time work than other EC countries (Figure 3.7). Since such workers often escape the labor standards required for other workers, there is a growing move within the EC bureaucracy to

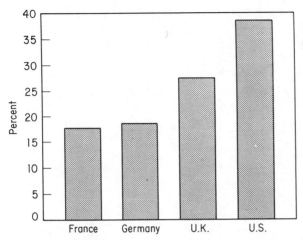

Figure 3.4. Percentage of workers with less than 2 years' tenure. *Source:* Organisation for Economic Cooperation and Development, *Flexibility in the Labour Market: The Current Debate* (Paris: OECD, 1986), Table II-1.

Figure 3.5. Employment–to–population ratio, 1967 (dotted bar) and 1987 (cross-hatched bar). *Source:* U.S. Bureau of Labor Statistics, *Handbook of Labor Statistics* (Washington: GPO, 1989), Table 143.

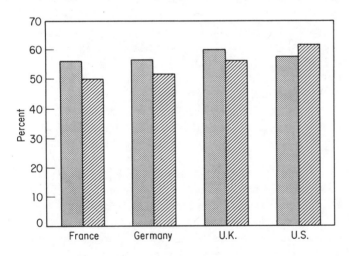

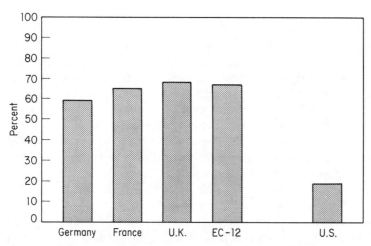

Figure 3.6. Percentage of job losers and leavers seeking work at least 6 months, 1987. *Source:* Office for Official Publications of the European Communities, *Labour Force Survey—Results 1987* (Luxembourg: EC, 1989), Table 69.

Figure 3.7. Part–timers as percentage of employment, 1987. *Source:* Office for Official Publications of the European Communities, *Labour Force Survey—Results 1987* (Luxembourg: EC, 1989), 68–69, 122–23, 126–27, 234–35.

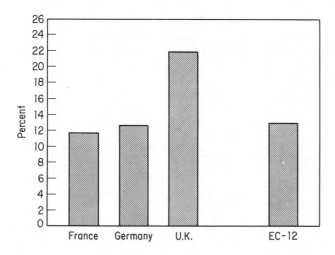

cover contingent workers by social insurance and other protections and to see that they receive the same employee benefits as other workers.

While European labor markets may seem less flexible than American, it also appears that these markets have been under more strain. Figure 3.8 presents an index of national structural adjustment based on employment shifts between industrial sectors. The index is computed by summing one half the absolute change in the percentage of employment over 1977–87 in the nine one-digit sectors used in the industrial classification system of the International Labour Organisation. This index suggests that Britain and France, especially, have been undergoing more substantial industrial restructuring than the United States (Figure 3.8). And that may account for their less happy labor market outcomes. But on the other hand, the index reinforces the impression that growing European integration is adding to the pressure for labor market flexibility and a social insurance and benefit system to go with it.

Although much has been said about workers crossing frontiers in the post-1992 EC, the right of employees to do so goes back to the original Treaty of Rome. In fact, however, there is relatively little cross-border mobility among nationals of the EC countries. Much of the international mobility that exists involves persons from outside the EC, e.g., North Africans in France (Figure 3.9). Apparently, barriers of culture and language keep intra-EC mobility to a very low level. Thus, although the idea of harmonizing social insurance and benefits in response to immigration may seem appealing, there is in fact relatively little pressure to do so. Any benefit and

Figure 3.8. Index of structural adjustment, 1977–1987. *Sources:* International Labour Office, *Yearbook of Labour Statistics,* various issues; U.S. Bureau of Labor Statistics, *Labor Force Statistics Derived from the Current Population Survey, 1948–87* (Washington: GPO, 1988), Table B11; *Employment and Earnings,* various issues.

Index calculated using the eight industrial sector classifications appearing in the yearbook: agriculture, mining, manufacturing, utilities, construction, commerce, transportation, finance, services. Employment not classified by sector was excluded. The U.S. index value is based on U.S. data, approximating *Yearbook* classifications. Index is equal to one-half the sum of the absolute changes in the percentages of employment in each sector.

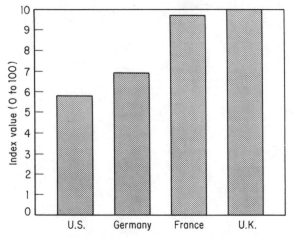

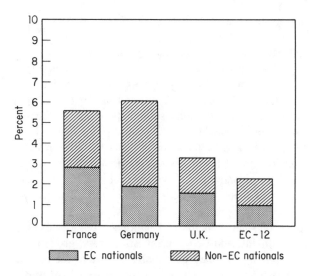

Figure 3.9. Foreign workers in EC countries as percentage of workforce, 1989. *Source: European Industrial Relations Review* (August 1990), 12.

social insurance reforms that are undertaken in the future are more likely to be in response to the need for more labor mobility *within* individual member countries.

NATIONAL BENEFITS AND ECONOMIC CONSIDERATIONS

Sometimes benefits and social insurance are seen as harmful to economic performance. Sometimes they are seen as helpful. Both perspectives can be found in the debates surrounding Europe 1992. So what can be said about the economic effects of social insurance and benefits?

Employee benefits are often seen as employer costs. From the viewpoint of the individual employer, getting rid of such costs would improve competitiveness relative to other employers. Thus, employers frequently complain about the cost side of the benefits they provide (or pay for via payroll taxes).

However, when viewed from the national perspective, a rather different picture emerges. If *all* employers are paying for benefits at about the same rate, than *none* is at a relative disadvantage on the cost side. This is especially true for payroll taxes which are commonly uniformly assessed. Obviously, there are exceptions to this generalization. But the important point is that it should not be assumed automatically that benefits are inherently disadvantageous. Each 1 percent of benefits is not 1 percent less competitiveness.

Of course, if firms spend money on voluntary benefits inefficiently, they will put themselves at a disadvantage. Providing benefits that employees do not value, or administering benefit plans ineffectively, will waste firm resources. In terms of administration, however, the most difficult benefits to manage are those relating to health care. These are generally not a problem for European firms because of the dominance of national health care systems. But they do pose problems for American employers.

From the international perspective, the cost approach to benefits must also be questioned. Benefits are not simply add-ons to labor costs. There is evidence that benefit costs are largely absorbed by employees. Employees located in countries with rich social insurance and benefit schemes paid by employers end up with less take-home pay than they otherwise would receive. Benefits should therefore not be assumed to make countries less competitive in world markets on a one-for-one basis.

The cost approach to benefits paints them as "bad things." But there are reverse arguments. Benefits, especially pensions, can also be seen as forms of saving. Saving is often viewed as a "good thing" for economic performance; if saving rates are higher, the reasoning goes, more investment will occur, raising growth rates and productivity. Hence, benefits are sometimes promoted to raise saving rates.

In fact, there is much slippage between benefits and national saving rates, between national saving rates and investment, and between investment and growth and productivity. Benefits *are* forms of saving but they potentially substitute for private saving which would otherwise occur. An extra unit of benefit or social insurance saving is not necessarily an extra unit of overall national saving. The empirical literature on this point is largely inconclusive.

Within the twelve EC countries in the 1980s, the top six in terms of gross saving rates out of GDP did have higher ratios of gross investment to GDP than the bottom six. But the investment advantage was smaller than the saving advantage because high-saving countries lend to low-saving countries. The top six savers had a slight advantage in growth rates but no advantage in productivity increases (Figure 3.10). The moral seems to be that public policy towards the mix of pay versus benefits cannot be assumed to be a strong lever on economic performance. Benefits are best considered on their own merits.

Somewhat related to the saving issue is the question of the use of benefit-related saving. In EC countries where retirement saving is largely done through a public social security fund, the business community is sometimes tempted to promote private pensions on the grounds that the assets will be invested in private securities rather than government securities. The argument is that this reallocation will promote more funds for business investment.

But the difficulty with this reasoning is that saving is fungible. If public funds invest in government securities, then there is that much less public borrowing to be supported by private saving. Private saving is thus freed for other purposes. Unless the government would borrow less in the absence of the public retirement plan, substituting a private system will not necessarily increase capital available for private investment. Again, the same moral returns. Benefits are best considered on their own merits and not on their supposed impact on national economic performance.

Ultimately, there is one key issue to consider in shaping public policy on social insurance and benefits: What is the relative role to be assigned to the state, the employer, and the individual in arranging for retirement, health, and other needs? The other arguments concerning the effects of benefits and social insurance—both pro and con—are generally substantially overstated given the limited evidence available.

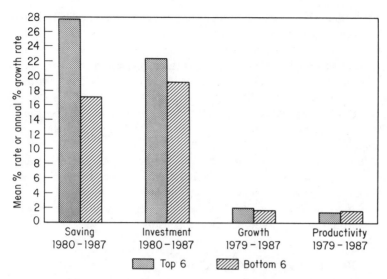

Figure 3.10. Saving, investment, growth, and productivity, top six and bottom six savers, EC12 countries. *Source:* Organisation for Economic Cooperation and Development, *Historical Statistics, 1960–1987* (Paris: OECD, 1989), 44, 65, 70; Organisation for Economic Cooperation and Development, *Labour Force Statistics, 1967–1987* (Paris: OECD, 1989), 25.

Saving and investment rates are in gross terms as a percent of GDP. Productivity refers to real GDP/Employment.

PUBLIC SOCIAL INSURANCE

Social security systems in Europe generally date from the late nineteenth and early twentieth centuries. The United States, which waited until the Great Depression to begin its system, was comparatively late in developing social insurance (Figure 3.11). In most countries, the pension element was the initial component of the system. Generally, the pension is earnings-related, although in a few countries flat amounts regardless of earnings are specified.

In all cases, social security is based in part on an employer tax. Generally in Europe, an employee tax plus a government subsidy also helps finance the system. The United States in contrast, limits government support to certain specialized programs.

Because of the implicit government guarantee behind social security systems, they can be funded on a pay-as-you-go basis. For firm-level pensions, such funding is more difficult or at least less credible. National quasi-private mandatory funds, such as used in France, can be funded on a pay-as-you-go basis since, if need arises, the mandatory contributions can be raised to support the system.

Where scope remains for private pensions, private pension planners must take account of the benefits to be expected from the government-run system. There may be formal recognition in the private formula of the amount to be received from social security. Some U.S. plans have this feature. Or there may simply be a net target for retirement replacement income with the private pension filling in the gap likely to be left over after social security for the typical retiree.

The British system of contracting out is the most formal linkage between social security and private pensions to be found in the EC. Originally, British social security payments were of the flat variety. Private pensions at larger companies, in contrast, were generally earnings-related. An earnings-related second tier of social security was added for employees at firms without pensions. Those firms which had pensions were allowed to opt out of the second tier if their plans met the minimum standards of the state earnings-related pension.

With the Thatcher government came an ideological commitment to greater personal initiative. Individuals were encouraged to contract out of either the public second tier or their private firm-level pension plans and open tax-favored savings accounts. It might be noted that these personal pensions are the ultimate in portability; individuals can move from job to job without loss of pension rights.

FIRM-LEVEL BENEFITS: GENERAL INTRODUCTION

Generally, where private firm-level benefits are extensive, some government promotion is involved. Often the promotion takes the form of tax incentives. For example, money paid into a pension fund on behalf of an employee is not taxed immediately upon receipt. Most European countries provide such tax-favored treatment to pensions. But it is rare for employer-provided health insurance.

Government can also promote private benefits by mandating them. For example, vacation plans may be specified by law, as in France. In contrast, in the United States, mandated benefits are not typically used; the tax-incentive route is the chief policy instrument. However, firms which elect to offer tax-favored benefits may be required to tailor those benefits in particular ways. For example, there are rules in American tax law prohibiting the offering of tax-favored benefits exclusively to higher-paid employees. Recently in the United States, there have been proposals

Figure 3.11. Public social security: pension types. *Source*: U.S. Department of Health and Human Services, Social Security Administration, *Social Security Programs Throughout the World—1989* (Washington, D.C.: HHS, 1988), various country pages.

Belgium (1924)	Earnings-related
Denmark (1892)	Flat, earn
France (1910)	Earn
Germany (1883)	Earn
Greece (1914)	Earn
Ireland (1908)	Flat
Italy (1919)	Earn
Luxembourg (1911)	Earn
Netherlands (1913)	Flat
Portugal (1935)	Earn
Spain (1919)	Earn
U.K. (1908)	Flat, earn
U.S. (1935)	Earn

to mandate the offering of certain benefits such as medical benefits and family leaves.

Whether firm-level benefits are promoted by tax subsidy or by mandate, they carry an implicit assumption about the employment relationship. The assumption is that the employee should be dependent on the employer for such needs as retirement income. There is an obvious paternalistic element in this approach. It stems from an older view of the employer-employee relation. Moreover, benefit design may be based on the assumption of a continuing employment relationship. But this assumption may not hold up under the economic pressures previously described.

In both the United States and Europe there was a history of pensions prior to World War II, but only covering a small fraction of the workforce. Often the plans were paternalistic in nature and were enacted in the hope of securing employee loyalty and gratitude. Europeans referred to these programs as "occupational pensions," a name which continues for all firm-level pensions including those not confined to a specific occupation. If there was a tradition of occupational pensions, the plans were often continued in the postwar period, even as the public social security system became more generous. However, in Europe—in contrast to the United States—the development of national health systems largely preempted the market for private firm-level health insurance. Where firms offer such insurance, it is often for higher-paid employees such as executives who prefer to opt out of the public plan.

FIRM-LEVEL PENSIONS

Europeans often talk about "three pillars" of retirement income: social security, private pensions, and individual saving. In recent years, there has been a growing emphasis on enhancing the second two pillars. Part of the reason for this emphasis is the anticipation of the retirement of the post-World War II baby boom early in the twenty-first century. Public pension programs which are relying in whole or in part on pay-as-you-go will be forced to raise taxes or contribution rates to meet the burden. The thought, therefore, is to encourage baby boomers to do more on their own (or to have their employers do more for them) to finance their retirement benefits.

Moving from public pay-as-you-go systems to private prefunded arrangements, however, will not lessen the overall cost of the baby boom's retirement. Disposable income will have to be reduced one way or another to finance the promised pensions. Nonetheless, the idea of private financing has been reinforced by the movement toward privatization generally in Europe. Private pensions are sometimes seen as more in line with the spirit of this movement than public social security.

The importance of private firm-level pensions varies across countries. In France, almost all retirement income comes from social security and national funds. Countries where firm-level pensions are prominent, such as Germany and the United Kingdom (and the United States) still feature significant reliance on public social security. However, as one moves up the income scale, the private pension tends to become more important as an income source relative to social security (Figure 3.12).

Private firm-level pensions come in two varieties: defined benefit and defined contribution. Under the former, the employer promises an eventual pension based on a formula commonly involving earnings history, age, and seniority at the firm. Under the latter, the employer simply creates what amounts to a savings account for the

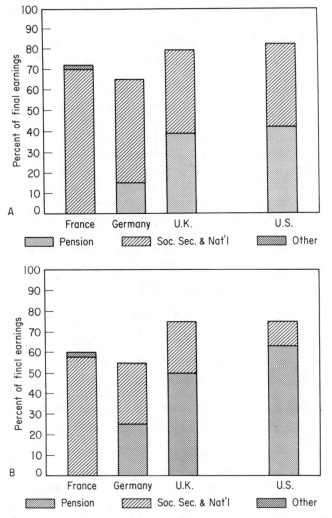

Figure 3.12. Retirement income: career male factory worker (**A**) and middle manager (**B**), 1989. *Source:* Towers, Perrin, *Retirement Income Throughout the World* (New York: Towers, Perrin, 1990), various country pages. NOTE: Lump–sum and saving plan distributions are converted into equivalent annual income. Figures based on estimates from graphic presentations.

employee and contributes a specified sum annually (say, as a percentage of pay). Personal pensions are similar to defined contribution plans, except that the employee rather than the employer administers the account.

Defined benefit plans shift risk from the employee to the employer. It is the employer which must ultimately come up with the resources to meet the pension promise. What level of resources that may be cannot be known in advance with certainty. The eventual cost will depend partly on such factors as interest rates, which the employer cannot control. However, defined benefit plans are more difficult to make portable than defined contribution plans and personal pensions. European pensions are mainly of the defined benefit variety. Only Britain seems actively to be promoting the personal pension concept.

DEFINED BENEFIT PENSIONS: RETENTION AND RECRUITMENT

The lack of 100 percent portability that is often associated with defined benefit pensions is sometimes defended as a virtue for employers. Employees will become tied to the firm by "golden handcuffs." Costs associated with employee turnover will be reduced. Firms will have less difficulty retaining employees, especially more senior ones.

But the strength of the retention argument surely varies with economic conditions. In tight labor markets with chronic labor shortages, retaining employees is an important employer objective. Thus, during the tight labor markets of the 1960s, defined benefit pensions were defended by German employers and others as a valuable human resource strategy. The problem is that economic circumstances change. Labor markets were much looser in the 1970s and 1980s, making retention incentives less important. Indeed, with competitive pressures and corporate restructuring increasing since 1992, many firms may need to downsize. Given such conditions, having benefit plans that make it painful and difficult for employees to leave or be laid off is not a sensible policy.

Moreover, even in tight labor markets, the retention argument is overstated. Yes, defined benefit pensions can help tie existing employees to the firm. From the individual employer perspective, that is valuable. But if all employers have such plans, they largely nullify each other. Each tied-down employee is an employee made more difficult for some other employer to recruit. One employer's gain is another's loss. If employees are in short supply, no firm-level strategy can succeed for all employers.

DEFINED BENEFIT PENSIONS: PLAN ATTRIBUTES

Defined benefit pensions have two key attributes that influence their retention incentives: vesting and backloading. Figure 3.13 shows a hypothetical defined benefit (DB) plan with vesting after five years, retirement at age 65, and a benefit formula providing an annual pension of 1.5 percent of final earnings for each year of seniority with the firm. Final earnings are defined as an average of the last three years of service. An employee is assumed to start working at age 25, vest at age 30, and continue with the firm until retirement. The price inflation rate is assumed to be 4

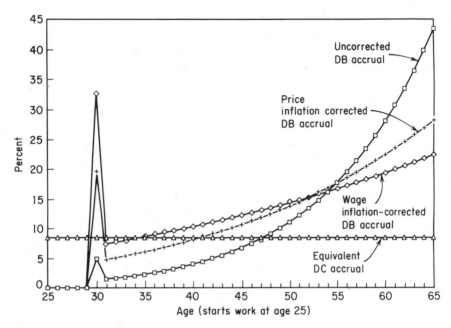

Figure 3.13. Pension accrual as percentage of quitting wage.

percent per annum and annual interest rates are assumed to be 7 percent. It is assumed in addition that the employee's nominal wage rises at 5.5 percent per year.

Figure 3.13 shows the pension value accrual achieved by staying one additional year with the firm rather than quitting. Pension value is calculated on a presented discounted basis. It is assumed that the individual will live for ten years after retirement. If no adjustment is made for price or wage inflation, the accrual curve is at zero for the first five years, shows a small upward spike at the five-year vesting point, and then gradually rises thereafter. By age 50, the gain from staying one more year rises to over 10 percent of the wage. By age 55, the gain rises to around 20 percent. Towards the end of the career, the gain is about 40 percent. In short, there is a mild incentive to stay until vesting and a strong incentive to remain with the firm for high seniority workers.

Three factors cause the accelerating slope of the accrual curve. First, the pension comes at age 65. Discounting back to earlier years will reduce the pension's present value. Second, the rise in the nominal wage is partly due to general price inflation. Early retirement means that the eventual pension will be based on final earnings which have been eroded in purchasing power by price inflation. Third, nominal wages will also reflect increases in real wages. Quitting before retirement age means forgoing the growth in the final earnings base that would come from future real wage increases.

Some European countries have sought to provide for transfers between defined benefit plans when employees change jobs—notably the Netherlands and the United Kingdom. If defined benefit plans are not coordinated, job changing will put employees at a significant disadvantage. Working for two employers for twenty years each will produce a combined pension well below what working for one for forty years would have produced. The objective behind the transfer schemes is to coordinate pensions so that the employee will collect from the final employer what he/she would have collected had he/she been with that employer for an entire career. Each employer's transfer payment to the next employer is supposed to pay fully for service previously accrued.

Achieving this goal is technically complex. As Figure 3.13 shows, merely correcting for price inflation will flatten the accrual curve somewhat, but will still leave some of the golden handcuff effect in place. And the vesting spike will increase, making the retention effect bigger at low seniority levels. Correcting for the full wage inflation effect (price effect plus real wage growth) creates still more flattening—but not total flattening—and further enlarges the vesting spike. Put another way, transfer payments between employers that reflect these corrections will not completely convert these plans into the aggregate equivalent of a national system.

The ultimate transfer system would be to calculate the defined contribution (DC) equivalent (with immediate vesting) to the defined benefit promise and require employers to make that DC-equivalent contribution into their funds. These funds could then follow the individual from job to job. Firm-level funds which experienced deficits because of atypical employment patterns would be compensated by those with surpluses. At the industry level, such systems can be found in multiemployer pension plans in the United States in certain sectors such as unionized construction and apparel manufacturing. Indeed, social security systems essentially are supported in this manner.

While transfer payments raise complex issues, it is comparatively easy for countries to move toward quicker plan vesting. In the United States, the basic vesting rule dropped from ten years to five years in the 1980s. British vesting is now down to two years. But German vesting remains at ten.

DEFINED BENEFIT PENSIONS: PLAN PROTECTION

Defined benefit pensions are essentially future promises. What is the guarantee these promises will be kept? A worker who discovers at retirement that an expected pension is not going to be fully paid is not easily able to offset the adverse impact. His/her life decisions about work and saving have already been made, premised on the promise.

In the early days of pensions, the plans were essentially contingent on the financial health of the firm; if the firm went bankrupt, the pension would not be delivered. Effectively, firms operated on a pay-as-you-go basis, paying pensions out of current revenues. But since few workers were able to qualify for pensions, the expenses entailed were not great.

Germany has essentially continued this procedure for many of its pension plans under the "book reserve" system. Accrued pension liabilities are charged against company profits as they are incurred, thus reducing corporate tax liability. However, no separate and independent fund is actually created to accumulate pension assets. The liability is just carried on the books of the firm as an accounting formality.

In other countries such as the United Kingdom (and the United States), independent pension funds are created and financed by ongoing contributions of the employer. The employee thus has some assurance that the pension will be paid, even if the employer eventually goes bankrupt. However, the guarantee is not absolute; employers in poor financial condition may not adequately fund their pensions. Thus, assets in the independent fund may not cover full pension liabilities.

To protect pension promises, it is possible for governments to sponsor official insurance funds. Germany has such an official fund, as does the United States. Potentially such funds can leave governments with responsibilities for inadequately funded pension promises, a growing problem in the United States. If Europe 1992 entails corporate failures and bankruptcy, similar difficulties could arise in the EC. Thus, defined benefit pensions again entail substantially more administrative and regulatory complexity than defined contribution plans and personal pensions. They promise stability in an unstable world and the risk has to be absorbed somewhere.

Even if pensions are paid as promised, there remains the question of what the benefits will be worth in purchasing-power terms. Benefits specified in nominal amounts can be eroded by inflation. German pension benefits are generally adjusted annually with the cost of living. But this type of inflation protection is not always present in other countries.

In Britain, some employers provide cost-of-living adjustments, but others do not. Private employers in the United States almost never have formal pension escalation, but sometimes *ad hoc* pension increases are provided. But these adjustments do not typically fully offset price inflation. Thus, even defined benefit plans do not completely shield retirees from risk. Unless there is formal escalation, no one can be sure what their pension will be worth. In contrast, public social security system pensions are generally indexed to inflation.

Employees with private defined contribution plans or personal pensions ultimately can buy annuities upon retirement. In Britain, the annuity market can provide inflation-protected pensions for those who want them. Development of such financial instruments can be assisted if governments offer inflation-protected securities with which to back them. If a significant market can be developed for inflation-protected annuities, defined contribution plans and personal pensions could be used to shield against inflation risk.

THE FINANCIAL SIDE OF PENSIONS

Europe 1992 envisions more integrated markets for services as well as goods. Included are financial services and insurance. This objective has an obvious link to pensions. Defined benefit pensions with independent trust funds can accumulate substantial assets. They can be major financial intermediaries. Multinational firms operating in the EC which have country-level pensions have noted the analogy between financial service enterprises and their own pension systems.

What multinationals such as IBM have been seeking is the right to set up "European pension funds." Such funds would be integrated on the financial side, not the benefit side. Benefits provided at each subsidiary would continue to be paid in accordance with national law. But the funds accumulated could be invested in any EC country and payments into such EC-wide trusts would receive the same tax benefits as payments into national-level trusts. Directorate-General XV of the EC is moving toward such a concept. Ironically, more progress on integrating pensions is being made on the financial side than on the social side within the EC's political machinery.

HEALTH INSURANCE

Firm-level health insurance plans, as are commonly found in the United States, raise issues of portability similar to those of pensions. Naturally, individual employers and their insurance carriers are anxious to avoid taking on risky clients. Thus, new employees or their dependents may be denied health insurance if they have "preexisting" illnesses. For example, a new employee with a heart condition might be denied coverage for a specified period. Of course, employees with preexisting conditions will be reluctant to leave their current employers—where they have coverage.

In effect, there is a selective golden handcuffs effect of health insurance. But it is more difficult to defend as a good human resources strategy than the one associated with pensions. Can it really be said that firms especially want to retain those workers with health problems? In the European context, of course, the issue does not generally arise because of the prevalence of national health systems.

The United States finds itself spending a larger fraction of its GDP on health care than the EC countries. But this spending does not seem to be associated with better health outcomes such as longer life expectancy (Figure 3.14) or reduced infant mortality. Possibly, there are intangible elements of health care service quality which

Figure 3.14. Health expenditure/GDP, 1987. NOTE: Life expectancy at birth, 1988. *Sources:* U.S. Bureau of the Census, *Statistical Abstract of the United States, 1989* (Washington, D.C.: GPO, 1989), 817–18; Organisation for Economic Cooperation and Development, *Health Care Systems in Transition: The Search for Efficiency* (Paris: OECD, 1990), 10.

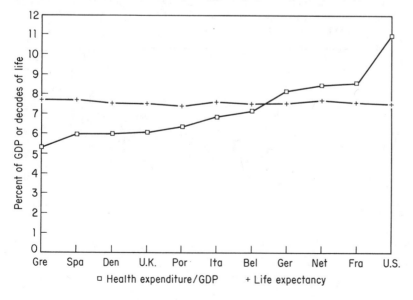

Americans obtain for their larger expenditure. It is often said that Americans would not tolerate the waiting lists and rationing associated with, say, the British system. But in fact the American system has been moving toward less choice and *de facto* rationing in an effort to contain health care cost through arrangements such as health maintenance organizations (HMOs).

Many countries have complained about the growth in health care costs. This growth has two elements: inflation and usage. Costs can rise if the unit price of health care rises faster than the general price level. This phenomenon has been a problem in the United States and in some (but not all) of the EC countries (Figure 3.15). Costs will also rise if more usage is made of health services. Usage is a more universal problem and the one most likely to lead to rationing and queues.

In short, paying for health care is a general problem in all countries. But only in countries where health insurance is mainly provided by employers does it become a special problem for human resource managers. European human resource managers have not been diverted in the way their American counterparts have to dealing with health care cost containment and administration.

CONCLUSIONS

There is a paradox which emerges from this brief review. Lower-mobility Europe has an employee benefit system more accommodating to labor turnover than the higher-mobility United States. The European advantage, which will be accentuated in this post-1992 period, consists of heavier reliance on national rather than firm-level systems and a more proactive response to the issue of benefit portability and transferability.

Figure 3.15. Medical care and health service inflation. *Sources:* Organisation for Economic Cooperation and Development, *Historical Statistics, 1960–1987* (Paris: OECD, 1989), 79; U.S. Department of Health and Human Services, *Health Care Financing Review: 1989 Annual Supplement* (Washington, D.C.: GPO, 1989), 133.

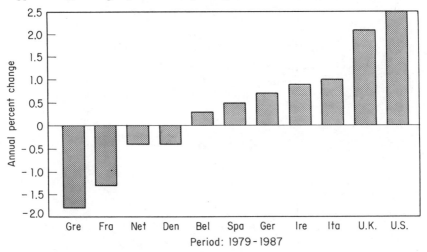

Some lessons for managers also emerge. First, national norms have tended to dominate the specifics of employee benefit provision. Second, public policy toward benefits and social insurance plays a large and shifting role in determining what kinds of benefits firms provide.

A choice for managers is also posed. One option is simply to play "follow the leader" and offer benefits which are similar to the average package offered in a particular country. There are numerous guide books available from management consulting firms which provide examples of typical national packages which can be emulated. A second option, however, is to examine the employment relationship which is being sought and to design benefits around that relationship. In particular, unless a firm is really prepared to offer lifetime employment, it should not build its benefits around that model.

Finally, there are some lessons for public policy at the national level. Public policy makers should examine the employment relationship, just as human resource managers should. Benefits should not be promoted or mandated which are out of date in terms of the modern employment relationship. If the prognosis presented here of greater needs for flexibility and mobility is correct, then there should be emphasis on either national systems or devices to make benefits portable and/or transferable. It may be difficult technically to make decentralized firm-level systems function as if they were part of a centralized national plan. But it isn't impossible.

NOTES

Material in this chapter is drawn from a larger study by the author and Jacques Rojot. Details on sources of data may be obtained from the author.

4

The End of Corporatism?
Wage Setting in the Nordic and
Germanic Countries

PETER LANGE, MICHAEL WALLERSTEIN, and MIRIAM GOLDEN

The discovery of corporatism and its successes in the 1980s fueled a "growth indus-try" for comparative political economy. By the early 1990s, its decline and even collapse shifted the terms of debate. Whereas initially interest was sparked by the need to investigate corporatist success, the new focus centered on the causes and consequences of corporatism's seeming demise.

The analysis of Swedish political economy is paradigmatic of this shift. In the 1970s, Sweden embodied *the* model corporatist country. Its highly centralized bar-gaining between densely representative organizations of labor and capital was encour-aged by government, which used social and economic policies to underpin and facili-tate such arrangements. The outcomes were apparently beneficial for all concerned: the economy was efficient, as indicated by Swedish competitive success internation-ally, but also relatively equitable, as evidenced by the country's record of redistribu-tion. The cooperative tripartism found in Sweden thus offered a template against which other countries were measured for adherence to the corporatist formula.

Not surprisingly then, the apparent collapse of the Swedish model sometime in the 1980s and 1990s was often taken to indicate a more general crisis of corporatism. The cumulative evidence of such a crisis in Sweden was substantial. The country's system of centralized wage setting appeared to have broken down, a collapse seem-ingly rendered irreversible by the employers' association's, the *Svenska Arbetsgivar-eförening*, or SAF's, decision in 1990 to dismantle its central bargaining unit.

Just as Sweden proved the modal case of corporatism in the 1960s and 1970s, so later events there were believed to represent a more general trend towards the decay of corporatist practices and institutions. The collapse, while perhaps more dra-matic and extreme in Sweden, apparently threatened all those countries generally identified as corporatist. Thus, despite ongoing definitional vagaries attached to the concept, a general consensus seemed to emerge that corporatism was under stress, and indeed that industrial relations and wage setting were undergoing considerable fragmentation and decentralization more generally.

Analyses of the causes for the collapse of centralized collective bargaining in Sweden reinforced the conclusion that the purported crisis of corporatism must have become widespread. Analysts often focused on two primary changes in the international political economy, changes affecting the conditions necessary for employers and countries to remain internationally competitive in manufacturing. The first has been the increased openness of the international economy, particularly the integration of capital and labor markets associated with the creation of a single market in Europe. The second change in the international economy said to affect domestic wage setting processes has been the shift in technology allowing for flexible specialization and reducing the role of mass, batch production goods in international trade. Both changes altered the strategic calculations and orientations of employers while simultaneously weakening and internally dividing labor movements. The result, it is said, has been that employers have wanted to dismantle centralized wage setting and have had the institutional opportunities to do so. Given that increased openness and changes in technology affect Western European countries generally, this diagnosis of the causes of corporatist collapse in Sweden suggests that corporatist arrangements should be in decline everywhere.

In this chapter, we present empirical evidence showing no general trend towards the decay or collapse of corporatist institutions in those countries most often identified as highly corporatist. We present a preliminary analysis of data on the coordination of collective bargaining in six countries between 1970 and 1992: specifically, those six most often identified as exemplars of corporatist wage setting. Five of these countries are small, open economies: Sweden, Norway, Austria, Denmark, and Finland. The first three constitute the *loci classici* of corporatism, and the latter two generally enjoy high rankings on comparative scales of corporatism.[1] We also include data on Germany, a large, open economy whose collective bargaining practices are similar in effect—although only partially in structure—to those of the smaller countries.

As a preliminary descriptive presentation of a larger project, the present chapter makes no pretense of offering an alternative explanation for the demise of corporatism in Sweden, or indeed of trends in collective bargaining and industrial relations occurring across Europe.[2] Our purpose is, more modestly, to offer empirical evidence to contest the widely held view that a uniform trend characterizing the most corporatist of European countries exists at all. We will show, instead, that the six countries analyzed fall into at least three separate groups, only one of which exhibits clear signs of corporatist breakdown. In four of the six countries that we analyze, preexisting corporatist institutions remain largely intact. Moreover, even those countries that have experienced substantial changes in the scope of wage setting exhibit stability and continuity on some dimensions of corporatism.

CONCEPTUAL CONSIDERATIONS

Corporatism, as a characteristic ascribed to national political economic systems, can be thought of as a collection of features that have tended to covary, although the balance of features has been somewhat different from case to case (as well as from analyst to analyst).[3] The assembly includes organizational characteristics of the major trade union and employer organizations, and characteristics of how these various bodies interact with one another and with the government in the wage setting process. Operationally, then, analysis falls naturally into two parts: one concerning the organizational characteristics of the trade unions, and a second regarding the interactions of unions, employers, and government in the wage setting process.[4]

Organizational characteristics of the trade unions that are often considered important in operationalizing the concept of corporatism include the following: (1) *associational monopoly,* or the extent to which unions are united in a single peak association or divided among competing associations; (2) *centralization,* or the authority of the leadership of peak organizations to enact and implement decisions that prove binding on their affiliates; (3) *concentration,* or the extent to which peak organizations are divided into a relatively small number of affiliates with a substantial portion of the total membership in each; and (4) *encompassingness,* or the proportion of potential members who are actual members. Below, we present data for all six countries on these four aspects of union organization.

The characteristics of the wage setting process covered in our study include: (1) *the level of wage setting,* or the extent to which national agreements covering the whole economy or whole industries determine or frame wage bargaining outcomes; and (2) *the involvement of the government,* or the degree to which national political authorities set wages by fiat or in other ways use their offices to establish or influence bargaining outcomes. Below, we present annual measures of these two variables for the years between 1970 and 1992 for our six countries.

These various indicators of the institutional structure and operation of the collective organizations of labor and capital together suggest the extent to which wage setting can be nationally coordinated. This, we believe, lies at the heart of the corporatist phenomenon, regardless of the variations in the indicators and measures of corporatism scattered throughout the literature. But, as the data presented below indicate, the relationships among these various structural and behavioral aspects of collective bargaining are highly variable even within single countries. Change in one does not necessarily imply changes in other measures. In what follows, we present cross-national and longitudinal comparisons of the six countries along all six dimensions since 1970.

ORGANIZATIONAL CHARACTERISTICS

Organizational Encompassingness

Declining union membership is often taken as a sign of a decay in the institutional underpinnings of corporatism. Aggregate union membership did indeed fall in the 1980s in many advanced industrial societies (Visser, 1991). Figure 4.1 displays the number of active union members as a percentage of the total dependent labor force for the six countries of our study.[5]

As the data presented in Figure 4.1 demonstrate, there is no common trend to union membership across these six countries. In Austria, union density has been

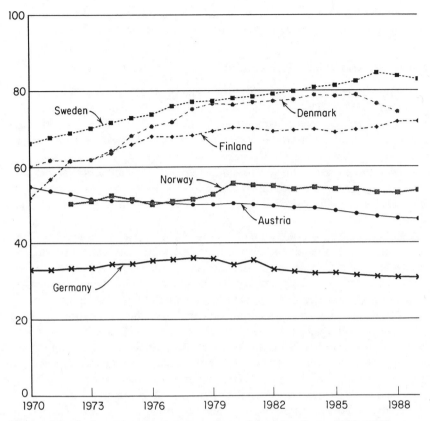

Figure 4.1. Active union members as a share of the labor force, 1970–1989.

gradually falling during the entire twenty years. German union members by contrast, grew slightly as a share of the labor force during the 1970s, and then declined slightly in the 1980s. In the Nordic countries, union density either remained stable (Norway) or continued to increase until the late 1980s (Denmark, Finland, and Sweden). The growth of union membership in these last three countries is likely influenced by the powerful selective incentives provided by union unemployment funds in a period of rising insecurity about employment (Rothstein, 1992).[6] Thus, the evidence shows no general decline in the unions' positions as encompassing organizations.

Membership figures are, however, only one indicator of the degree of organizational encompassingness. The proportion of the labor force covered by collective agreements is also important, and in many countries extends well beyond the number of union members. In Germany, the coverage of union contracts greatly exceeds the share of the workforce belonging to unions, as government proclamations routinely require all employers in an industry to abide by contract provisions. In Austria, all private employers are legally required to join the Chamber of Commerce, and all members of the Chamber of Commerce are obligated to comply with the collective agreements its affiliates sign. In Norway, although extension laws do not exist, pay increases negotiated by the unions effectively set the standard for all firms, even those in the nonunion sector. The proportion of the labor force covered by collective agreements appears to be high and stable in all our countries since 1970.

Associational Monopoly and Concentration

Unions not only face potential competition from unorganized workers, but may also compete with each other. The extent to which union confederations compete with other confederations, and affiliates within each confederation compete with other affiliates in the same confederation, may affect unions' willingness and capacity to cooperate in wage policy. Lash (1985) traces the collapse of centralized wage restraint in Sweden to increased competition among unions. Golden (1993) argues that the presence or absence of competition among unions is the single most important of the multiple aspects of industrial relations that are typically joined together in definitions of corporatism.

We examine whether or not the unions in our six countries have become more or less fragmented and competitive since 1970, using various measures. The simplest is the number of union confederations and the number of affiliates in each. Windmuller (1981) observed a general tendency for the number of independent unions to decline over the postwar period. We update Windmuller's figures for our six countries to see if any such trend is evident among them over the past two decades. A second measure, labeled associational monopoly by Visser (1989), is the percentage of all union members who belong to the largest confederation. Concentration ratios, or the share of each confederation's membership that belongs to the largest x number of affiliates, are a third type of measure. Here we report concentration ratios for the largest single and largest three affiliates. Concentration ratios are useful indicators of the extent to which a confederation is dominated by a few large unions. Changes in the extent of competition among unions might be reflected in one or all of these measures.[7]

Our six countries can be divided into two groups. Both in terms of the average level of concentration and in terms of changes over time, Austria and Germany are distinct from the four Nordic countries. The Austrian union movement is probably the least competitive in the world, as illustrated by the data presented in Table 4.1 (on Austria, see Kindley, 1992). The *Österreichischer Gewerkschaftsbund*, or ÖGB, is the sole union in Austria. Following a merger of two branches in the service sector in 1978, the

Table 4.1. Union Concentration in Austria

Confederation	Year	Share of total union membership	Number of affiliates	Share of membership in largest affiliate	Share of membership in largest 3 affiliates
ÖGB	1970	100.0	16	n.a.	n.a.
	1975	100.0	16	19.2	48.5
	1980	100.0	15	20.4	48.7
	1985	100.0	15	20.8	49.3
	1990	100.0	15	20.5	49.1

ÖGB has been divided into fifteen branches, most of which are organized along industrial lines. The ÖGB branches are not free-standing organizations that have chosen to affiliate, as in most other countries, but administrative subunits of national confederation. No unions with collective bargaining functions exist outside the ÖGB.

The main union confederation in Germany, the *Deutscher Gewerkschaftsbund,* (DGB) does not enjoy the absolute monopoly of the ÖGB. A general union of white-collar workers, *the Deutsche Angestellten Gewerkschaft* (DAG) has remained outside the DGB in order to preserve its occupational basis of organization (Visser, 1990: 138). The DGB also faces competition from a public sector confederation, the *Deutscher Beamtenbund* (DBB), as well as from a Christian confederation, the *Christlicher Gewerkschaftsbund Deutschlands* (CGB). Yet the preeminent position of the DGB has been stable over time, in spite of employment trends that would seem to favor its rivals. The large share of DGB members in the largest affiliate, the metalworkers, accurately captures the importance of the metalworkers within the DGB.[8] The metalworkers' share of DGB members has also remained surprisingly constant since 1970. Neither Austria nor Germany shows much evidence of change since 1970 in measures of associational monopoly or union concentration (Table 4.2).

The stability of the DGB's position among German unions, and of the metalworkers within the DGB, contrasts sharply with the experience of the Nordic countries. The latter all exhibit a common pattern marked by a relative decline of the major union confederation found in each as well as a relative decline of the metalworkers (or, in Denmark, of the general union of unskilled workers) within the major confederation. Measures of associational monopoly and concentration ratios for the Nordic countries are presented in Tables 4.3–4.6.

On one dimension—the number of affiliates of the major blue-collar confederation—the Nordic countries are moving toward their Germanic counterparts. The number of separate unions in the Danish, Norwegian, and Swedish *Landsorganisation,* or LO, and the Finnish *Suomen Ammattiliittojen Keskusjrjest* (SAK), has declined significantly since 1970, although none yet approaches the small number of affiliates in either the Austrian ÖGB or the German DGB. This trend toward consolidation within the main confederations, however, is offset by the growing share of union members who remain outside the main confederations, either in other confederations or in unaffiliated unions. All of the Nordic countries have multiple confederations distinguished by occupation. Among blue-collar workers in both private and public sectors, the main confederation in all four countries maintains a monopoly position. But in all four countries, separate confederations for white-collar workers (the *Fælles-rådet for danske Tjenestemands-og Funktionærorganisationer* [FTF] in Denmark, the *Yrkesorganisasjonenes Sentralforbund* [YS] in Norway, *Tjänstemännens centralorganisation* [TCO] in Sweden, and the *Toimihenkilö-ja Virkamiesjärjestöjen Keskusliitto* [TVK] in Finland) and workers with university degrees (the *Akademikernes Centralorganisation* [AC] in Denmark, *Akademikernes Fellesorganisasjon* [AF] in Norway, the *Sveriges akademikers centralorganisation* [SACO-SR] in Sweden, and the *Akademikersammanslutning* [Akava] in Finland) have emerged and grown in importance. In Denmark and Finland, there is also a separate confederation for foremen and technicians. Finally, in Denmark and Norway, there are a substantial number of workers in unions that are unaffiliated with any confederation. As a result of these various factors, the main blue-collar confederation in each of the Nordic coun-

Table 4.2. Union Concentration in Germany

Confederation	Year	Share of total union membership	Number of affiliates	Share of membership in largest affiliate	Share of membership in largest 3 affiliates
DGB					
	1970	83.0	17	33.1	56.6
	1975	83.8	17	34.7	57.8
	1980	83.1	17	33.3	56.2
	1985	82.8	17	33.1	56.8
	1990	82.5	17	34.4	58.6
DAG					
	1970	5.7	8		
	1975	5.4	8		
	1980	5.2	8		
	1985	5.4	n.a.		
	1990	6.0	4		
CGB					
	1970	2.4	n.a.		
	1975	2.6	n.a.		
	1980	3.0	n.a.		
	1985	3.3	n.a.		
	1990	3.2	n.a.		
DBB					
	1970	8.9	n.a.		
	1975	8.3	n.a.		
	1980	8.7	n.a.		
	1985	8.5	n.a.		
	1990	8.3	n.a.		

tries is significantly less able to dominate collective bargaining today than it was in 1970.

Another significant change in the Nordic countries is only partly visible from the data reported in Tables 4.3–4.6, namely, the relative decline of private sector workers in manufacturing and the growing importance of public sector unions. While there is no common trend in the membership share held by the largest single or largest three affiliates in each country's blue-collar confederation, there is a common trend in the identity of the largest affiliates. In 1970, the single largest affiliate of the main confederation in Norway, Sweden, and Finland was the metalworkers. In 1990, it was the union of local government employees. By 1980, Norwegian metalworkers had fallen into third place behind both the local and central government employees unions. Only by merging with four other private sector unions in 1988 to create the *Fellesforbund* could metalworkers regain their position as second largest union. Indeed, the perceived need of private sector unions to maintain their relative size (and power within the LO) vis-à-vis the public sector unions was the major motive behind the merger.

The unions in the Danish LO are unique among our six countries in their resistance to organizing along industrial lines. In spite of numerous appeals for reorganization into industrial unions by the LO's leadership, and in spite of a large number

Table 4.3. Union Concentration in Denmark

Confederation	Year	Share of total union membership	Number of affiliates	Share of membership in largest affiliate	Share of membership in largest 3 affiliates
LO					
	1970	76.7	45	28.7	56.0
	1975	74.4	40	27.3	55.1
	1980	73.0	38	25.0	56.6
	1985	71.0	31	22.6	54.7
	1990	69.4	30	22.7	54.6
FTF					
	1970	13.4	34	19.9	49.2
	1975	16.5	34	20.3	50.2
	1980	16.2	40	21.1	43.6
	1985	15.7	38	21.0	44.4
	1990	15.8	30	19.4	44.3
FR					
	1970	2.6	7		
	1975	1.7	7		
	1980	1.4	7		
	1985	1.2	6		
	1990	3.4	5		
AC					
	1970	2.4	n.a.		
	1975	3.5	13		
	1980	4.1	n.a.		
	1985	3.8	14		
	1990	5.0	16		
Unaffiliated					
	1970	5.0	n.a.		
	1975	3.9	n.a.		
	1980	5.4	n.a.		
	1985	8.3	n.a.		
	1990	6.3	n.a.		

Table 4.4. Union Concentration in Finland

Confederation	Year	Share of total union memberhip	Number of affiliates	Share of membership in largest affiliate	Share of membership in largest 3 affiliates
SAK					
	1970	68.8	31	16.2	39.0
	1976	64.6	27	15.6	38.8
	1980	62.7	29	15.2	40.4
	1985	59.0	28	17.0	41.1
	1990	55.9	24	18.8	42.8
TVK					
	1970	22.3	29	17.6	42.0
	1976	19.0	22	20.6	45.3
	1980	19.7	19	21.1	48.6
	1985	21.0	15	18.4	51.2
	1990	20.2	15	22.3	50.9
STTK					
	1970	2.9	4		
	1976	6.0	11		
	1980	7.0	13		
	1985	7.3	15		
	1990	8.1	16		
Akava					
	1970	4.5	41		
	1976	9.9	51		
	1980	9.9	48		
	1985	12.0	45		
	1990	14.5	34		
Unaffiliated					
	1970	1.5	n.a.		
	1976	0.4	n.a.		
	1980	0.7	n.a.		
	1985	0.8	n.a.		
	1990	1.2	n.a.		

of mergers, the Danish LO affiliates remain divided among industrial, craft, and general unions (Visser, 1990: 141).[9] The largest single union is the general union of unskilled and semi-skilled workers, the *Specialarbejderforbund i Danmark,* or SiD. As the data reported in Table 4.3 show, however, SiD's share of LO membership has been declining, just as the once-central metalworkers' unions have undergone relative decline in Sweden, Norway, and Finland.

To summarize our data, the composition, concentration, and associational monopoly of the union movements in Austria and Germany have been remarkably stable over the past two decades, in spite of substantial shifts in the composition of the labor force. In contrast, the Nordic countries have experienced significant changes since 1970. The changes, however, do not all point in the same direction. At the same time as the unions affiliated with the main blue-collar unions have undergone mergers, thereby becoming more consolidated, an increasingly large share of union members have joined unions in rival white-collar and professional confederations: union concentration has thereby increased whereas monopoly has undergone decline. Finally, the relative position of private-sector industrial workers within the blue-collar confederations has declined as public sector workers have grown in importance in all of the Nordic countries, but not in Austria and Germany.

The Centralization of Authority

The authority of central confederations may be measured in a variety of ways, including the following: (1) whether the peak organization appoints officials at lower levels;

Table 4.5. Union Concentration in Norway

Confederation	Year	Share of total union memberhip	Number of affiliates	Share of membership in largest affiliate	Share of membership in largest 3 affiliates
LO					
	1970	79.8	35	15.1	36.6
	1975	76.6	35	16.4	40.0
	1980	68.6	36	19.2	48.4
	1985	63.9	34	21.8	49.8
	1990	60.8	29	25.4	61.6
YS					
	1980	8.9	14	23.9	54.6
	1985	10.6	15	23.0	56.1
	1990	14.3	17	18.6	52.5
AF					
	1975	8.3	34		
	1980	9.4	34		
	1985	11.4	36		
	1990	16.1	40		
Unaffiliated					
	1970	20.2	n.a.		
	1975	15.1	n.a.		
	1980	13.0	n.a.		
	1985	14.1	n.a.		
	1990	8.8	n.a.		

Note: The YS was founded in 1977. The AF was founded in 1974.

Table 4.6. Union Concentration in Sweden

Confederation	Year	Share of total union membership	Number of affiliates	Share of membership in largest affiliate	Share of membership in largest 3 affiliates
LO					
	1970	66.2	29	22.0	46.4
	1975	62.8	25	23.7	50.7
	1980	62.3	25	24.2	54.9
	1986	59.6	24	28.1	57.7
TCO					
	1970	28.3	23	28.9	49.0
	1975	31.2	24	27.7	49.8
	1980	30.6	21	28.3	54.6
	1986	32.3	20	24.2	49.3
SACO-SR					
	1970	4.5	30		
	1975	5.4	27		
	1980	6.6	26		
	1986	7.7	25		
Unaffiliated					
	1970	0.9	n.a.		
	1975	0.6	n.a.		
	1980	0.5	n.a.		
	1986	0.4	n.a.		

(2) whether the peak organization controls industrial action or strike funds; and (3) whether the peak organization is required to sign collective agreements negotiated by lower levels.

Austria's central confederation exercises exceptional authority within organized labor; indeed, the greatest among our six countries. The ÖGB has powers well beyond those held by any other union confederation in Europe. For instance, it is unique in having the power to appoint the leaders of its branches. In addition, strike action cannot be initiated without the ÖGB's consent, although occasional wildcats may occur (Karlhofer, 1983; Kindley, 1992). The confederation controls all strike funds. Finally, ÖGB consent is required before any wage agreement is concluded, since only the ÖGB has the legal authority to sign a contract.

The German case differs considerably from the Austrian. The central German confederation has no authority over affiliates: it maintains no strike funds, is not able to vet wage demands or sign agreements, and exercises no authority over appointments. The DGB lacks coercive controls over its industrial unions.

The Danish central confederation also enjoys limited authority, albeit slightly more than its German counterpart. The LO maintains no strike funds of its own and cannot require members to participate in a strike unless the strike is approved by a majority of the workers who would be involved. The confederation does have the power to order an affiliate to end or avoid a strike that threatens the continuity of work for other affiliates, but only with a vote of at least 75 percent at a union congress. In practice, however, it seems that the LO has little effective control over industrial conflict. The LO also has no authority to sign contracts or vet the bargaining demands of its affiliates.

The Danish national employers' organization, however, is substantially more centralized than the LO. Employers who belong to the *Dansk Arbejdsgiverforening* (DA) are prohibited from signing a wage agreement without the DA's approval. The DA can (and does) levy fines on employers who make concessions without permission. Finally, the DA has strike funds of its own.

In comparison with the Danish LO, the Norwegian and Swedish LO exercise substantial authority. In both countries, participation in strikes requires the LO's prior consent.[10] In addition, the LO of both countries controls 25 percent or more of strike funds. While neither LO has the statutory power to veto the bargaining demands of its affiliates, both confederations may impose an industrial peace obligation on its affiliates when it signs a national agreement.

Leaving aside Finland for lack of information, a comparative ranking of the five countries on a scale measuring the authority of central officials over affiliates would order them as follows: Austria at the highest level, Norway and Sweden next, then Denmark with Germany at the bottom. More importantly for present purposes, we found no evidence of any changes in the authority relations between central confederations and affiliates in any of the countries since 1970. On this measure of corporatism, all six countries exhibit stability.

THE LEVEL OF WAGE BARGAINING AND GOVERNMENT INTERVENTION

The centralization of wage bargaining and the extent of government involvement—typically in the form of incomes policies—constitute the core of what many mean by the label "corporatist." In this section we examine the extent to which centralized wage negotiations and government involvement declined, if decline they did, among our six countries from 1970 to the present. We analyze the level of wage setting separately from government involvement. While in some countries the two go hand in hand, in others there is little relationship between them. We present data on both together to avoid repetition. Throughout, our analysis refers to the level of wage setting and government involvement in the private sector.[11]

Our index of the centralization of wage setting consists of the following ordered categories:

0. Industry-level bargaining without coordination. (There are no cases as decentralized as this among the six countries analyzed here)
1. Industry-level bargaining with informal coordination (for example, a particular union acts as the pattern setter which the rest tend to follow)
2. Industry-level bargaining with a centralized ratification procedure (for example, all agreements are linked in a centralized ratification vote)

3. Peak-level talks without a peak-level agreement
4. Peak-level agreement without an industrial peace clause (that prohibits industrial action in subsequent bargaining at the industry level)
5. Peak-level agreement with an industrial peace clause
6. Peak-level agreement with a ban on subsequent bargaining at the industry or local level

The categories were given numbers between zero (for the least centralized) and one (for the most centralized) and each country was given a score for each year from 1970 to the present.[12] The ranking is purely ordinal. We made no attempt to judge the relative differences between different categories of increasing centralization. The scale is designed to be comparable across countries.[13]

The index of government involvement in private sector wage setting consists of the following categories:

0. No government involvement
1. The government extends industry-level wage contracts to cover all workers in the industry
2. The government provides statistical information to be used as the basis for wage bargaining
3. Government offers policy concessions to influence wage bargaining without directly participating in the negotiations
4. Government participates in wage negotiations, offering policy changes in exchange for desirable wage settlements
5. Government arbitrator imposes industry-level wage contracts where industry-level bargaining reaches an impasse or extends one union's wage contract to cover other unions
6. Government arbitrator imposes national wage contract when peak-level bargaining reaches an impasse
7. Parliament passes a peak-level wage settlement that was negotiated by the union and employers' confederation that does not prohibit local bargaining
8. Parliament passes a peak-level wage settlement that was negotiated by the union and employers' confederation that does prohibit local bargaining
9. Parliament passes a peak-level wage settlement that was not negotiated by the union and employers' confederation, but does not prohibit local bargaining
10. Parliament passes a peak-level wage settlement that was not negotiated by the union and employers' confederation and prohibits local bargaining

Again, we scored each country between zero (for the least government involvement) and one (for the most) for every year. The easiest way to present results is by country.

Austria

As in the other aspects of industrial relations that we have already reviewed, not much change is apparent in the process of wage setting in Austria since 1970. What

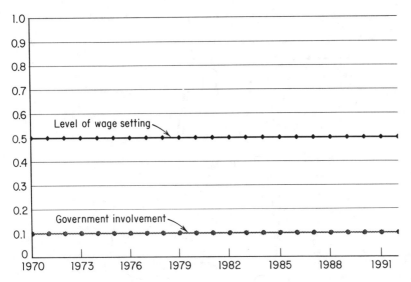

Figure 4.2. The level of wage setting and government involvement in Austria, 1970–1992.

may be more interesting, given how often Austria is held up as a "pure" corporatist system, is the moderate degree of the centralization in wage setting and the low level of government involvement displayed by the data reported in Figure 4.2.[14] Unlike the Nordic countries, there are no peak-level wage negotiations in Austria. Collective agreements are all negotiated at the industry, regional, or plant level. However, the unions' initial bargaining demands are discussed by the ÖGB and the Chamber of Commerce in the Subcommittee on Wages of the Joint Commission prior to the initiation of bargaining. The Joint Commission (composed of representatives of the unions, employers, and the government) has the power to refuse to delay bargaining until the two sides have agreed on a new contract. The Austrian case thus represents a system with regular peak-level discussions regarding the appropriate range of wage settlements but without a formal peak-level agreement.

Direct government involvement in Austria is low. Although the government has representatives on the Joint Commission (and hence can veto proposals since all decisions must be unanimous), the discussion of wage demands takes place in the Subcommittee on Wages where the government is not represented. All firms are legally required to belong to the Chamber of Commerce, however. Since all members of the Chamber of Commerce are obliged to abide by collective agreements signed by the Chamber, this amounts to an automatic extension of industry-level contracts to all workers in the industry.

Denmark

Denmark represents the clearest case of declining centralization in wage setting among our six countries. Even here, however, the situation has fluctuated consider-

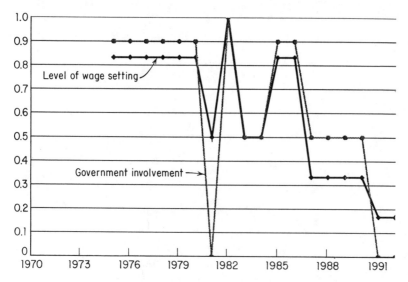

Figure 4.3. The level of wage setting and government involvement in Denmark, 1975–1992.

ably, as the data reported in Figure 4.3 demonstrate. Between 1975 and 1980, industry-level wage increases were determined by Parliament.[15] In 1981, the pattern changed and bargaining took place largely at the industry level. The LO and the peak association representing Danish employers, the DA, imposed settlements in a few smaller industries where the two sides could not come to an agreement. In 1982, however, a return to centralization occurred as the government imposed a general wage freeze. In 1983–84, some industries settled separately, but most were referred by the LO and DA to the state mediator, whose proposal was accepted in a centralized ballot. In 1985–86, Parliament prolonged all contracts when peak-level negotiations reached an impasse.

Since 1987, these fluctuations have ceased and wages in Denmark have been set exclusively in industry-level bargaining. In 1987 and again in 1989, the contracts were linked by the state mediator such that the ratification vote was centralized. This feature did not recur in 1991–92. Hence the coding portrayed in Figure 4.3 shows a further decline in the level of wage bargaining and the degree of government involvement in it for the final two years considered.

A central feature of Danish wage setting is the close correspondence between centralization and government intervention. From 1973 through 1979, wages were determined by Parliament. In most years from 1979 through 1990, wage agreements were negotiated at the industry level but the ratification process was centralized by the state mediator. In those years when the government has not intervened, the unions have bargained separately. Indeed, the unions and employers in the metalworking sector have agreed, as of 1993, to decentralize further and allow unrestricted bargaining at the plant and company level (EIRR, April 1991: 20). The Danish case since 1973 is thus one of no central wage determination without government participation in the process.

Finland

The level of centralization of wage setting in Finland has fluctuated during the last two decades, but without any noticeable long-term trend, as the data displayed in Figure 4.4 show. Since 1968, wage bargaining in Finland has been characterized by tripartite negotiations between the SAK, the *Soumen Tyoenantajain Keskusliitto* (STK—the employers' confederation), and the government. Wage settlements have been regularly linked to changes in tax and social policies. In most years since 1968, the SAK and STK have negotiated a central agreement. These central agreements are not binding, however. The industry-level bargaining that follows is not covered by an industrial peace clause. Strikes, in fact, occur frequently in the subsequent industry negotiations. Since the end of the 1970s, it has become routine for one or more affiliates to negotiate contracts with wage increases above the level specified in the central agreement. Moreover, in 1973, 1977, 1980, 1983, and 1988–89, the SAK and STK failed to agree. In those years industry-level bargaining proceeded without centrally negotiated guidelines.

The government has rarely used its powers to impose wage settlements on the unions and employers in spite of the government's regular participation in tripartite bargaining. Exceptions occurred in 1968–70 and 1978. In 1968–70, the government enacted emergency legislation giving it the power to regulate wages and prices. In 1978, the government requested the SAK to defer a previously agreed upon wage increase. When the SAK agreed, the government acted to require a similar deferment by the confederation of white-collar workers, the TVK, and the confederation of supervisors, the *Suomen Teknisten Toimihenkilöjärjestöjen Keskusliitto* (STTK).

Nothing about developments in Finland suggests that it is undergoing a substantial decentralization of its wage setting practices. Finland's version of centralized but nonbinding bargaining appears to have operated without much change since 1968.

Figure 4.4. The level of wage setting and government involvement in Finland, 1975–1992.

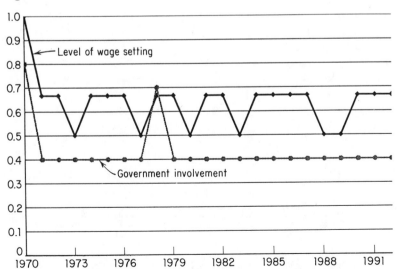

Germany

In Germany, collective bargaining occurs at the industry level (and often at the *land* level as well). The DGB has no authority over its affiliates in industrial conflict, nor does the DGB have any statutory power over the bargaining demands of its affiliates. From 1967 through 1976, however, the DGB, the employers' association, the government, and the *Bundesbank* participated in annual talks, dubbed "concerted action sessions." The talks never produced a formal wage agreement. Since the DGB withdrew from the talks in 1976, the peak associations have not participated in collective bargaining. The role of the government is limited to extending union contracts to cover all workers in the industry and providing statistical information to the bargaining actors through the Council of Economic Experts. The unions affiliated with the major confederation, the DGB, have been successful in maintaining a large share of white-collar union members (over 50 percent since 1970 [Visser, 1990: 151]) while maintaining their near monopoly position among blue-collar workers. Thus the majority of white- and blue-collar workers bargain jointly. Bargaining is coordinated, with the metalworkers consistently the first to settle, thereby setting the standard for the rest.

German bargaining practices appear strikingly stable (Figure 4.5). Although the peak associations have not played much of a role in wage setting since the end of concerted action, the metalworkers' position as the pattern-setter seems secure. In this way, a significant degree of coordination may be achieved even though collective bargaining occurs exclusively at the industry level.

Norway

Apart from 1974 and the early 1980s, wage setting in Norway has been highly centralized during the last two decades, as inspection of the data in Figure 4.6 shows.

Figure 4.5. The level of wage setting and government involvement in Germany, 1970–1992.

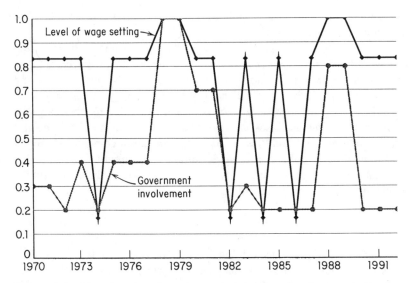

Figure 4.6. The level of wage setting and government involvement in Norway, 1970–1992.

Most bargaining rounds have been dominated by central agreements between the LO and the national employers' association, the *Norsk Arbeidsgiverforening* or NAF, with a peace obligation that covers subsequent industry-level and local bargaining.[16] Two-year contracts are the rule, with renegotiations after one year. Even when the two-year contracts were negotiated at the industry level—1974, 1982, and 1984— the second year renegotiation was conducted at the national level between the peak associations. In 1986, the NAF insisted on purely local bargaining while the LO demanded a centralized wage agreement with special increases for low-wage workers and reductions of working time. The unions emerged victorious after the failure of a general lockout by employers. The subsequent industry-level settlements embodied the original demands of the LO and the leader of the NAF was forced to resign. After 1986, bargaining has remained centralized as unemployment climbed rapidly and the unions and government cooperated in a series of extraordinary wage controls.

The role of the government in wage settlements has varied greatly. Since 1966, a committee of experts drawn from the government and the two peak associations has provided background information and forecasts of the economic consequences of different wage settlements. In addition, the government has often used policy changes to influence bargaining outcomes. The wage agreement of 1970–71 was affected by government price controls. Tripartite bargaining, with the LO, NAF, and the government negotiating comprehensive income agreements including tax and benefit concessions along with wages and salaries, began in 1973 and continued in 1975–77. In 1978–79, Parliament enacted a mandatory wage and price freeze when tripartite negotiations failed. In 1980–81, Parliament extended the LO-NAF agreement to all workers as part of a tripartite agreement. In 1983, the government promised job creation programs if wage guidelines were followed. (The wage guidelines were exceeded.) In 1988–89, the

LO-NAF agreement was made contingent upon government action to prohibit drift and extend the contract to the entire labor market.

Centralized wage setting in Norway appears to have been under stress during the 1980s, a fact reflected in the direct if occasional role played by government in the bargaining process. Because other union confederations were frequently unwilling to abide by centralized agreements, particularly given LO's policy of favoring low-wage workers, the LO sought government involvement in order to prevent other confederations from obtaining increases above the standard set in the LO's central agreement. Yet, in spite of the difficulties posed by the increased competition among unions, no trend toward decentralization of wage setting is apparent so far. A period of relatively decentralized wage setting in Norway characterized the early 1980s. Since 1985, however, centralized wage setting has returned.

Sweden

The Swedish system of collective bargaining looks remarkably stable from 1956 through 1982, as examination of the data analyzed in Figure 4.7 reveals. Wages for private-sector blue-collar workers in Sweden were covered in centralized bargains between employers organized in the SAF and the LO. Although the national bargains were legally only recommendations for subsequent industry-level negotiations, they were binding in the sense that subsequent negotiations took place under industrial peace obligations. Although the government sometimes attempted to influence wage settlements by offering policy concessions, it never formally participated in the negotiations between the LO and the SAF. In the Haga agreements of 1974–76, for example, the government promised to lower income taxes (and raise payroll taxes) in exchange for union wage restraint. In 1980, the government attempted to exchange tax reductions for moderate wage increases without success.

Figure 4.7. The level of wage setting and government involvement in Sweden, 1970–1992.

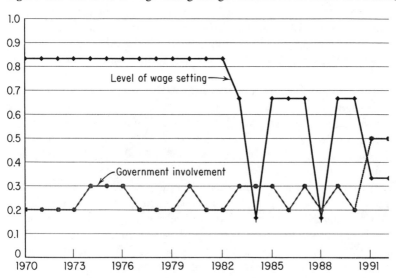

Since 1982, the system has been much less stable. In 1983, the metalworkers withdrew from the central negotiations and signed their own agreement. In addition, the central agreement, covering unions and employers outside the metalworking sector, lacked the customary peace clause. In 1984, there was only industry-level bargaining. Centralized bargaining was reestablished in 1985 and 1986–87, partly in reaction to the assassination of Olof Palme, but without an industrial peace obligation. Bargaining was fully decentralized to the industry level in 1988. In 1989–90 the metalworkers again refused to participate in central negotiations. Also in 1989–90, as in all central agreements since 1983, the central agreement carried no obligation to refrain from strikes at the industry level. Most recently, the LO and SAF accepted the wage guidelines proposed by a government commission in industry-level bargaining with a ban on local bargaining. With the prohibition of increases at the plant level, central negotiators have attempted in the latest bargaining round to gain more centralized control over wages than they have had at any time in the past. Yet the commission's proposals do not have the character of an agreement that would carry an industrial peace obligation.

Throughout the 1980s, as in the early 1970s, the social democratic government instituted tax and social policy changes to encourage moderate wage settlements. In the Rosenbad consultations of 1985, the government offered a one-shot tax rebate if wage increases remained within a specified target. In 1987, the government temporarily froze prices in exchange for the unions' agreement not to reopen negotiations. In 1989, income tax reductions were again promised in exchange for moderate wage increases. An attempt by the government to directly control rising labor costs with a wage freeze and strike ban in 1990 was defeated in Parliament and led to the government's resignation.

Bargaining in Sweden has certainly become less centralized since 1983. But the most notable characteristic of the past decade is ongoing instability rather than any clear trend toward decentralized bargaining. In 1990, the employers' confederation, SAF, announced the dissolution of its bargaining unit, ostensibly to make it impossible to return to centralized negotiations. Only a year later, Swedish employers accepted the centralized wage guidelines recommended by the Rehnberg Commission. The most durable feature of the post-1982 collective bargaining system in Sweden is its chronic instability.

CONCLUSION

In conclusion, we summarize our findings with respect to each of the dimensions of corporatism that we examined.

Encompassingness

There is no general trend toward declining union density among these six countries, nor is there evidence of change in the coverage provided by collective agreements. Only in Austria was union density in 1990 significantly lower than it was in 1970. In Germany, unionization rose slightly during the 1970s and fell slightly during the 1980s. In Norway, union density shows little trend, and in Denmark, Finland, and

Sweden, union membership continued to grow relative to the labor force through most of the past two decades. Moreover, the coverage of wage contracts shows no change over the period.

Concentration

In the Nordic countries, there has been a decline in the number of unions affiliated with the main blue-collar confederation, increasing the concentration of the union movement according to this measure. In most countries, there has been little change in the proportion of members in the largest single or largest three affiliated unions. The most notable change concerns the identity of the largest union. Throughout Northern Europe, metalworkers have ceded their position as the largest blue-collar union to unions representing local government employees. In Austria and Germany, by contrast, there has been surprisingly little change in either the concentration or composition of the union movement.

Associational Monopoly

Again, there is divergence between the Nordic and the Germanic countries. In the former, the relative position of the blue-collar confederation has declined due to the rapid growth of unions affiliated with separate white-collar and professional confederations. In Austria and Germany, on the other hand, there has been no change in the relative position of the major union confederation.

Centralization of Authority

Although considerable variation characterizes the six countries, the extent of statutory authority exercised by confederal offices has not changed in any of the countries under consideration between 1970 and 1992.

Government Participation in Private-Sector Wage Setting

In Austria and Germany, where government involvement was low in 1970, there has been little change since then. Nor has there been much change in Norway, Finland, and Sweden, where governments frequently attempt to influence the outcome of wage negotiations through policy concessions and talks with the peak associations. Only in Denmark, where wages were set in Parliament through most of the 1970s, has there been a decline in the role of the government involvement in wage setting in the 1980s.

Level of Private-Sector Wage Setting

There does not appear to be any common trend across all six countries. The coordinated industry-level bargaining characterizing wage setting in Austria and Germany has proven stable. The centralized wage setting in Norway and Finland, although fluctuating since 1970, exhibits no clear trend. Only in Denmark and Sweden did wage bargaining clearly become more decentralized in the 1980s and early 1990s.

Moreover, the impetus for decline in these two countries appears different. In Sweden, the central conflict concerned solidaristic bargaining. Employers in the metalworking industry sought to escape the egalitarian wages schedules demanded by the LO (Pontusson and Swenson, 1992). In Denmark, decentralized bargaining was adopted in 1981 in order to make government intervention more difficult after a decade in which wages were set in Parliament (Andersen and Risager, 1990). Even among the countries with a similar trend, the story of corporatist decline is surprisingly differentiated.

Such diversity of national experiences is not necessarily inconsistent with claims that corporatist institutions and practices are being buffeted by underlying changes in the nature of production or the international integration of national economies. But our findings reveal that the impact of changes is strikingly different in different countries, even those who entered the current period with relatively similar collective bargaining practices and institutions.

Instead of evidence of a general trend toward declining corporatism in the 1980s, our data reveal contrasts among three groups of countries. First, Austria and Germany exhibit stability on all but one of our measures of peak organization and collective bargaining practices. In both cases, the only change concerns moderate declines in union density. The Scandinavian countries, by contrast, look similar on measures of union structure. In all four, there has been a decline in the monopoly position of the central confederation and an increasing fragmentation of central organizations but at the same time an increased concentration among affiliates and (with the exception of Norway) a growth of union membership. Differences exist, however, regarding the practice of collective bargaining in the four Nordic countries. Sweden and Denmark reveal relatively clear declines in the centralization of wage setting, although even here the decline is less pronounced and more variable than might be expected. Norway and Finland, by contrast, are marked by fluctuating but continued high centralization of the wage setting process. Of course, the content of wage negotiations may have changed even where the level of bargaining has not. Although our indicators do not capture such processes, subsequent statistical analysis will be designed to test for the importance of such omitted variables.

The one dimension of corporatism where decline is evident in all four Nordic countries is the increasing number of actors in collective bargaining. Even in Norway and Finland, where wage agreements continue to be negotiated at the confederal level, there are now multiple confederations on the union side. In addition, the Nordic blue-collar confederations have become less unified as public sector unions have grown larger than the traditionally dominant metalworkers. The Austrian unions remain controlled by the ÖGB. Collective bargaining in Germany is still dominated by the union of German metalworkers, *IG Metall*. In the Nordic countries, in contrast, no single union organization can play such a role any longer.

This preliminary analysis suggests greater diversity in institutional changes affecting wage setting and industrial relations in the highly corporatist countries than is usually imagined. The importance that this diversity might have for the kinds of real economic outcomes that motivated the corporatist debate in the first place has still to be demonstrated. This will require statistical testing of the relationships between the independent variables presented here and such dependent variables as changes in inflation, unemployment, wage rates, and wage dispersion. Only this later analysis will allow us to verify the real importance of the measures presented in this chapter.

APPENDIX: DATA DESCRIPTION AND SOURCES

Number of Affiliates per Union Confederation

Data reported are from the statistical yearbooks for each country.

Union Membership by Confederation and Affiliate

Union membership figures by union and confederation are from the statistical yearbooks for each country, with the following exceptions: Austrian membership figures are from the *ÖGB Annual Report (Taetigkeitsbbericht),* various years. Membership figures for the AC and unaffiliated Danish unions for 1970 are from Visser (1989: Table DE 1/2). Membership figures for the German CGB for 1970 through 1985 are from Visser (1989: Table GE 1/2). Membership in unaffiliated unions in Norway from 1970 through 1983 is from Colbjørnsen, Fennefoss, and Hernes (1985: 76). The figures are those reported by the unions. Retired and self-employed members are generally included.

Net Union Density

The numerator is the total number of active union members (i.e., union members who are neither retired nor self-employed). The denominator is the total number of wage and salary earners plus the unemployed. Source: Visser (1992).

Centralization, Level of Wage Setting, and Government Involvement

Data were gathered by Jonathan Moses, David Ellison, and Torben Iversen on the basis of a lengthy codebook prepared in conjunction with this project. Sources consulted include secondary materials and government and union publications. Additional information is available from the authors upon request.

NOTES

An earlier version of this paper was delivered at the 1992 annual meetings of the American Political Science Association, Chicago, September 3–6. We thank Torben Iversen, Jonathan Moses, and David Ellison for collecting the data reported here, and Randall Kindley for helpful comments. Financial support was provided by the National Science Foundation, SES-9110228 and SES-9108485. At UCLA, additional support was provided by the Center for International Business Education and Research and the Institute of Industrial Relations. Peter Lange acknowledges the hospitality of the Center for the Advanced Study in the Behavioral Sciences.

1. Finland is usually ranked highly corporatist, while the position of Denmark varies from one scale to another. Headey (1970), Schmitter (1981), Crouch (1985), and Cameron (1984) contain perhaps the most frequently cited measures of corporatism used in political science.

2. The larger project, currently under way at both Duke University and UCLA, consists of collecting and analyzing data on wage setting practices and institutions for seventeen advanced industrial societies from 1950 to the present.

3. Schmitter's initial (1974) presentation of the concept encompassed characteristics which ex-

tended well beyond political economy, much less wage setting practices. Much of the subsequent literature, however, narrowed the concept to a focus on the organizations representing workers and employers and their interaction with national government, and the processes through which wage setting was conducted and coordinated with other aspects of national demand management and supply-side policies. It is this latter conceptualization which we employ here. Effectively, we are interested in what has been happening to the "corporatist" organization of economic interests and to the "concerted" peak-level wage and economic policy bargaining between them and with government.

4. In principle, the organizational characteristics of the employers' associations are equally important. In this chapter, we largely follow the standard but unfortunate practice of concentrating on organizational characteristics of the unions for lack of sufficient information regarding employers. We hope soon to have data for employers' associations that match the data we have collected on the unions.

5. Active union members refer to union members who are neither retired nor self-employed. Both adjustments are important. In older blue-collar unions, retired workers frequently constitute as much as 15 percent of union members, while self-employment is common among members of unions organizing persons with university or professional degrees. Visser (1989) has a full discussion of union membership figures and the adjustments that need to be made in order to determine the number of currently working employees who belong to unions. The dependent labor force is defined as the sum of wage and salary earners plus unemployed.

6. These three countries, together with Belgium, are the only countries to utilize the "Ghent system," in which the unions administer a state-subsidized unemployment insurance system.

7. For similar arguments, see Kindley (1992).

8. The seventeen affiliates of the DGB are organized strictly along industrial lines.

9. A recent reorganization plan in Denmark, adopted by the LO Congress in 1989, called for the creation of five new cartels: building and construction, industry, local government, central government, and commerce, transportation, and services. But strong disagreements over the number of cartels—the metalworkers wanted more, the SiD wanted fewer—and the authority of the new cartels—the metalworkers wanted more, the SiD wanted less—resulted in a deadlock. Rather than risk a split of the LO, the reorganization plan was tabled by the LO leadership in the 1991 Congress (EIRR, January 1992: 17–18).

10. In Sweden, the LO's prior approval is required for any strike that involves more than 3 percent of LO members or where "vital interests" are threatened.

11. At least in the Nordic countries, public sector wage setting follows a pattern of its own.

12. Thus, category 0 was scored as 0, category 1 as .17, category 2 as .33, and so on.

13. Note that the categories all refer to the level at which the base or tariff wage is negotiated. In all countries, increases above the base wage, called wage drift, are regularly obtained in subsequent negotiations at the local level. Local bargaining always takes place under the constraint of an industrial peace obligation. The available evidence indicates that the variance of aggregate wage growth is largely determined by the increase in the base wage (Holden, 1989; Hibbs and Locking, 1991). See Moene, Wallerstein, and Hoel (1993) for a theoretical exposition of the relationship between increases in the base wage and wage drift, with and without an industrial peace clause at the local level.

14. See Kindley (1992) for a discussion of the "informal" degree of central control exercised in Austria.

15. We have insufficient information to categorize Danish wage setting prior to 1975.

16. In 1989, the NAF merged with other employers' organizations to form the *Naeringslivet Hovedorganisasjon*, or NHO.

REFERENCES

Andersen, Torben, and Ole Risager. 1990. "Wage Formation in Denmark." In Lars Calmfors, ed., *Wage Formation and Macroeconomic Policy in the Nordic Countries*. Oxford: Oxford University Press.

Cameron, David R. 1984. "Social Democracy, Corporatism, Labour Quiescence, and the Representation of Economic Interest in Advanced Capitalist Society." In John H. Goldthorpe, ed., Order and Conflict in Contemporary Capitalism: Studies in the Political Economy of Western European Nations. Oxford: Oxford University Press.

Colbjørnsen, Tom, Arvid Fennefoss, and Gudmund Hernes. 1985. *Så Samles Vi på Valen*. Oslo: FAFO.

Crouch, Colin. 1985. "Conditions for Trade Union Wage Restraint." In Leon N. Lindberg and Charles S. Maier, eds., *The Politics of Inflation and Economic Stagnation*. Washington, DC: Brookings Institution.

EIRR. 1991. "Denmark: Collective Bargaining and the 1991 Round." *European Industrial Relations Review* 207 (April): 20–23.

EIRR. 1992. "Denmark: LO Congress Fails on Future Cartels Structure." *European Industrial Relations Review* 216 (January): 17–18.

Golden, Miriam. 1993. "The Dynamics of Trade Unionism and National Economic Performance." *American Political Science Review* 87: 439–54.

Headey, Bruce W. 1970. "Trade Unions and National Wage Policies." *Journal of Politics* 32: 407–39.

Hibbs, Douglas A., Jr., and Håkan Locking. 1991. "Wage Compression, Wage Drift, and Wage Inflation in Sweden." FIEF Working Paper No. 87. Stockholm: FIEF.

Holden, Steinar. 1989. "Wage Drift and Bargaining: Evidence from Norway." *Economica* 56: 419–32.

Karlhofer, Ferdinand. 1983. *'Wilde' Streiks in Oesterrich*. Vienna: Boehlan Verlag.

Kindley, Randall Wayne. 1992. "Rational Organization: Labor's Role in the Emergence and Reproduction of Austrian Neo-Corporatism." Ph.D. dissertation, Department of Political Science, Duke University.

Lash, Scott. 1985. "The End of Neo-Corporatism?: The Breakdown of Centralised Bargaining in Sweden." *British Journal of Industrial Relations* 23: 215–39.

Moene, Karl Ove, Michael Wallerstein, and Michael Hoel. 1993. "Bargaining Structure and Economic Performance." In Robert Flanagan, Karl Ove Moene, and Michael Wallerstein, eds., *Trade Union Behavior, Pay Bargaining and Economic Performance*. Oxford: Clarendon Press.

Pontusson, Jonas, and Peter Swenson. 1992. "Markets, Production, Institutions, and Politics: Why Swedish Employers Have Abandoned the Swedish Model." Paper presented at the Eighth International Conference of Europeanists, Chicago, March 27–29.

Rothstein, Bo. 1992. "Labor Market Institutions and Working-Class Strength." In Sven Steinmo, Kathleen Thelan, and Frank Longstreth, eds., *Structuring Politics: Historical Institutionalism in Comparative Analysis*. New York: Cambridge University Press.

Schmitter, Philippe C. 1974. "Still the Century of Corporatism?" *Review of Politics* 36: 7–52.

Schmitter, Philippe C. 1981. "Interest Intermediation and Regime Governability in Contemporary Western Europe and North America." In Suzanne D. Berger, ed., *Organizing Interests in Western Europe: Pluralism, Corporatism, and the Transformation of Politics*. Cambridge: Cambridge University Press.

Visser, Jelle. 1989. *European Trade Unions in Figures*. Deventer, Netherlands: Kluwer Law and Taxation Publishers.

Visser, Jelle. 1990. *Bulletin of Comparative Labour Relations* 18: *In Search of Inclusive Unionism*. Deventer, Netherlands: Kluwer Law and Taxation Publishers.

Visser, Jelle. 1991. "Trends in Trade Union Membership." In OECD, *OECD Employment Outlook, July*. Paris: OECD.

Visser, Jelle. 1992. "Trade Union Membership Database." University of Amsterdam: Unpublished manuscript.

Windmuller, John P. 1981. "Concentration Trends in Union Structure: An International Comparison." *Industrial and Labor Relations Review* 35: 43–57.

5

Strikes Around the World:
A Game Theoretic Approach

GEORGE TSEBELIS and PETER LANGE

The bargaining power of labor vis-à-vis capital declined in the 1980s. A series of conditions contributed to this decline. Unemployment rose in most OECD countries; left-wing governments were replaced by the political right; internal differentiation weakened labor in negotiations; increased capital mobility strengthened the bargaining position of capital. However, these generalized conditions did not have a consistent impact on a central feature of the interaction between labor and capital in industrialized countries: strike activity. Days lost to strikes increased substantially in some OECD (Organization for Economic Cooperation and Development) countries, declined in others, and remained stable in still others (see Table 5.1). Why did similar trends in underlying conditions (decline of labor strength) produce different outcomes in strike activity?

Existing theories do not provide an adequate response to this question; some theories would expect increases and others would predict decreases in strikes, but none of them would expect differences in the direction of response. For example, while the literature on neocorporatist systems correctly foresees labor quiescence—". . . infrequent strike activity and wage restraint" (Cameron, 1984: 170; also Hibbs, 1978)—it remains silent as to why strike rates in corporatist countries like Norway and Sweden would increase in the 1980s.

Another literature expects strike activity to decline with bargaining centralization (Roomkin, 1976). Thus, a generalized increase in strike activity in the 1980s would be anticipated (due to the increase in labor differentiation).

Other theories drawn from economics (Ashenfelter and Johnson, 1969) and political sociology (Tilly, 1978; Snyder, 1975; Shorter and Tilly, 1974) expect a positive association between the strength of unions, and worker militancy and strikes. Such theories would expect a generalized decline in strike activity in the 1980s.

In fact, most existing theories hypothesize a monotonic relation between labor strength and strike activity. Thus, they lead one to expect a movement of strike

INDUSTRIAL RELATIONS CONSEQUENCES

Table 5.1. Strikes in the 1970s and 1980s, Corporatism, and Government by the Left in OECD Countries

| Country | Workdays lost[a] | | Corporatism[b] | | | Left[c] |
	1970s	1980s	C&D	S	C	W
Austria	23	6	1	1	3	49
Australia	3,146	2,050	10	—	10	34
Belgium	826	216	8	7	4	43
Canada	7,321	5,772	16	10	13	0
Denmark	507	450	4	4	6	90
Finland	1,062	976	5	4	5	59
France	3,374	1,207	11	11	14	9
Germany	1,165	744	6	8	8	35
Italy	20,490	11,103	13	13	12	0
Japan	4,443	465	14	—	15	2
Netherlands	166	78	7	6	7	32
New Zealand	292	542	9	—	—	60
Norway	64	204	2	2	2	83
Sweden	161	745	3	2	1	112
Switzerland	5	2	15	9	11	12
U.K.	12,870	8,037	12	12	9	44

[a] Average of thousands of workdays lost due to strikes or lockouts (source: *Yearbook of Labor Statistics*). The United States is omitted because in the 1980s data, strikes involving fewer than 1,000 people are excluded, so the numbers are not comparable.
[b] According to Calmfors and Driffill (C&D) (1988), Schmitter (S) (1981), and Cameron (C) (1984), respectively. The overall index of corporatism is the average of the three indicators. The ranking of some noncorporatist countries may have changed to reflect the omission of the United States from our data set.
[c] According to Wallerstein (W) (1989).

activity in the same direction for all countries in association with uniform changes in political and economic conditions.

Finally, variations in the direction of change of strike activity would be produced by simply hypothesizing that strike rates regress to the mean. If strike activity is random or has a strongly random component, then high or low measurements are less likely to be repeated than intermediate ones. Consequently, countries with high strike activity in the 1970s (like Italy) had nowhere to go but down, and countries with low strike activity (like Norway) were bound to experience an increase in strikes. If such an explanation were consistent with the data, it would eliminate the puzzle. Yet, as the data in Table 5.1 show, other countries do not follow the regression to the mean pattern. Despite the plethora of theories, therefore, we are left without a systematic explanation of the differences in the level and direction of change in strike activity.

This chapter presents a model of bargaining between labor and management that explains the differences in the trends in strike activity for different countries under consistent changes in the underlying conditions. The bargaining model we propose produces a curvilinear relationship between labor bargaining power and strikes. Countries with strong or weak labor have low strike rates, while countries with intermediate levels of labor strength have high levels of strikes. A uniform reduction of labor strength moves countries formerly in the zone of high strength to the intermediate level, leading to an increase in strike activity, while countries from the intermediate level now move to the level of weak labor strength, producing a decline in strikes. Initially low-strength labor movements suffer a further decline in strength, and in strikes.

The argument that strike patterns vary in a curvilinear fashion with the bargaining power of labor has a general, and possibly controversial, policy implication: such a relationship challenges the conventional notion that conflict in democratic capitalist political economies is a direct function of the strength of the workers' movement. This notion underlies many of the commonplace assumptions about the kinds of policies toward labor and the union movement which can be expected of parties of the Left and Right when in government and should be pursued by such parties. In fact, to the extent that such governments are ultimately concerned with their own reelection and, as a result, with the performance of the economy and the negative impact of strikes, it may well be that, under certain conditions defining the strategic interaction between labor and capital, governments of the Right would do better to strengthen labor and governments of the Left to weaken it. Whether political pressures from their core constituencies will permit them to undertake such policies is, of course, another matter. To the extent they cannot, however, our analysis highlights the contradictory situation in which they find themselves, and why such a situation exists.

The chapter is organized into three sections. Section 1 reviews the relevant theoretical literature and compares its predictions regarding strike activity with the actual strike levels of the 1970s and 1980s. Section 2 presents a bargaining game with incomplete information between labor and management. The model predicts high strike activity at intermediate levels of labor strength and low levels at high and low levels of labor strength. Section 3 compares the expectations generated by this model to the actual record of strike activity in OECD countries.

POWER AND INFORMATION: A REVIEW OF SOME LITERATURE

There are primarily three theoretical approaches to the explanation of strikes in the existing literature.[1] The *bargaining power* approach[2] stresses the relative resources unions and employers can bring to bear as they bargain. The *information* approach focuses on the role of information in reaching efficient (and possibly strike-free) agreements. The *game theory* approach stresses the interaction between bargaining parties in an equilibrium context, but it has not been systematically applied to the analysis of labor-capital relations with the possibility of strikes. All three lines of analysis provide useful insights into why strikes occur, but each has theoretical and/ or empirical limitations. We discuss each of these in turn.

Bargaining Power

The bargaining power approach, as we define it, includes all those theories of strikes that explain them as a function of the relative balance of resources (defined differently by different theories) which labor and capital bring to the process and through which they define the wage and other terms of the labor contract.[3] These theories develop hypotheses—sometimes relatively *ad hoc* or inductive—about how different states of the world—economic, political, social—affect the expectations and/or tactical opportunities of the bargaining adversaries. These hypotheses are then tested through time series regression analyses of aggregate strike behavior. The better of these models explain very high degrees of the variance in strike frequency.

Shalev (1980) makes an important distinction between two streams of theory, both of which fall within the bargaining power approach as we define it. First, some theories—predominantly in economics, which we refer to as "bargaining strength" theories—stress the role of economic variables and their effects on wage expectations and employers' willingness to pay. Strikes result from failures in bargaining due to workers' demands that exceed the employers' willingness to pay.

The *locus classicus* of this type of theory is that of Ashenfelter and Johnson (1969). In their model, workers pressure their leaders—who must be responsive for organizational reasons—for a wage increase which exceeds, and which the leaders understand to exceed, the level of wages their employers are willing to offer. If the employer judges the costs of a strike to be less onerous than paying the union's demand, a strike results. But the strike leads to a gradual reduction of the minimum wage workers are willing to accept until it reaches the level at which the strike can be brought to a close. Thus, strikes are the result of a "misalignment" between what workers expect from a contract and what employers are willing to give.

Operationally, strikes are expected to vary with unemployment levels, recent employer profitability, and past changes in real wages, all of which affect workers' wage expectations and/or employers' willingness to pay.[4] Strikes result from economic conditions which make labor more aggressive, leading it to make demands which employers cannot accept. The role of strikes is to realign workers' demands. The power of labor matters, but only because it leads to demands which are economically excessive, given the economic condition of employers.

The second stream of bargaining power explanations of strikes is found primarily in sociology and political science. It emphasizes a far broader range of variables affecting the "power resources" of labor and capital. In some of these theories, manifest conflict becomes more likely as the power resources of labor increase (Tilly, 1978; Snyder, 1975; Shorter and Tilly, 1974). In others, as the balance of power becomes more favorable, unions are expected to exploit their tactical advantages to improve their economic situation. Whether this is done through strikes, however, depends on the relative advantage of using the market versus political means to achieve the greatest gains. As the political arena becomes more advantageous as a result of the strength of workers' parties, a shift of the distributional conflict from the market to politics is anticipated. Thus, labor strength, as manifested in both the labor market and in politics, is expected to give rise to low strike rates (Korpi and Shalev, 1980; Cameron, 1984; Hibbs, 1978; Shalev, 1980; Korpi, 1978, 1983).[5]

Some of the factors considered in this broader conception of the distribution of power resources overlap with the explanatory variables used in the narrower bargaining strength models. However, political and institutional conditions enter fully into the set of explanatory variables so that factors such as the stance of government toward unions and employers and toward strike action, the density of unionization, the capacity of the unions for collective action, the ability of the government to repress, etc., need to be incorporated. More important from a theoretical standpoint, open conflict and strikes are explained as a manifestation of the "continuous struggle for influence and advantage" (Shalev, 1980: 154) between labor and capital, rather than just as an indicator of the alignment of wage expectations with employers' willingness to pay. Moreover, the approach stresses the relative advantages for unions and employers of pursuing their goals through struggle in the political institutions and/or market.

This broader formulation seems to be the more satisfactory line of analysis, for it is more theoretically sound to recognize that it is not only what workers expect or would like to get from wage negotiations but their ability to pursue those expectations which should be considered (Shalev, 1980: 155). This is all the more the case given that wage expectations themselves are likely to be influenced by workers' perceptions of the balance of power between themselves and their employers. Finally, a number of quantitative and more qualitative studies have demonstrated the power of such political and institutional variables in explaining variances in aggregate strike frequency, especially in contexts outside the United States (Shalev, 1980; Korpi and Shalev, 1980; Hibbs, 1978; Snyder, 1975). Thus, political and institutional—and not just economic—variables should certainly be included in any model of strike behavior.

Despite its empirical success, even the more expansive power resources approach to strikes has both empirical and theoretical limitations. Empirically, all existing arguments posit a monotonic relationship between resources and strikes. This relationship is either decreasing (in the neocorporatist literature) or increasing (particularly for single country studies). The authors have good results because they have restricted the universe of countries to which they apply their theories (those at either the high or low end of the scale of labor strength).[6]

The more serious problem with the power resources literature is theoretical: it is rooted in what has been dubbed the "Hicks paradox" (Kennan, 1986), a direct outgrowth of the theory of wage bargaining developed by John Hicks (1963). Hicks argued that the wage settlements arrived at through bargaining are entirely predictable. Using a simple deductive model that relies exclusively on the economic considerations of the union and the employer operating as a bilateral monopoly, he showed that wage settlements are the product of the interaction of the employer's desire to minimize the wage bill but willingness to make wage concessions in the face of a strike threat, and the union's desire to maximize some wage function and consequent resistance to wage concessions, counterbalanced by the costs of a strike. The intersection of two curves, one expressing the union's and the other the employer's trade-offs, produces a determinate outcome on which the bargaining parties cannot simultaneously improve. The problem with this explanation of strikes, however, is that, given any determinate solution, if the actors are rational and fully informed, strikes should never occur:

> . . . if one has a theory which predicts when a strike will occur and what the outcome
> will be, the parties can agree to this outcome in advance, and so avoid the costs of a
> strike. If they do this, the theory ceases to hold . . . strikes are apparently not Pareto
> optimal, since a strike means that the pie shrinks as the employer and the workers argue
> over how it should be divided. If the parties are rational, it is difficult to see why they
> would fail to negotiate a Pareto optimal outcome (Kennan, 1986: 1091).

Thus, if strikes occur, it must be "the result of faulty negotiation . . . adequate
knowledge will always make a settlement—without a strike—possible" (Hicks, 1963:
147).[7] As this suggests, when labor and capital are considered as rational, fully
informed actors, it is not clear why their relative power however measured and however changed from the preceding negotiation should affect the probability of strikes.
Bargaining outcomes reflecting the prevailing balance of power resources should be
attained without recourse to a strike[8] which can only reduce joint net utility without
improving relative payoffs. So, bargaining power theory lacks a fully credible theory
of the behavior of the actors—that is, microfoundations. It seems likely that political
and institutional, and not just economic, variables affect the likelihood of strikes, but
we do not have a satisfactory explanation of why and how.

Information Models

Information models take the Hicks paradox as their starting point, but seek to resolve
it by loosening the perfect information assumption. They have principally argued that
strikes become more likely either when the "informational environment" within
which bargaining takes place becomes more uncertain or less tractable (Cousineau
and Lacroix, 1986);[9] or when one or both of the bargaining actors have private
information to which the other actor does not have easy or immediate access (Hayes,
1984; Mauro, 1982).

While these theories are significantly dissimilar in many of their details,[10] they
share some important features. First, all the theories within this approach seek to
build up from microfoundations. The issue in evaluating these models, therefore, is
the adequacy of their microfoundations, empirically (how well do they incorporate
real world variables) and theoretically (how well do they capture the processes they
are trying to model).

Second, all of these theories consider a relatively narrow range of variables in
discussing the kinds of misinformation which lead to strikes, focusing on "the collective bargaining dynamics internal to the firm" (Cohn and Eaton, 1988:24). They,
therefore, ignore any uncertainty or incomplete information which arises from
changes in the political or institutional environment.[11] This is unsatisfactory in an
effort to build a cross-nationally generalizable theory of strikes.

Third, information models share the view that strikes "result essentially from
misjudgment in a world of imperfect information" (Cousineau and Lacroix, 1986:
385). This approach, then, recognizes that the relative level, or changes in the relative level of power resources cannot, if the actors are fully rational and informed,
explain strikes (Cousineau and Lacroix, 1986: 382).[12]

Yet, information-based theories cannot address the empirical puzzle of this chapter and fail fully to meet the requirements of a satisfactory theoretical treatment of
strikes. They do not incorporate what seem to be empirically important variables

relating to the political and institutional environment in which collective bargaining takes place, nor do they provide an argument connecting uniform change in conditions with both increase and decrease of information (and therefore strikes).

They contain as well an underlying theoretical weakness, for they are premised on the idea that the function of the strike is to transmit information and correct the misperceptions of one or both parties about the other (Mauro, 1982: 536). Strikes, therefore, are treated as mistakes, the result of misjudgment in the presence of incomplete information.

Such an explanation, however, is itself incomplete for it fails to capture a critical distinction between nonstrategic and strategic bargaining. Strikes in the incomplete information models presented thus far are "mistakes" in the sense that each actor would prefer that they did not occur and would act differently if confronted with the same situation again. They are not equilibrium outcomes produced by the actors undertaking appropriate strategic behavior given the information available to them at the time they had to make their decision.

The difference may seem relatively minor, even linguistic, but it is not. Two points illustrate why this is so. First, in the information theories, imperfect information of the actors is treated solely as a source of error and suboptimal outcomes. In a more strategic understanding of the problem, however, the uncertainty or partial information of the adversary is not only a source of potential suboptimality; it can also become a resource in bargaining. For instance, knowing that the opponent does not know with certainty whether one is strong or weak can provide a strategic opportunity better to advance one's interests. A clear example is the bluff in poker with a potentially good hand showing in one's face-up cards. What this suggests is that in a more fully strategic and interactive framework strikes would not be assumed to be the result of "faulty negotiation" or a way to communicate the truth.

Moreover, a strikes-as-equilibria approach has the ability to answer conditional questions, like what would be the effect on the behavior of rational agents if some condition were altered and, thus, to lead to empirically testable predictions. If strikes are mistakes, it is difficult to specify the conditions that lead to these mistakes, and even more difficult to predict what would have happened if some of the parameters of the model were different. The advantages of an equilibrium approach to strikes, therefore, are considerable. Discussion of some contemporary developments in game theory allow us to pursue this approach.

Game Theoretic Models

The third stream of literature relevant to the explanation of strikes includes noncooperative game theoretic models of bargaining. As in Hicks' argument, under complete information, that is, if the players know each others' payoffs (or, more precisely, if the payoffs are common knowledge), there is no possibility of strikes,[13] and the outcomes are efficient. It is impossible to improve the situation of one player without making the other worse off. The reason is that only reasonable demands (justified by the payoffs of the players) are made, and so, the demands are perfectly anticipated and met. The possibility of strikes or disagreements and inefficient outcomes exists only if one or both of the players does not know some of the opponents' payoffs. The situation then is resolved by trial offers, which are sometimes turned down, or sometimes, in the case of labor-management negotiations, by strikes. All of these game theoretic models share with our model the characteristic that they focus on the micro level, and that trial offers (or by extension strikes) are not mistakes, but part of the equilibrium strategies of the players.

These models are precise in the description of the institutional features of the bargaining game itself (who makes the offer, who knows what at each point in time, etc.). They remain, however, abstract in terms of the contextual and empirically relevant factors which, as the empirical literature indicates, influence the outcomes of the bargaining game.[14] Furthermore, most of these models speak about bargaining in general, or about the interaction between seller and buyer, and, therefore, do not include explicitly the possibility of strikes.

The archetypical models of noncooperative bargaining are two models by Rubinstein (1982, 1985, 1986), the first with complete information, the second with one-sided incomplete information (one player knows only his/her own payoffs, while the other knows the payoffs of both). Rubinstein (1986) solved the problem of the division of one dollar between two players. He noted that any division of the dollar is a Nash equilibrium (that is, that any unilateral deviation from the partition is either nonfeasible, or nondesirable). Since there is an infinite number of equilibria in the "divide the dollar" game, Rubinstein tried to find a partition with some characteristics of stability. He considered that each player is impatient, and that this impatience would drive the process of bargaining to its final outcome. Each player makes an offer, which is either accepted or rejected by the opponent. If the offer is accepted, the game ends; if the offer is rejected, the other player makes a new offer which is in turn either accepted (game ends) or rejected (game continues). Rubinstein modeled impatience by a discount factor: in each period of time, the dollar shrinks by a different percentage for each player. He proved that under perfect information this process converges to a unique perfect equilibrium. The first player (whoever it may be) makes an offer which is immediately accepted.

In another paper, Rubinstein (1985) introduced incomplete information (one of the players did not know the other's discount rate). In this case, the first player's offer was not always accepted, and the negotiations could continue for several rounds. Crampton (1983) and Sobel and Takahashi (1983) produced similar bargaining models with one-sided complete information, where only one player could make offers. Fudenberg and Tirole (1983) introduced a model with two-sided uncertainty, but with a finite number (two) of rounds.

We will briefly discuss only two other models which provide important ideas for our own model which follows. Shaked and Sutton (1984) introduce the idea of an "outside option." Their model is a bargaining model with complete information, where one or the other player has the possibility, if he/she wants, to choose an "outside option." If one player chooses the outside option, then with some probability p the game ends, and prespecified payoffs are distributed to the players; with a probability $(1-p)$ the bargaining continues, and a player makes an offer which gets accepted (game ends) or rejected (the game continues), another outside option becomes available, it is taken or not, etc. We will use the concept of outside option to model strikes explicitly. In our model, labor will have the outside option of a strike. If the option is taken, the government steps into the negotiation process with probability p, and gives some payoffs to the players. Empirically, this does not require that the government actually dictate the terms of the agreement between capital and labor but only that with probability p the government will intervene and thereby assure an agreement that will be more, or less, favorable to labor. The agreement itself could still be reached between the bargainers for capital and labor. If the government does not step in to terminate the game, the negotiations continue.

A second model, that of Grossman and Perry (1986), is very similar to the one we subsequently present. Its major innovation over the game theoretic models already presented is that it not only presents a bargaining problem with infinite rounds, but it also introduces the possibility of one-sided or asymmetric information. The situation is that of a seller and a buyer, where the buyer's valuation of the transaction object is unknown. Grossman and Perry's model presents all the desirable properties for a labor-management negotiation game, except for two: (1) it does not include the possibility of strikes and the strategic alternatives generated by this option; (2) it includes only one-sided uncertainty.

As we will see, the model we propose resolves only the first of these problems. Labor and capital bargain over the division of their economic output through negotiations at the factory level, the branch, or the whole country. Strikes are possible and therefore, the actors, especially labor, have expanded possibilities for strategic action. Furthermore, capital is considered to have incomplete information about the strength of labor. To simplify the presentation, we rescale the output so that the negotiation is, in the model, over one dollar.

We present the model in two steps, in order to facilitate understanding. The first discusses a bargaining model with complete information and an outside option (the strike); in this model, strikes never occur. The second step introduces incomplete information which makes strikes possible and helps us understand the reasons why bargaining between capital and labor may lead to strikes.

A MODEL OF STRIKES

Step 1. Bargaining with Complete Information and an Outside Option

There are two players, Labor and Capital. Capital makes a proposal of how to split the dollar; if the offer is accepted, the game ends; if not, Labor has an outside option available. Labor may interrupt bargaining and choose an outside option (the strike). If labor makes this choice, then the bargaining game stops, and each player receives, with probability p, a prespecified payoff of which both are aware; call these payoffs o_C for Capital and o_L for Labor.[15] The bargaining continues with probability $(1-p)$ and Labor makes an offer. Capital can accept, and the game ends; or refuse, and make a new offer.[16] The game repeats until it is terminated by the choice of the outside option, or until there is an agreement.

Both players are impatient, which means that the dollar shrinks in the eyes of each one of them in each period of time by different amounts. Call d_C and d_L the time discount factors of Capital and Labor, respectively. It means that one dollar in period one is worth only d_C to Capital and only d_L to Labor in the next period.

The political meaning of these time discount factors is what generates the impatience of the actors, and, therefore, what drives the negotiation process to its end.

Capital is pressed because of the potential loss of profits with the passage of time, so d_C of a firm can be conceptualized as such a potential due, for instance, to intense competition in the presence of high demand or the absence of inventories in the presence of the prospect of sales. In the case of national bargaining, d_C could represent the level of international competition: the more competitive international markets and the greater the possibility of lost sales if negotiation is prolonged, the more Capital is eager to conclude bargaining. Labor, on the other hand, is pressed to present tangible results to its internal organizational structure. Leaders who do not produce desirable outcomes can face internal challenges and the possibility of replacement or organizational decay. Thus, Labor has a time discount factor. As this implies, the discount factor can be conceptualized in terms of the level of control the leadership possesses over the organization. The higher this level, the less Labor leaders feel pressed to conclude negotiations rapidly.

This rendering of time discount factors permits us to introduce other arenas, and thereby other actors into the model.[17] When Labor, for example, increases its organizational discipline, or solidifies its jurisdictional boundaries, or, in Hirschman's (1970) terms, when there is a reduction in the potential for exit or voice without a commensurate increase in the other, its time discount factor increases and, therefore, *ceteris paribus,* its share of the output (of the dollar) rises. Or, when Capital faces a more competitive economic environment, its time discount factor decreases, it feels pressure to conclude an agreement more quickly, and, consequently, is willing to give up more in order to finish sooner rather than later.

Appendix 1 calculates the equilibrium of the bargaining model between Capital and Labor with outside options. Here we will explain the logic of the outcomes. Labor will choose the outside option only if o_L is greater than the share it would otherwise receive. So, although a strike is always an available outside option for Labor, it will be chosen only if its value is over a certain threshold. Knowing that, Capital will not be affected if the value of the outside option is less than this threshold. If, however, the value of the outside option is greater than the threshold, Capital has to make an offer which will be at least as attractive to Labor as the (discounted for impatience) combination of strike and possible counteroffer.

Here we can report the results and introduce terminology which will be useful in the next and final step. We will call "Strong Labor" (SL) the Labor player with an outside option big enough to be taken whenever the opportunity arises. We will call "Weak Labor" (WL) the Labor player with an outside offer smaller than what would result from the bargaining process (and who, therefore, never selects the outside offer). The outcomes will be reported in the following way: x is the equilibrium share of Capital, and it will be indexed by the order in which the two players take turns in making offers.[18] The first line indicates Capital's share when it goes first and plays against Weak Labor (1). The second line indicates Capital's share when it starts the negotiation process against Strong Labor (2).

$$x_{C,WL} = (1-d_L)/(1-d_L d_C) \tag{1}$$

$$x_{C,SL} = [1 - p o_L - (1-p)d_L]/[1 - (1-p)d_L d_C] \tag{2}$$

Note that in every case, despite the fact that there is the possibility of infinite bargaining, the players' impatience, on the one hand, and complete information on the other, terminate the process in one period: the first offer is such that it is immediately accepted, and the game ends. If Labor is weak, it does not have a credible threat to strike; if it is strong, its strength is anticipated and Capital makes an offer which preempts a strike. Moreover, the value of the outside option does not figure into the solution of the bargaining game between Capital and Weak Labor because under perfect information both players know that such an option will not be exercised, so they disregard it.

Step 2 introduces incomplete information and not only the possibility but also the occurrence of strikes. Moreover, as we shall see, the value of Weak Labor's outside option figures into the solution since it determines the possibility for Weak Labor to bluff and pretend that it is strong in order to extract more from Capital.

Step 2. Bargaining with Incomplete Information

Consider now the case where Capital does not know the value of the outside option for Labor. That is, discount factors are common knowledge, and Labor knows the value of striking, but Capital knows the value of the outside option only as a probability. Labor has a probability w of being weak (value of outside option o_W) and $(1 - w)$ of being strong (value of outside option o_S). The model will examine in detail the case where o_W is less than, and o_S is more than, the value indicated by (1). So, Strong Labor would always strike, while Weak Labor would never strike. This is by far the most interesting case. In the final discussion, we will examine several variations of the model, where some of the assumptions we make here will be relaxed.

The situation can be conceptualized as in Figure 5.1. Labor and Capital must divide the dollar. Labor's share is measured from left to right, while Capital's share is the remainder and is measured from right to left. Strong Labor will strike a deal which is toward the right of Figure 5.1, while Weak Labor will not be able to push the outcome very much to the right. According to our assumptions, o_W, the outside option of Weak Labor, is less than it would obtain through negotiation $(1 - x_{C,WL})$. On the other hand, Strong Labor can obtain more $(1 - x_{C,SL})$ than Weak Labor through negotiation, and the value of its outside option o_S is even higher.

Appendix 2 presents the analytic solution to the problem. Here we will present only the logic of the model. Let us study the problem that each one of the actors faces. As we said, Capital does not know whether it deals with Strong or Weak Labor. However, there is a probability w that Labor is weak, and this probability is common knowledge. Capital knows that any offer which gives Labor less than $(1 - x_{C,WL})$ will be rejected by both Weak and Strong Labor. Thus, because it is pressed for time, it will not make such offers. On the other hand, Capital knows that any offer giving Labor more than what Strong Labor would get (that is, more than $(1 - x_{C,SL})$) would be accepted by both Weak and Strong Labor. Moreover, Capital

Figure 5.1.

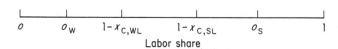

Labor share

knows that if it has to deal with Strong Labor, it will not be able to concede less than $(1 - x_{C,SL})$. In fact, if Capital's offer is any less than $(1 - x_{C,SL})$, Strong Labor will immediately go on strike. So, Capital has to make an offer somewhere in between the two extremes, so that the offer will be accepted by both possible types of Labor, or at least by Weak Labor.

Strong Labor has easy choices. It knows that it can get $(1 - x_{C,SL})$, so it will accept nothing less. If an offer is made, it will accept it only if it grants this share, and go on strike otherwise.

Weak Labor faces a more complicated problem. If Capital knows that it is facing Weak Labor, it will give only $(1 - x_{C,WL})$. However, Capital does not know which opponent it is facing, so there is a possibility for Weak Labor to bluff and behave as if it were strong. That is, if it is offered anything which is considered unacceptable, it will strike first and then make the same counteroffer that Strong Labor would make. One could imagine that Weak Labor could behave exactly as Strong Labor and always strike unless it is offered $(1 - x_{C,SL})$. However, there are costs of such behavior. As we have stated, if the outside option is taken, there is a probability p that the outcome for Weak Labor will be o_W, which is less than it could get through negotiation under perfect information. Hence, Weak Labor's bluffing capacity is limited. If the offer is big enough, Weak Labor will be better off accepting it rather than bluffing and striking.

Knowing all that, Capital will be able to make an offer that makes bluffing by Weak Labor costly. In other words, Capital will be able to make an offer attractive enough to be immediately accepted by Weak Labor. Such an offer is

$$1 - x_{C,L} = \max \{ [po_W + (1-p)d_L(1 - d_C x_{C,SL})], \ (1 - x_{C,WL}) \} \quad (3)$$

which will be accepted by Weak Labor and rejected by Strong Labor. This is the *separating equilibrium* offer of Capital. It manages to separate between the two possible types of Labor. Weak Labor immediately accepts it, while Strong Labor rejects it, strikes, and either receives the outside option (with probability p), or makes a counteroffer (with probability $(1-p)$).

An alternative strategy for Capital would be to make an offer acceptable to both types of Labor. The *pooling equilibrium* offer:

$$1 - x_{C,SL} = 1 - \{ [1 - po_L - (1-p)d_L] / [1 - (1-p)d_L d_C] \} \quad (4)$$

will be immediately accepted by Labor whether weak or strong. Equation (4) leads to a partition of the dollar identical to that in equation (2); that is, the equilibrium that results when Capital is facing Strong Labor and makes an offer first. The calculation of equation (3) is given in Appendix 2. The logic that leads to this equation is to dissuade Weak Labor from bluffing. Weak Labor might be tempted to bluff if the first quantity in the right hand of (3) is greater than the second. In this case, Weak Labor is willing to take the risk of a strike (which is likely to produce unfavorable results since o_W is by definition less than $(1 - x_{C,WL})$) in order to persuade Capital that it is strong and receive $(1 - x_{C,SL})$ in the next round. If the second quantity in the right hand side of equation (3) is greater than the first, then Weak Labor has no bluffing potential. If Weak Labor has no bluffing capacity and Capital wants to probe whether its opponent is strong or weak, it will make the offer $(1 - x_{C,WL})$.

Now it is time to spell out the implications of the model for strike activity. It is obvious from the previous account that strikes occur with probability $1 - w$ only when Capital chooses a separating equilibrium strategy. In pooling equilibria, strikes do not occur. Therefore, we are able to calculate the overall probability of strikes by multiplying the probability that Capital will select the separating equilibrium strategy by $(1 - w)$ (the probability of a strike conditional upon the selection of a separating equilibrium). So, the question of strikes is closely connected to the question of when Capital selects a separating equilibrium.

The logic of equilibrium selection from Capital's viewpoint is the following: The pooling equilibrium strategy gives a sure (low) payoff to Capital. The separating equilibrium offers a gamble. If Labor is weak, it will accept the lower offer. If, however, Capital is facing Strong Labor, it will have to pay the higher price along with the additional penalty of the strike. So, in the face of uncertainty, Capital makes a calculated choice (not at all a "mistake"); it selects the outcome with the highest payoff:

$$x_{C,SL} \geq w x_{C,L} + (1 - w) d_C x_{C,SL} \qquad (5)$$

If (5) holds, Capital will select the pooling equilibrium (no strike). If (5) is false, Capital will select the separating equilibrium which produces strikes with probability $(1 - w)$.

Equation (5) should be read in the following way: If the probability that Labor is strong is high, or if the time discount factor for Capital is low, that is, if Capital is pressed for time, it will give in immediately, and make a proposal acceptable by both Weak and Strong Labor. If, on the contrary, the time discount factor is high, and/or the probability of facing a strong Labor is low, then Capital will pay the price to probe whether the opponent is strong or weak.

To recapitulate:

1. If (5) holds, Capital will treat Labor as if it were strong with probability 1. It will offer $(1 - x_{C,SL})$, and the offer will be accepted immediately. Equation (5) indicates that an immediately acceptable offer becomes more likely when the probability that Labor is strong is high, and when Capital is pressed for time.
2. If (5) does not hold, Capital will make an offer which will be accepted by Weak Labor and rejected by Strong Labor, which will immediately strike. There are two possibilities:
   2a. If the second term in the right-hand side of (3) is greater than the first, then Weak Labor has no bluffing capacity, so the offer will be $(1 - x_{C,WL})$. Weak Labor will accept immediately.
   2b. Otherwise, Weak Labor has bluffing capacity, so it has to be bought by a higher offer. Capital will make the offer $(1 - x_{C,L})$ of equation (3), which will be accepted immediately by Weak Labor.

In this model, strikes occur only when Strong Labor faces an offer which is less than $(1 - x_{C,SL})$. The reason that Capital may make such offers is not due to some miscalculation, but rather to the fact that Capital's time discount factor is sufficiently high, or the probability that Labor is strong sufficiently low, so that it is in the interest of Capital to probe the strength of its opponent. Note also that in this model, Weak Labor never strikes. Its bluffing potential is anticipated and neutralized by Capital.

These formal characteristics of the model prompt some more general observations which serve as preliminaries to an examination of the model's empirical relevance. First, the distributional impact of incomplete information should be underlined. Because Capital is incompletely informed, it has to pay a price. Its offer has to prevent Weak Labor from pretending that it is strong; and if Capital's discount factor is low, or the probability of facing Strong Labor is high, it has to make an offer acceptable to Strong Labor, regardless of whether it is facing a strong or a weak opponent. No such conclusions about the distributional impact of misinformation can be drawn from the information theory discussed earlier.

Second, because of incomplete information, Weak Labor is sometimes able to bluff and pretend it is strong, and extract more concessions from Capital. Equation (3) is crucial in determining the bluffing potential of Weak Labor. If the first term in the right-hand side is greater than the second, Capital has to worry about the bluffs of Weak Labor. If Weak Labor can bluff, then the outside option can be used, and the solution of the game includes the value of this outside option. Note that in equilibrium, Weak Labor never bluffs, because Capital makes a higher offer, precisely in order to prevent it from bluffing. But the absence of evidence of bluffing does not mean that the potential for bluffing, with its distributional consequences, does not exist. Both this potential and its distributional implications are entirely absent from the information theories.

Third, the game does not necessarily end after the first offer, as was the case in the complete information model. It is possible that Capital finds it more profitable to take the risk and probe the identity of its opponent. If it is facing a weak opponent, the offer will be accepted; if the opponent is strong, then a strike will result, and the bargaining game will end in the next round. Therefore, if Capital decides to probe, a strike results with probability $(1-w)$. As we have already said, such behavior is not a mistake, or a miscalculation, or the result of misinformation. It is the best course of action for each one of the actors, given the information that he/she possesses.

Fourth, when a strike occurs, there is a resulting loss of welfare for both actors. In the models of perfect information, the first offer is immediately accepted, so the two actors divide the whole dollar between them. In the model of incomplete information, there are three possible cases: (1) Capital makes an offer acceptable by both Weak and Strong Labor; (2) Capital makes an offer acceptable only by Weak Labor, and is actually facing Weak Labor; (3) Capital makes an offer acceptable only to Weak Labor, while it is actually facing Strong Labor. Only in the first two cases do the players share the whole dollar. In the third case, there is a strike, which may end by the government stepping in and giving to both players their outside option (with probability p), or by continuation of bargaining and loss to both actors because of their time preferences. So, in the third case, one way or the other there is a loss in aggregate welfare. Again, this results from both players pursuing the best course of action available to them in the given situation.

Fifth, it will be useful to our discussion below to offer comments here about the impact of variations in the six parameters of the model (d_L, d_C, o_S, o_W, p, and w) on three characteristics of the outcome of the model: the share of Capital, the bluffing capacity of Weak Labor, and the first offer made by Capital. We remind the reader that Capital's first offer determines whether there will be a strike (with probability $(1-w)$) or not.

The bluffing potential of Weak Labor is directly related to Labor's discount factor (d_L) and the value of the outside options of both Strong and Weak Labor (o_S and o_W); it is inversely related to the time discount factor of Capital (d_C) and the probability that the outside option will be materialized (p).

When the bluffing potential of Weak Labor increases, the share of Capital shrinks, because it has to make an offer acceptable at least to Weak Labor. Moreover, when this potential becomes very high, it may be profitable for Capital to make an offer acceptable to both Weak and Strong Labor instead of probing.

The share of Capital in general increases when its time discount factor (d_C) increases, and when the probability that Labor is weak (w) increases; it decreases with increases in all the other parameters of the model.

Whether Capital will make an offer acceptable to just Weak Labor (which results in a strike with probability $(1 - w)$), or to both Weak and Strong Labor, depends on how close the two offers are to each other, the time discount factor of Capital (d_C), and the probability (w) that Labor is weak. Capital is more likely to make the offer that ends the game immediately rather than wait the closer the two offers are to each other, the lower its discount factor (d_C), and the lower the probability that it faces Weak Labor (w).

Strikes are a function of the probability that Labor is weak w. As we said in the previous paragraph, the selection of the separating equilibrium is an increasing function of w (the probability that Labor is weak). However, once this strategy is selected, the probability that a strike will follow is $(1 - w)$. Combination of these two propositions indicates that strikes will be more likely for intermediate values of w. Indeed, when w is high, separating equilibria will be frequently selected, but Labor will not strike because it is weak. Similarly, when w is low, the strength of Labor will be anticipated and higher offers (preventing strikes) will be made.

As the share of Strong Labor ($1 - x_{C,SL}$) increases, Capital becomes less tempted to test Labor, and therefore, the probability of strikes decreases. Conversely, as the share of Weak Labor ($1 - x_{C,WL}$) increases, Capital becomes more tempted to test Labor, so the probability of strikes increases.

The above discussion indicates that in cases of high Labor strength—whether this is indicated by a low w (a high probability that Labor is strong), a high outside option (o_S), or a high share in the negotiations ($1 - x_{C,SL}$)—reduction of labor strength leads to an increase in strikes. On the contrary, in cases of low labor strength—whether this is indicated by a high w (a high probability that Labor is weak), a low outside option (o_W), or a low share in the negotiations ($1 - x_{C,WL}$)—reduction of labor strength leads to a decrease in strikes. This is the proposition we will test empirically.

STRIKES IN THE 1970s AND 1980s

The game theoretic model presented in the previous section predicts a curvilinear relationship between labor strength and strikes, and is therefore consistent with both lines of analysis found in the corpus of the bargaining power theories— the one that, focusing on noncorporatist countries, predicts an increase in strike activities when labor power increases; and the literature on corporatism that predicts a decrease in strikes in countries where labor is very strong both politically and in the market. In fact, our model provides a synthesis of the two lines of analysis found in the bargaining power literature.

In addition, parts of this model are consistent with the predictions of information theories, which maintain that strikes will increase with lack of information. Consider the curvilinear relation between w (the probability that Labor is weak) and strikes that was discovered in the previous section. Now assume that the two different types of Labor derive from a binomial distribution with probability w. The highest variance of this distribution (that is, the lowest level of information) comes from intermediate values of w. Our findings thus provide a rationale for applying information theories to the empirical question of strikes in the 1970s and 1980s. The difference in our account, however, is that nothing is regarded as a mistake: both actors are rational and attempt to achieve their best outcome in the situation. In particular, Weak Labor tries to make strategic use of Capital's lack of information, and Capital selects its equilibrium strategy in order to prevent such maneuvers from Weak Labor. Similarly, the selection of a separating equilibrium (which leads to strikes) or a pooling one (which avoids them) is made as a maximizing decision by Capital.

One test of our theory would be to try to explain the level of strike activity in different countries. Our theory would predict a curvilinear relationship between strike activity and labor power such as the one presented in equation (6):

$$s = a + cP - dP^2 + e \tag{6}$$

where s is the level of strike activity, c and d are positive constants, and P is some measure of the power of Labor in different countries. The form of the equation (quadratic) captures the curvilinear form of the hypothesis: countries with Strong or Weak Labor (a high or low probability that Labor will be weak) will have low levels of strike activity; countries with intermediate strength (an intermediate probability that Labor will be weak) will have high levels of strike activity.

Figure 5.2 presents two different quadratic curves of strikes. If our theory were a unicausal explanation of strikes, different countries would be placed along one of the parabolas of Figure 5.2 (parabola 1). However, we do not claim to have explained all aspects of strike activity and discovered all its determinants. It is possible that high strike activity in Italy and France can be explained by the existence of strong Communist parties, in the United Kingdom by political conditions, in Canada by labor decentralization, etc. In order to control for such possible explanatory variables one would have to include all the factors operating at the national level in one equation of the form:

$$s = a + \Sigma b_i X_i + cP - dP^2 + e \tag{7}$$

where X_i are (the many) factors we have not included in our model, and for some of which data are not available, and the rest of the equation is the same as in (6). Equation (7) would have countries bounce all around parabola 1 of Figure 5.2. In fact, these other factors influence strike activity so much that the actual plot of strike activity as a function of power does not look like a parabola at all, and regres-

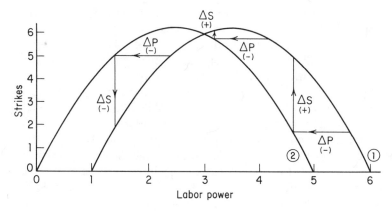

Figure 5.2.

sions do not produce significant results. However, this test does not necessarily suggest that our theory is wrong, but rather that the omitted factors are many and important.

Consider now the same equation (7) applied in the 1970s and 1980s, and take the differences in the left- and right-hand sides. In this case, if we assume that the variables X_i that are omitted from our theory have the same value for each country (which is in itself a heroic assumption), they cancel each other out, and we are left with an equation of the form

$$ds = k - 1(dP) + e \tag{8}$$

A visual representation of the argument is offered in Figure 5.2: we select three points on parabola 1, and trace the change in strikes when labor power decreases. The uniform reduction of labor power P is represented by the horizontal lines connecting parabola 1 with parabola 2; the corresponding change in strikes is represented by the vertical segments connecting parabola 2 with parabola 1. The figure illustrates that this change is positive and significant in the first case (Strong Labor), positive but not significant in the second (intermediate labor power), and negative in the third (Weak Labor).

We will test equation (8). In fact, in Table 5.2 we use a series of different specifications of the dependent variable. We consider the difference in strikes (strikes of the

Table 5.2. Change in Strikes and Labor Power: Regression Results

Dependent variable	Labor strength	t-stat	p	R^2
str80 - str70	444	2.1	.05	.24
str80/str70	.33	4.82	.000	.62
ln(str80/str70)	.09	3.6	.003	.48
(str80-str70)/str70	.32	4.83	.000	.62

1980s minus strikes in the 1970s), the ratio of strikes (strikes in the 1980s over strikes in the 1970s), the relative difference of strikes (strikes in the 1980s minus strikes in the 1970s divided by strikes in the 1970s), and the natural logarithm of the ratio of strikes.[19] It is easy to see that all of these specifications produce qualitatively the same results: Strikes increase in countries with high strength of labor, decrease in countries with low strength of labor, and remain the same in countries in between. Those models that have relative change in strikes as the dependent variable produce better results. The probable cause is that they control for the size of the workforce of a country.

We used the interaction between two indicators to approximate labor strength. The first is the level of corporatism.[20] It is widely believed that labor is stronger the more centralized and concentrated it is, so societal corporatism is a measure of the strength of labor in wage negotiations.[21] The second is the strength of the Left in the political arena.[22] Regressions including only one of these variables come to the same qualitative results with lower fit and are omitted, although participation of the Left in government is a better predictor of strike activity than corporatism.

Of all these specifications, the best, for theoretical and empirical reasons, is the relative difference of strikes: for theoretical reasons, because it eliminates the influence of other variables, such as size of the country or strong influence of particular organized groups (communists, anarchists, etc.) on the dependent variable; for empirical reasons, because the residuals of this regression come closest to a normal distribution (standard assumption for application of least squares models).

The results of the model with relative difference of strikes are plotted in Figure 5.3. The R^2 of the model is .65 (adjusted $R^2 = .62$). The probability that the overall results are due to chance (F-statistic) is less than .0005 and so is the positive coefficient between strength of the Left and increase in strikes (t-statistic = 4.77).

CONCLUSIONS

We presented and preliminarily tested a game theoretic model of strike activity. We showed that the existing literatures on strikes have important strengths and weaknesses. Bargaining theories have a very good fit with the countries they study, but their observations are often skewed to cases most likely to fit their arguments. However, they do not explain the mechanisms by which strikes occur, nor do they have strong theoretical foundations. Our model improved upon both features: it explained the contradictions in the bargaining power literature through a curvilinear relation between labor power and strikes; and more importantly, this curvilinear relationship was *derived* out of the assumption of rationality of the actors involved instead of being posited, as is often the case in the bargaining power literature.

Information theories possess much better theoretical foundations than bargaining power theories, but they ignore important institutional variables and consider strikes as mistakes. Because of the first flaw, it is difficult to formulate expectations about the differential impact of a uniform reduction in labor power on strike activity. Our model improved upon these theories by considering the strategic features of incomplete information, and by presenting an explanation which incorporates a broad set of political, economic, and institutional variables.

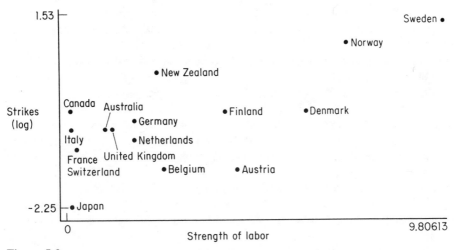

Figure 5.3.

Game theoretic applications to macropolitical economy issues are relatively rare. Most of the models also remain abstract and their connection with actual situations questionable. Our model is part of this game theoretic literature and demonstrates the potential empirical relevance of such models. We do so by investigating possible empirical referents to abstract mathematical concepts and by using the model to resolve the puzzle of differential responses of both capital and labor to uniform reduction of labor power in the 1980s.

Further empirical research along the lines indicated in this chapter is necessary. Most important is the relaxation of the very restrictive assumption that there was a uniform reduction of labor power in the 1980s. While the direction of this change is the same for all countries, the magnitude may have been different. For example, in some countries (like the United Kingdom), the Left lost power in the 1980s; whereas in others (like Sweden), labor power decreased because of decentralization of bargaining. We are in the process of re-estimating the model in order to eliminate this simplifying assumption. The enterprise presents a series of theoretical and empirical difficulties. Some of the indicators of change in labor strength such as changes in unemployment or left-wing government readily exist, but others such as change in decentralization of bargaining remain to be measured.[23] Moreover, assumptions about normal distribution of error terms are much more difficult to satisfy. Our preliminary results with changes in unemployment and left-wing government produce a model with four independent variables and all coefficients with the correct sign but not significant (which is to be expected since the independent variables are highly colinear). Consequently, the qualitative results of our model are quite robust and indicate strong support for the curvilinear relationship between labor strength and strikes. However, further data gathering and empirical research are necessary in order to raise the power of the empirical tests for our model.

Nonetheless, some of the policy implications of our initial findings should be underlined. The most general is that little in the potentially conflictual, but also potentially cooperative, world of capital-labor relations can be fully understood without paying close heed to the strategic character of the relationship and how it is affected by the institutional setting in which it is played out. To base policies on ideological predispositions which generally prescribe unique policies without attending to the strategic setting is to invite policy failure.

Second, it means that policy makers seeking to divine the implications of contextual changes affecting the relative strength of capital and labor should not assume linearity, either nationally or cross-nationally. In fact, such changes are likely to have different effects depending on the particular strategic situation in the bargaining unit with which the analyst/policy maker is concerned. This implication of our findings is particularly relevant in the 1990s when many have argued that the increasing interdependence of the world economy has been weakening the power of labor in national economies and specific sectoral or other markets. Many have drawn the conclusion that such trends, if true, should decrease the frequency and intensity of strikes and other forms of labor militancy. This certainly has broadly been the case, but as we have shown, it is not universal and is a strategically contingent, rather than "necessary," outcome. To the extent that policy makers at the firm, sectoral, or national levels choose the course to follow based on expectations about how contextual changes are affecting the relative power of capital and labor, they would do well to recognize this contingency and adopt policy—whatever their goals—to it.

Finally, as we indicated at the outset, once we recognize that strikes and, more generally, the tenor of capital-labor relations are a function of institutionally embedded strategic interactions, simple nostrums about the appropriate policies for governments of the Left and Right lose their power. Instead, to the extent such governments are interested in their own reelection and thus in the stability and health of the national economy, they will have to pursue policies which may not fit conventional expectations but which are, instead, adapted to the national setting and the strategic balance between capital and labor. Failure to do so, we would suggest, may not only make their policies ineffective for, but even damaging to, their ultimate goals.

APPENDIX 1

Bargaining with outside option (strike) and perfect information

Notation

> call x the share of Capital. x is indexed by the two players, with the player making the offer first.

> call d_L and d_C the time discount factor of Labor and Capital, respectively.

> call o_S and o_W the outside option of Strong and Weak Labor, respectively. Note that o_S is greater than the bargaining share, while o_W is less. As a result o_S is always taken by Strong Labor and appears in the formulas, while o_W is never taken and never appears.

Case 1: Capital + Weak Labor; Capital moves first.

time				$C \geq$ (at least)	$WL \leq$ (at most)
time	0	C	offer	$1 - d_L(1 - d_C x_{C,WL})$	
			accept		$d_L(1 - d_C x_{C,WL})$
time	1	WL	offer		$1 - d_C x_{C,WL}$
			accept	$d_C x_{C,WL}$	
time	2	C	offer	$x_{C,WL}$	
			accept		$1 - x_{C,WL}$

Assume that Capital at time 2 receives at least $x_{C,WL}$. This share is equal to $d_C x_{C,WL}$ at the previous time period. So, Weak Labor can receive at most $1 - d_C x_{C,WL}$ at time 1. Therefore, in the previous time period, Weak Labor can receive at most $d_L(1 - d_C x_{C,WL})$, which leaves at least $1 - d_L(1 - d_C x_{C,WL})$ for Capital.

The same argument can be made by interchanging the terms "at least" and "at most." So, Capital at equilibrium receives exactly $x_{C,WL}$. To calculate $x_{C,WL}$, we equate Capital's share at time 2 with time 0, and solve for $x_{C,WL}$:

$$x_{C,WL} = 1 - d_L(1 - d_C x_{C,WL}) \geq x_{C,WL} = (1 - d_L)/(1 - d_L d_C)$$

Note: In the next case, the table will be presented, and the repetition of the argument will be left to the reader.

Case 2: Capital + Strong Labor; Capital moves first

		C	SL
C	offer	$1 - [p o_S + (1-p)d_L(1 - d_C x_{C,SL})]$	
	accept		$[p o_S + (1-p)d_L(1 - d_C x_{C,SL})]$
			(strike)
SL	offer		$1 - d_C x_{C,SL}$
	accept	$d_C x_{C,SL}$	
C	offer	$x_{C,SL}$	
	accept		$1 - x_{C,SL}$

In equilibrium the initial offer of Capital should be equal with the offer after one round of negotiation. Solving for $x_{C,SL}$ gives:

$$x_{C,SL} = [1 - p o_S - (1-p)d_L] / [1 - (1-p)d_L d_C]$$

Note: Capital and Strong Labor could have such attractive outside options that they are tempted to make unacceptable offers to each other, waiting for the government to intervene. In this case, the expected value for Labor will be:

$$po_S + pd_L(po_S) + p^2 d_L{}^2(po_S) + \ldots = po_S/(1-pd_L) = o_S$$

and

$$po_C + pd_C(po_C) + p^2 d_{C2}(po_C) \ldots = po_C/(1-pd_C) = o_C$$

in order to eliminate this implausible possibility, we assume

$$o_S + o_C < 1$$

Moreover, we assume that $o_C < x_{C,SL}$ (otherwise Capital would choose to have a lockout before making its next offer).

APPENDIX 2

Bargaining with outside option (strike) and incomplete information

Notation. In addition to the notation of Appendix 1, there is probability w that Labor is weak and $(1-w)$ that it is strong.

The solution concept applied here is that of sequential equilibrium (Kreps and Wilson, 1982). Application of this concept requires that strategies are optimal responses to each other for the remainder of the game (subgame perfection) given the players' beliefs; and beliefs are updated along the equilibrium path by Bayes' rule. This concept is not restrictive enough (it leads to too many equilibria), because how a player updates his beliefs off the equilibrium path is not specified. We will assume optimistic conjectures (Rubinstein, 1986). That is, any time Capital sees Labor making a choice off the equilibrium path, it infers that it is confronting Weak Labor. This restriction leads to a unique outcome.

Lemma 1: Any offer greater or equal to $1-x_{C,SL}$ is immediately accepted by Labor.

Proof: See Case 2 in Appendix 1.

Lemma 2: Any offer less than $1-x_{C,WL}$ is rejected by Labor.

Proof: See Case 1 in Appendix 1.

Lemma 3: Strong Labor rejects any offer less than $1-x_{C,SL}$, strikes, and makes a counteroffer of $1-d_C x_{C,SL}$ which is accepted.

Proof: See Case 2 in Appendix 1.

Lemma 4: If Weak Labor rejects an offer, it strikes first, and makes the counteroffer $1-d_C x_{C,SL}$.

Proof: The offer will be at least $1 - x_{C,WL}$ by Lemma 2. If Weak Labor rejects and reacts differently from Strong Labor (either does not strike first, or does not counter-offer $x_{SL,C}$ afterwards), Capital identifies the opponent as weak with probability 1. Consequently, it will never offer more than $1 - x_{C,WL}$. However, several rounds have gone and the share is accordingly discounted.

Lemma 5: An offer which is rejected by both Strong and Weak Labor is a dominated strategy for Capital.

Proof: If both Strong and Weak Labor reject, Capital gains no information, and when it is its turn to make an offer, it finds itself in the initial situation while the dollar has been discounted by d_C^2.

Lemma 6: There are only two undominated equilibrium strategies for Capital.
1. Make the offer $1 - x_{C,SL}$ (pooling equilibrium).
2. Make an offer $1 - x_{C,L}$ which is acceptable by Weak Labor but not by Strong Labor (separating equilibrium).

Proof:
1. An offer more than $1 - x_{C,SL}$ is dominated because $1 - x_{C,SL}$ is accepted by Labor (Lemma 1).
2. An offer in the $[(1 - x_{C,L}), (1 - x_{C,SL})]$ interval is dominated by $(1 - x_{C,L})$. Indeed both of these offers are accepted by Weak Labor and rejected by Strong Labor.
3. Any offer in the $(0, 1 - x_{C,L})$ interval is rejected by both Weak and Strong Labor (Lemma 5).

Theorem 1: The value of $x_{C,L}$ is given by

$$x_{C,L} = \max \{[po_W + (1-p)d_L(1 - d_C x_{C,SL})], (1 - x_{C,WL})\}$$

Proof:

	C	WL
C	$1 - po_W - (1-p)d_L(1 - d_C x_{C,SL})$	
L		$d - d_C x_{C,SL}$
C	$x_{C,SL}$	

From the table it follows that the share of Weak Labor is

$$po_W + (1-p)d_L(1 - d_C x_{C,SL})$$

The rest of the theorem follows from Lemmas 2 and 5.

Theorem 2: Capital offers $1 - x_{C,SL}$ if

$$wx_{C,L} + (1 - w)d_C x_{C,SL} < x_{C,SL} \text{ (pooling); } 1 - x_{C,L} \text{ otherwise (separating).}$$

Proof: Capital has the option of making an offer $(1 - x_{C,SL})$ which will be accepted immediately; or an offer $(1 - x_{C,L})$ which will be accepted by Weak Labor (that is, with probability w), and rejected, followed by a strike and a counteroffer by Strong Labor (with probability $(1-w)$). Capital chooses the expected utility maximizing option.

Note: The belief of Capital is that Labor is strong with probability $(1-w)$ in the beginning of the game; if Capital makes a separating equilibrium offer, it immediately infers with probability 1 what type of Labor it faces. Off-equilibrium beliefs act as a deterrent here so that no player deviates from his equilibrium strategy. Alternative off-equilibrium belief formation would lead to less intuitive equilibria. For example, if Capital has pessimistic beliefs (inferred from an off-equilibrium path move that the opponent is Strong Labor), then Weak Labor will have an incentive to deviate all the time, and therefore, the only equilibrium would be the pooling one.

NOTES

The authors would like to thank Brian Loynd for research assistance. Tsebelis gratefully acknowledges financial support from the UCLA Institute of Industrial Relations. Lange is grateful for financial support provided by the National Science Foundation (#BNS–8700864) through the Center for Advanced Studies in the Behavioral Sciences.

1. We concentrate much of our attention on the relevant literature in economics. We are entirely ignoring the "pluralistic industrialism" approach to strikes which represented the mainstream only ten years ago. Our reason for doing so is that recent work such as that of Hibbs (1978) and Korpi and Shalev (1980) has shown that the arguments found in this literature concerning strikes cannot be sustained.

2. We have adopted a descriptive title for each approach.

3. In keeping with other discussions (Cousineau and Lacroix, 1986), we are including the strike theory of Ashenfelter and Johnson (1969) within the bargaining power approach, despite the fact that it is more deductive and the range of relevant variables is narrow.

4. At the end of their article, Ashenfelter and Johnson (1969) recognize the possible effects of changes in the institutional framework within which bargaining takes place.

5. Lange and Garrett (1985) make a different argument which is, however, congruent with the corporatist literature: that as unions become encompassing (Olson, 1982), they have the interest to contribute to the public good through regulating their wages, but that this will only occur where the government is also favorable to labor.

6. When Paldam and Pedersen (1982) compare seventeen OECD countries, they find both positive and negative coefficients (particularly for unemployment) and divergences from the expectations of the corporatist literature (left-wing governments are sometimes associated with more conflict) *and* of Ashenfelter and Johnson (1969). However, Paldam and Pedersen do not propose a theoretical explanation for their findings. Even Korpi and Shalev (1980) who present a table (Table 3) with a curvilinear relation between labor power and strikes fail to provide an argument for such a relationship. They focus rather on the high end of the scale, underlining the importance of left-wing governments for lower strike rates.

7. Actually, Hicks (1963: 146–47) proposed two basic explanations for strikes in light of his model: imperfect or private information or reputation building. We will not discuss the latter.

8. Cousineau and Lacroix (1986: 377) make the same point when they write that if one assumes that ". . . the parties involved in wage negotiations are informed about changes in the relative bargaining power . . . it would be reasonable to expect changes in relative bargaining power to be reflected in the terms of the wage agreements rather than in strikes."

9. Cousineau and Lacroix (1986: 377) stress that "both the quantity and reliability of information needed to assess relative bargaining power do have significant value in predicting strike incidence."

10. Although all are basically deductive in their construction, Hayes (1984), for instance, relies exclusively on extensive formal modeling while most of the others construct models which are then given empirical referents and tested through regression techniques.

11. It should be underlined that there is nothing inherent in these models which should restrict the range of variables which they consider. For a critique of the narrowness of these models, see Cohn and Eaton (1988).

12. Cousineau and Lacroix (1986: 385) provide evidence showing that economic variables reflecting instability in the informational environment of collective bargaining significantly explain interindustry differences in strike frequency "better than do interindustry differences in relative bargaining power or union militancy."

13. For a model where strikes occur without incomplete information, see Fernandez and Glazer (1991).

14. For a review see Kennan and Wilson (1989).

15. The payoff o_L of Labor includes costs of strike. Such costs are variable, depending on Labor organization, strike funds, etc.

16. One can introduce the possibility of a lockout, but without any additional analytic power. In order to simplify calculations, we introduce a lockout option for Capital which gives lower payoff than the bargaining game, so it is never taken.

The calculations replicate Sutton (1986). The reader should consult that article for more details.

17. In other words, we can study strikes as a game "nested" inside broader political games (Tsebelis, 1990).

18. One can replicate the calculations in Appendix 1 and see that the outcome of the game is not the same if Labor makes an offer first. In fact, there is an advantage to having the first move in this game. We will not pursue the issue further. (For discussion of this issue in a different institutional setting, see Money and Tsebelis, 1992).

19. The reader can verify that three of these specifications produce similar results. It is not accidental. The second and fourth models produce virtually identical results because the relative difference is equal to the ratio minus 1; the second and third produce similar results because $d(\ln x)/dx = dx/x$.

20. As measured by the average of three different measures: Schmitter (1981), Cameron (1984), and Calmfors and Driffill (1988).

21. For a criticism of this point of view, see Golden (1992).

22. As measured by Wallerstein (1989). Wallerstein considers only government participation, so scores countries like Italy and France extremely low. An alternative measure would take into account political strength of the Left even when it is in the opposition.

23. See Lange, Wallerstein, and Golden (Chapter 4, this volume) for such an attempt.

REFERENCES

Ashenfelter, Orley, and George Johnson. 1969. "Bargaining Theory, Trade Unions, and Industrial Strike Activity." *American Economic Review* 59.

Calmfors, Lars, and John Driffill. 1988. "Bargaining Structure, Corporatism and Macroeconomic Performance." *Economic Policy* 3: 13–61.

Cameron, David R. 1984. "Social Democracy, Corporatism, Labor Quiescence and the Representation of Economic Interest in Advanced Capitalist Society." In John Goldthorpe, ed., *Order and Conflict in Contemporary Capitalism*. Oxford: Oxford University Press.

Cohn, Samuel, and Adrienne Eaton. 1988. "Historical Limits of Neoclassical Strike Theories: Evidence from French Coal Mining 1980–1982." *Industrial and Labor Relations Review* 42.

Cousineaux, Jean-Michel, and Robert Lacroix. 1986. "Imperfect Information and Strikes: An Analysis of Canadian Experience, 1967–1982." *Industrial and Labor Relations Review* 39: 3.

Crampton, P. 1983. "Bargaining with Incomplete Information: An Infinite Horizon Model with Continuous Uncertainty." Research Paper 680, Graduate School of Business, Stanford University.

Fernandez, Raquel, and Jacob Glazer. 1991. "Striking for a Bargain Between Two Completely Informed Agents." *American Economic Review* 81 (March).

Fudenberg, D., and J. Tirole. 1983. "Sequential Bargaining under Incomplete Information." *Review of Economic Studies* 50: 221–47.

Golden, Miriam. 1992. "The Dynamics of Trade Unionism and National Economic Performance." Paper presented at the Midwest Political Science Association.

Grossman, S., and M. Perry. 1986. "Sequential Bargaining under Asymmetric Information." *Journal of Economic Theory* 39: 120–54.

Hayes, Beth. 1984. "Unions and Strikes with Asymmetric Information." *Journal of Labor Economics* 2: 57–83.

Hibbs, Douglas A., Jr. 1978. "On the Political Economy of Long-Run Trends in Strike Behavior." *British Journal of Political Science* 8.

Hicks, John R. 1963. *The Theory of Wages,* 2nd ed. London: Macmillan.

Hirschman, Albert O. 1970. *Exit, Voice and Loyalty: Responses to Decline in Firms, Organizations, and States.* Cambridge: Harvard University Press.

Kennan, John. 1986. "The Economics of Strikes." In Orley Ashenfelter and Richard Layards, eds., *Handbook of Labor Economics,* Vol. 2. Amsterdam: North Holland.

Kennan, John, and Robert Wilson. 1989. "Strategic Bargaining Models and Interpretation of Strike Data." *Journal of Applied Econometrics* 4: 87–130.

Korpi, Walter. 1978. *The Working Class in Welfare Capitalism: Work, Unions and Politics in Sweden.* London: Routledge & Kegan Paul.

Korpi, Walter. 1983. *The Democratic Class Struggle.* London: Routledge & Kegan Paul.

Korpi, Walter, and Michael Shalev. 1980. "Strikes, Industrial Relations and Class Conflict in Capitalist Societies." *British Journal of Sociology* 30: 164–87.

Kreps, David M., and Robert Wilson. 1982. "Sequential Equilibria." *Econometrica* 50: 863–94.

Lange, Peter, and Geoffrey Garrett. 1985. "The Politics of Growth: Strategic Interaction and Economic Performance in the Advanced Industrial Democracries, 1974–1980." *Journal of Politics* 47:792–827.

Mauro, Martin. 1982. "Strikes as a Result of Imperfect Information." *Industrial and Labor Relations Review* 35: 522–38.

Money, Jeannette, and George Tsebelis. 1992. "Cicero's Puzzle: Upper House Power in Comparative Perspective." *International Political Science Review* 13: 25–43.

Olson, Mancur. 1982. *The Rise and Decline of Nations: Economic Growth, Stagflation, and Social Rigidities.* New Haven: Yale University Press.

Paldam, Martin, and Peder J. Pedersen. 1982. "The Macroeconomic Strike Model: A Study of Seventeen Countries, 1948–1975." *Industrial and Labor Relations Review* 35: 504–19.

Roomkin, Myron. 1976. "Union Structure, Internal Control, and Strike Activity." *Industrial and Labor Relations Review* 29: 198–217.

Rubinstein, Ariel. 1982. "Perfect Equilibrium in a Bargaining Model." *Econometrica* 50: 97–109.

Rubinstein, Ariel. 1985. "A Bargaining Model with Incomplete Information About Time Preferences." *Econometrica* 53: 1117–32.

Rubinstein, Ariel. 1986. "The Choice of Conjectures in a Bargaining Game with Incomplete Information." In Alvin Roth, ed., *Game-Theoretic Models of Bargaining.* Cambridge: Cambridge University Press.

Schmitter, Philippe. 1981. "Interest Intermediation and Regime Governability in Contemporary Western Europe and North America." In S. Berger, ed., *Organizing Interests in Western Europe.* New York: Cambridge University Press.

Shaked, A., and J. Sutton. 1984. "Involuntary Unemployment as a Perfect Equilibrium in a Bargaining Model." *Econometrica* 52: 1351–64.

Shalev, Michael. 1980. "Trade Unionism and Economic Analysis: The Case of Industrial Conflict." *Journal of Labor Research.* 1: 133–69.

Shorter, Edward, and Charles Tilly. 1974. *Strikes in France, 1830–1968.* London: Cambridge University Press.

Snyder, David. 1975. "Institutional Setting and Industrial Conflict: Comparative Analyses of France, Italy and the United States." *American Sociological Review* 40: 259–78.

Sobel, J., and I. Takahashi. 1983. "A Multi-Stage Model of Bargaining." *Review of Economic Studies* 50: 411–26.

Sutton, J. 1986. "Non-Cooperative Bargaining Theory: An Introduction." *Review of Economic Studies* 53: 709–24.

Tilly, Charles. 1978. *From Mobilization to Revolution.* New York: Random House.

Tsebelis, George. 1990. *Nested Games: Rational Choice in Comparative Politics.* Berkeley: University of California Press.

Wallerstein, Michael. 1989. "Union Organization in Advanced Industrial Democracies." *American Political Science Review* 83: 481–501.

6

The Impact of Foreign Investment on U.S. Industrial Relations: The Case of California's Japanese-Owned Plants

RUTH MILKMAN

The workers of the world are less united today than a century ago, when labor was international and capital national in orientation. Labor movements around the world now operate primarily on a national (or, in some cases, local) basis, even though capital has become increasingly internationalized. In recent years, as transportation and communication costs have dropped and barriers to international trade and investment have collapsed in nation after nation, capital's increased mobility has dramatically weakened organized labor in virtually every country.

The United States, which did so much to foster economic globalization, has become increasingly dependent on the reinvigorated economies of Western Europe and Japan. With relatively few barriers to foreign trade and even fewer to investment (the legacy of its former economic hegemony), the United States has been flooded with imports and with both direct and indirect foreign investment in the last two decades.[1] Once the world's largest creditor, it is now justly famous for its enormous trade and budget deficits; and total foreign direct investment inside the United States now exceeds U.S. direct investment abroad.[2]

This chapter explores a critical aspect of the changed position of the United States in the age of economic globalization: the growth of Japanese direct investment (JDI) and its impact on American workers and organized labor. Although still considerably smaller than direct investment from Western Europe, JDI in the United States has attracted disproportionate attention, both because of its high visibility, linked to persistent anti-Japanese racial prejudice, and because of its spectacular recent growth. From less than $5 billion in 1980, or 6 percent of worldwide direct investment in the United States, JDI skyrocketed to $83.5 billion (21 percent of the total) in 1990, the most recent year for which figures are available. Japan is now second only to Britain as a foreign direct investor in the United States; as recently as 1980 it ranked seventh among investing nations (U.S. Department of Commerce, various issues). JDI is also of special interest from a labor perspective because of its association—which, as we shall see, may be more imaginary than real—with "Japanese" industrial relations and human resource practices, such as quality circles and teamwork.

Against the background of an overview of the growth of JDI in the United States, this chapter explores the implications of JDI for American workers and unions in the manufacturing sector. It shows that while a few high-profile Japanese-owned plants have cooperated with established American unions and have introduced a wide range of "Japanese" managerial practices, these cases are not representative of Japanese-owned plants in the United States. On the contrary, most Japanese firms which have established factories in the United States have resolutely opposed unionism, and have adopted human resource practices that more closely resemble those of traditional nonunion American plants than those of their companies' plants in Japan.

THE GROWTH OF JDI IN THE UNITED STATES

Almost twenty years ago, Richard J. Barnet and Ronald E. Müller (1974: 213–53, 303–33) warned of the impending "LatinAmericanization of the United States." As industrial production (much of it controlled by U.S.-based multinationals) moved to the Third World, they noted, the United States was increasingly faced with the classical dilemma of underdeveloped nations: it was becoming more and more dependent on exports of primary products to maintain its balance of payments while increasingly importing manufactured goods. Barnet and Müller also pointed to the growing polarization of income distribution and the expanding political power of corporations in the United States as symptoms of "LatinAmericanization." They suggested, prophetically, that the accelerating international mobility of capital was undermining the power of organized labor in the United States, creating a new imperative for transnational forms of unionism.

Barnet and Müller were primarily concerned with the consequences of outward investment. In the period since they wrote, however, international capital has increasingly flowed *into* the United States. "The tables have turned on foreign investment in America," the London *Economist* noted in 1988. "For decades it was American firms that bought foreign rivals and set up factories around the world. Now it is the foreigners writing the cheques." (*Economist,* 1988: 74) The bulk of foreign direct investment in the United States still originates in Europe, but in the 1980s Japan emerged as an increasingly important source. In the 1970s, JDI in the United States was modest, totaling only $600 million in 1975 (compared with $18.6 million from Europe that year). However, by 1981 JDI had multiplied more than tenfold, to $7.7 billion; that was also the first year in which JDI in the United States exceeded U.S. direct investment in Japan. During the 1980s, JDI expanded even more rapidly. While the magnitude of the increase is difficult to measure precisely, due to the dramatic weakening of the dollar in relation to the yen during this period, by any standard JDI soared during the 1980s. By 1990 it stood at $83.5 billion, according to U.S. Department of Commerce figures. That was more than four times the level of U.S. direct investment in Japan and over one-third the amount of direct investment in the United States from all the nations of Western Europe combined (U.S. Department of Commerce, August 1991: 54).

JDI is present in many different sectors of the U. S. economy, from manufacturing, real estate, and banking to wholesale and retail trade. Throughout the 1980s, manufacturing accounted for about 20 percent of the total, increasing as rapidly as JDI in the United States generally. Over 11 percent of all foreign direct investment in U.S. manufacturing originated in Japan in 1989, compared with 5 percent as recently as 1987 (U.S. Department of Commerce, various issues).

The success of export-oriented industrialization in Japan in the 1960s and 1970s generated enormous amounts of capital, which made extensive direct investment abroad possible. As the largest single market for Japanese products, the United States became an especially attractive site for JDI. The growing trade friction between the United States and Japan played a critical role here, for JDI was basically a preemptive strike against protectionism. When the United States attempted to alleviate its trade deficit by manipulating the value of the dollar in the mid-1980s, the resulting cheapening of production costs further accelerated the growth of JDI. In addition, labor conditions in the United States made it attractive to foreign investors. By the late 1980s, wages were only slightly higher than in Japan, unionization rates were low by any standard, and labor was more tractable than in other nations with developed economies.

Nations with large internal markets have always been attractive sites for foreign direct investment, especially in the manufacturing sector. The United States, with the world's largest domestic market, was therefore a natural magnet for the Japanese capital that accumulated so rapidly in the 1970s and 1980s. This pattern was reinforced by the longstanding prestige of the United States as a market for Japanese goods, dating back to the days of unquestioned American economic supremacy in the immediate postwar period. In the 1960s, when Japanese exports to the United States began their rapid growth, the mark of success and prestige for a Japanese firm was to be able to sell its products to American consumers. By the 1970s and 1980s, Japanese manufactured goods were already being sold in vast quantities in the U.S. market, so that direct investment involved relatively few risks.

As early as 1975, the United States accounted for over a fifth of all JDI worldwide, according to Japanese government data.[3] The U.S. share has increased steadily ever since, even as JDI worldwide has skyrocketed. World JDI grew over 800 percent between 1980 and 1990, while JDI in the Unites Sates grew almost 1500 percent in that period. The U.S. share of worldwide JDI expanded from 24 percent of world JDI in 1980 to 42 percent in 1990. The North American share of world JDI in manufacturing rose even more sharply, from 19 percent in 1980 to *49 percent in 1990*.[4] In fact, by 1990, Japan had invested $40.3 billion in North American manufacturing, more than twice the level of manufacturing JDI in all of Asia ($18.7 billion, excluding Japan itself) and over three times the level ($12.5 billion) in Europe (Japan Ministry of Finance, June 1991: 22 and various earlier issues).

As JDI in North American manufacturing grew, it underwent a radical change in composition. At the beginning of the 1970s, the vast bulk (78%) of manufacturing JDI in North America involved the wood products industry. A decade later, JDI in North American manufacturing had become much more diversified, with wood products accounting for only 13 percent of the total and electrical products in the lead with 24 percent. By 1990, after a twentyfold increase in JDI in North American manufacturing relative to 1979, transportation equipment was in second place with 12 percent of the total, but electrical products retained their lead with 28 percent. Other important sectors were chemicals, with 12 percent of the total, and metals and machinery, each with 10 percent (Sebestyen, 1972: 20; Japan Ministry of Finance, August 1980: 18; Japan Ministry of Finance, June 1991: 22).

As the U.S.-Japan trade deficit widened in the 1970s and 1980s, the specter of protectionism posed an increasingly serious problem for which JDI quickly emerged as a solution. Much of the new JDI, especially in manufacturing, was essentially export substitution, whereby Japanese firms transferred production to the United States of goods that were formerly made in Japan and exported to the United States. In contrast to the import substitution industry that developed in the Third World in earlier decades, here it was the investing country rather than the host that took the initiative in making the switch from exports to direct investment. While there was ongoing American concern about the trade deficit, and continuing pressure to restrict imports, there was no significant opposition to the growth of JDI; on the contrary, it was widely embraced by policy-making elites as a welcome solution to the nation's trade problems. Organized labor, too, while critical of outward investment by U.S.-based multinationals because of the domestic job losses it usually produces, has generally welcomed inward investment. As Howard Samuel, president of the Industrial Union Department of the AFL-CIO, recently stated, "We support foreign investment. It can be extremely useful in maintaining jobs and improving company prospects" (Judis, 1991: 55–56).

In the mid-1980s, the Reagan administration deliberately depreciated the dollar, halving its value in relation to the yen and most other major currencies, hoping this would make imports more expensive and exports cheaper. As a strategy to resolve the trade problem, the depreciation was a dismal failure. Indeed, the dollar had already declined in value in relation to the Japanese yen and the German mark during the 1970s, yet the U.S. historical trade surplus had been replaced by a trade deficit in that very decade. By the time the government lowered the value of the dollar in the mid-1980s, many popular consumer products—such as videocassette recorders and other consumer electronics—were not even manufactured in the United States and thus continued to be imported regardless of price. Although the depreciation of the dollar did little to ameliorate the trade deficit, it did cut the cost of direct investment in the United States in half, as the yen-dollar ratio fell from 251 in 1984 to 124 in 1987 (United Nations, 1990: 184). This accelerated the existing trend toward growth of JDI and inward investment more generally. Foreign investors moved in rapidly in the late 1980s, acquiring existing firms, purchasing real estate, and setting up entirely new operations—all at bargain prices.

Indeed, as the *New York Times* (Nasar, 1991: 1) put it in a front-page story in the spring of 1991, "the United States, long derided as an industrial has-been, has become one of the world's low-cost manufacturers." Labor compensation costs (wages and benefits) in the United States, although still high by world standards, declined dramatically (i.e., rose less rapidly) relative to many other developed countries in the 1970s and 1980s. As Table 6.1 shows, in the 1960s U.S. workers were better compensated than those in virtually all other nations, but by 1988, workers in West Germany, Belgium, the Netherlands, and all of Scandinavia had higher compensation rates than those in the United States (U.S. Department of Labor, 1989: 572). In Japan as recently as 1980, compensation levels were only 57 percent of the U. S. level, but they rose to 95 percent of the U.S. level by 1988. Of course, this partly reflects the devaluation of the dollar, but the virtual disappearance of the wage gap is nonetheless a major spur to Japanese investment.

Foreign firms find other aspects of the U.S. labor climate attractive as well. In their 1980 book *The New International Division of Labour,* Folker Froebel and his colleagues identified several advantages the United States offered European investors that they lacked at home:

> . . . skilled and often non-trade union organised workers, good sites for export-oriented production, indirect and direct government investment assistance, "political stability," and, in addition, the great importance of the U.S. domestic market. . . . U.S. companies have on average relocated their production to quite a considerable extent . . . to the new sites abroad. This has led to the creation of chronically high open and hidden unemployment and stagnating or falling real incomes for workers. The USA has therefore become a favourable location for technologically advanced production for West European countries . . . . Alongside changes in the value of the dollar, lower social benefits and more hours worked per worker per year also play their part. The pace of work is somewhat higher and working hours per year longer (fewer holidays and days off), and it is easier to dismiss workers. The existence of different degrees of union organisation is also influential in the choice of site. The low level of union organisation is offered as an incentive to foreign companies. (Froebel et al., 1980: 251–52)

Indeed, as Table 6.1 shows, hours worked per year in the United States are much more extensive than in most of Western Europe (where vacations and other leaves customarily are far longer), and are exceeded only in Japan itself (see Landers, 1988: 314–22). Unemployment is low in the United States compared with Western Europe as well, but it is twice the Japanese level. The actual supply of labor for manufacturing industry is even more ample than these figures suggest, due to surging immigration combined with the decline of domestic manufacturing.

Another major attraction of the United States, from the viewpoint of foreign investors, is the low, and rapidly declining, rate of union membership. For many decades, the United States had lower union density than most other developed nations, but in the 1970s and 1980s its already low unionization rate declined dramatically. The aggregate figures shown in Table 6.1 conceal an even steeper decline in private sector unionization, which had fallen to 12 percent (for nonfarm wage and salary workers) by 1990. In manufacturing, the rate remains higher than for U.S. workers generally, with 21 percent unionized in 1989, but this is still a low figure by international standards.[5] The United States also compares favorably—from an investor's perspective—to many other countries in regard to time lost to work stoppages: of the countries shown in Table 6.1, only West Germany and Japan lost fewer hours per worker.

THE IMPACT OF JDI ON U.S. WORKERS: PROMISE AND REALITY

One reason for the lack of effective domestic opposition to increased foreign direct investment in the United States was the expectation that it would generate job

Table 6.1. Wages, Hours, Unemployment, Work Stoppages, and Unionization Levels, Selected Countries, 1960–1988

	Year	U.S.	Japan	France	FRG	U.K.	Italy	Sweden	Canada
Hourly compensation	1960	$2.66	$0.26	$0.82	$0.85	$0.84	$0.63	$1.20	$2.13
costs for production	1970	4.18	.99	1.72	2.33	1.49	1.76	2.93	3.46
workers in	1980	9.84	5.61	8.94	12.33	7.43	8.00	12.51	8.37
manufacturing(U.S. $)[a]	1988	$13.90	$13.14	$12.99	$18.07	$10.56	$12.87	$16.85	$13.58
Hours worked per	1960	1940	2509	1957	2079	2127	2046	1970	1881[b]
worker per year in	1970	1913	2269	1872	1889	1997	1905	1744	1918
manufacturing	1980	1885	2158	1713	1701	1838	1742	1508	1852
	1989	1956	2159	1610	1603	1851	1858	1487	1895
Civilian unemployment	1960	5.5	1.7	1.5	1.1	2.2	3.7	1.7	6.5
rate (%)	1970	4.9	1.2	2.5	0.5	3.1	3.2	1.5	5.7
	1980	7.1	2.0	6.4	2.9	7.0	4.4	2.0	7.5
	1988	5.5	2.5	10.5	7.1	8.3	7.9	1.6	7.8
Union membership as a	1960	32	34	24	39	45	55–60	68	31
percentage of all non-	1970	31	35	22	37	51	50–55	79	32
farm wage and salary	1980	25	31	28	42	57	43	90	36
workers	1987	17	28	10–19[c]	43[d]	50[d]	38[e]	96[e]	36
Days lost to work	1960	248	216	89	2	138	127	6	156
stoppages per 1000	1970	759	120	113	4	499	1554	48	951
nonfarm employees	1980	235	25	96	6	529	1002	1173	945
	1988	43	4	70	1[f]	169	174	01[f]	313

[a] Includes pay for time worked; for vacations, holidays, and leave; bonuses and special payments; and pay in kind, before payroll deductions. Also includes employer expenditures for legally required insurance programs and contractual and private benefit plans. For some countries, adjusted for payroll taxes and other factors that are regarded as labor costs.
[b] 1961 figure (1960 not available).
[c] 1988 estimate (1987 not available).
[d] 1986 figures (1987 not available).
[e] 1985 figure (1987 not available).
[f] 1987 figures (1988 not available).
Sources: Hourly compensation for 1980, 1988; unemployment, and work stoppages: U.S. Department of Labor, Bureau of Labor Statistics, *Handbook of Labor Statistics,* Bulletin 2340 (August 1989), pp. 554, 572, and 581; hourly compensation for 1960, 1970: U.S. Department of Labor, Bureau of Labor Statistics, *Handbook of Labor Statistics,* Bulletin 2271 (June 1985), p. 437; hours worked for all countries, and unionization except as noted below: unpublished data from the U.S. Department of Labor, Bureau of Labor Statistics, Office of Productivity and Technology, Division of Foreign Labor Statistics; other unionization data from: *Economist,* June 23, 1990, p. 62 (for France 1988 estimate); and for Italy in 1980 and 1985, computed from Guido Romagnoli, "Sindacalizzazione e rappresentanza," in Guido Baglioni, Ettore Santi, and Corrado Squarzon, eds., *Le Relazioni Sindacali in Italia: Rapporto 1981* (1982), p. 177; and Guido Romagnoli, "Sindacalizzazione e rappresentanza," in Guido Baglioni, Rinaldo Milani, and Ettore Santi, eds., *Le Relazioni Sindacali in Italia: Rapporto 1985/86* (1987), p. 181.

growth. However, foreign-controlled jobs from all countries account for only 4.8 percent of all U.S. employment, and 8.9 percent of employment in U.S. manufacturing. The number of U.S. residents who are directly employed by Japanese-owned companies remains surprisingly small—just over 500,000 people in 1989, the last year for which data are available. Firms based in the United Kingdom and in Canada both employ more people in this country than do firms based in Japan. Still, Japanese-based firms' employment is growing twice as rapidly as employment in foreign-based companies generally, and as JDI continues to grow, it will become a more significant part of the U.S. labor market.[6]

Another widespread expectation was that JDI would help the United States and its workers by establishing internationally competitive factories in the United States, and institutionalizing the human resource techniques and labor relations policies that are widely presumed to have contributed to Japan's recent industrial success. In the popular imagination and in the management literature and media representations that feed it, Japanese management is associated with efficient, "lean" production and with a variety of mechanisms designed to foster worker participation in decision making. Raw materials and parts are delivered "just-in-time" for their use in the production process; workers meet in quality circles or similar small groups to discuss problems that were traditionally in the managerial domain; manual jobs are rotated among teams of workers to encourage a flexible, multiskilled workforce; workers enjoy a high degree of job security, perhaps approximating "lifetime employment," and so forth.

Until recently, most commentators presumed that such "Japanese" management practices were culturally indigenous to Japan, or at least to Asia, and not readily transferable to the United States (or Europe). However, that claim cannot be sustained today, in view of the striking success of the Japanese "transplants" in the auto industry. It is now indisputable that the Japanese model is compatible with a U.S. workforce, and even with a unionized one. The best known example of this is the New United Motor Manufacturing Inc. (NUMMI) plant in Fremont, California, a joint venture of General Motors and Toyota, which has achieved levels of productivity and quality superior to that of any other U.S. auto assembly plant, and comparable to that of Toyota's plants in Japan (See Womack, et al., 1990: 83). NUMMI opened in 1984 at a plant GM had closed two years earlier, with a workforce drawn from the ranks of former GM employees, who continue to be represented by the United Auto Workers union (UAW).

Not only in its high productivity and quality, but also from the viewpoint of workers themselves, NUMMI compares favorably with the traditional American system of work organization that characterized the plant when it was run by GM. NUMMI's blue-collar workers are centrally involved in improving the production process. Production workers are organized into flexible teams that rotate jobs and meet regularly to discuss how the efficiency of the operations they perform could be enhanced. The Japanese word *kaizen* (continuous improvement) is part of every team member's vocabulary. In sharp contrast to the many markers of status at GM, managers and workers at NUMMI wear the same clothes and share the same parking and cafeteria facilities. At NUMMI management is defined not as supervision but as leadership: each team has a "team leader" and at the next level up there are "group leaders" (roughly equivalent to foremen at GM). Although it does not offer "lifetime employment," NUMMI's contract with the UAW includes a pledge that no workers will be laid off without first cutting management pay and taking other cost-cutting measures. To date, despite periods of slow sales, there have been no layoffs.[7] The union includes a dissident faction, but even this group prefers the team concept to the old GM system.

Although often touted as a model of labor-management cooperation in an age of intensified global competition, the NUMMI system has also been the object of serious debate among labor scholars. Its most prominent critics are Mike Parker and Jane

Slaughter (1988), who call the system "management by stress" and emphasize the fact that it greatly intensifies the pace of work. They warn that the "team concept" undermines unionism in the name of a dubious form of worker participation in management decisions. At NUMMI, they suggest, workers mainly "participate" in the intensification of their own exploitation, mobilizing their detailed knowledge of the labor process to help management speed up production and eliminate wasteful work practices. But even Parker and Slaughter acknowledge that workers themselves prefer the current setup to traditional "American" managerial methods. "Nobody says they want to return to the days when GM ran the plant," they report.[8]

Both critics and advocates of the team system often presume that NUMMI is representative of Japanese-owned plants in the United States. But a closer look reveals that this is generally not the case. Instead, most Japanese-owned manufacturing plants are resolutely opposed to unionism, and outside the auto industry most use American-style labor policies, rather than replicating the "Japanese" model. The Japanese-owned plants I studied in California bear little resemblance to their parent companies' operations in Japan. Instead, they are like the Japanese-owned firms Harley Shaiken and Harry Browne (1991) studied in Mexico, where managers "seem to be satisfied with using traditional quality control and work organization methods to achieve internationally competitive quality and costs, passing over the techniques that are credited with bringing their parent companies stunning success in both categories" (Shaiken and Browne, 1991: 48–49). Few of the managers Shaiken and Browne interviewed at Japanese-owned plants in Mexico had ever heard of *kaizen,* and very few of those plants had anything resembling quality circles. Similarly, Japanese-owned firms in Southeast Asia seldom use the participatory management practices their parent companies are known for (Maruyama, 1988).

JAPANESE-OWNED FACTORIES IN CALIFORNIA

I conducted detailed research on Japanese-owned factories in California, where almost a fifth of the nation's Japanese-owned plants are located.[9] In 1989, under the auspices of the UCLA Institute of Industrial Relations, I surveyed the sixty-six Japanese-owned manufacturing plants in the state with more than 100 workers, obtaining a 76 percent response rate.[10] Following the survey, in the spring of 1990 I arranged plant visits and interviews with managers at twenty of these plants. All of these were in Southern California, where almost three-fourths of the sixty-six plants are located. In the fall of 1990 I also visited five factories in Japan and interviewed managers there.[11]

California, and especially Southern California, attracts a disproportionate share of JDI for several reasons. Its long history as the main receiving station for Japanese exports to the United States is one important factor. In addition, like their domestic counterparts, many Japanese manufacturers find the state's ample supply of immigrant labor and the weakness of unionism highly attractive. "To many foreign firms, saving money on wage costs is far less important than control of the labor force," Norman Glickman and Douglas Woodward (1989: 209) point out in their authoritative study of foreign investment in the United States. "Along with proximity to growing markets, numerous surveys show that an absence of unions and positive 'worker attitudes' consistently rank at the top of foreign firms' state and regional preferences." Unionism is particularly weak in the California electronics industry, which accounts for over half (56 percent) of the state's Japanese-owned plants with more than 100 employees. Another 14 percent are in the metals and metal products industry, and 11 percent are in food products, with the rest in an assortment of other industries (derived from data in Japan Economic Institute, 1988).

The managers I interviewed frequently cited labor considerations when asked why their plants were located in Southern California. One American manager at a Japanese-owned electronics plant established in the mid-1970s, noting that "the Japanese are famous for location studies," recalled that in-depth research was done to select the site for the plant where he worked. "Cost was one concern," he said, "but other things were more important, especially the labor supply and a good working environment." Similarly, a manager employed by a large Japanese-owned electronics plant in San Diego, also built in the 1970s, said that in addition to its proximity to the Pacific Rim, San Diego was an attractive location for this firm because "the labor climate was good and availability of labor was ample." Another manager at a plastics plant located just east of Los Angeles attributed its site selection in the mid-1980s to low land and labor costs relative to other parts of Southern California, and to the perception that "the union situation seemed better here."

Just what is it about the labor situation in Southern California that is so attractive to these firms? The evidence suggests that they are looking for tractable, nonunion labor that is available at low wages. Their skill requirements are generally low, thanks to the routinized nature of most of the production processes carried out in these branch plants. In practice, this means that, like many of their domestically owned counterparts, Japanese-owned factories in Southern California rely heavily on the state's abundant supply of immigrant labor in recruiting production workers. Thus they combine foreign capital with foreign labor to produce goods "made in the U.S.A." The middle managers and clerical workers are typically the only native presence.

Depending on the composition of the population in the vicinity of their particular location, California's Japanese-owned plants employ Mexican, Salvadoran, Vietnamese, Thai, Filipino, and/or other immigrant workers from Asia and Latin America. In one plant located near the U.S.-Mexico border, a manager claimed that some workers actually live in Tijuana, Mexico, and walk across the border to come to work each day. Among the twenty plants I visited, none had a production workforce that was more than 50 percent native-born Caucasian. This upper limit was reported for only three plants; at the other seventeen at least two-thirds of the workforce was comprised of immigrants, and in many cases the figure was 90 percent or more. African-Americans, on the other hand, were conspicuously underrepresented in the workforce at most of these factories, and in many cases they were entirely absent.[12]

When asked what kind of criteria they used in selecting workers for employment, the managers I interviewed were careful to emphasize that they did not discriminate on the basis of race or ethnicity, and many cited the high proportion of "minorities" in their workforce in support of this contention. One manager volunteered that he thought the reason the plant had a largely immigrant workforce was because unlike native-born whites "like my kids, who think they should start at $10 or $15 an hour," immigrants "are willing to work their way up from the bottom."

None of the twenty plants had specific educational requirements for their production workers. While some managers reported that they gave preference to applicants with a high school diploma, almost all acknowledged that a substantial portion of their workforce had less than a high school education. While many said that they preferred workers with basic English language skills, this too was an ideal rarely realized in actual practice. The standard solution to the communication problem seemed to be to hire first-line supervisors from the same ethnic group as the workers they supervised, and these individuals were bilingual. In addition, on the factory tours I observed many bilingual signs.

The hiring process for production workers typically involved filling out an application form and a brief interview with either the personnel manager or the first-line supervisor. Few firms bothered to check workers' references. Only one of the twenty conducted any pre-employment aptitude testing (in this case for vision and manual dexterity). Five of the firms did pre-employment drug testing, usually as part of a general physical exam. Two firms relied on temporary employment agencies to recruit new workers, but most simply hired workers "off the street." While waiting in the plant's front office prior to interviewing a manager, I frequently noticed piles of blank application forms, and in a few cases I saw workers completing them. These plants rarely found it necessary to advertise job openings for production jobs; most could be easily filled by "walk-ins" and applications on file. Many firms relied on immigrant workers' networks to spread the word of any job openings. "Word spreads immediately if there's an opening," one manager told us. "We have never advertised for workers." Presumably this is what is meant by "labor force availability," that vague term so often mentioned by managers as a site selection criterion.

When pressed to specify the criteria they used in hiring, managers reported that they look for workers with "stable job histories," "reliability," "commitment," "willingness to work," "a manufacturing mentality," and "people who are not looking to set the world on fire." Some admitted straightforwardly that "we have no special criteria." One manager laughed outright at the question. "With what we pay," he said, "if they wear shoes, we'll hire 'em." In fact the Japanese-owned plants I surveyed paid wages significantly below the state average. In electronics, the Japanese plants averaged $7.19 an hour, compared with $11.18 statewide; for all manufacturing, the figures were $9.22 and $11.20, respectively.[13]

These Japanese-owned firms bear little resemblance to the Japanese management model. Relatively few have quality circles or other forms of worker participation; flexible teams (as at NUMMI) are even more exceptional; and many managers chuckled when asked about "just-in-time" delivery and the like. Moreover, while their parent firms in Japan are normally unionized, almost all of the Japanese-owned firms in California are nonunion, and are deeply committed to "union avoidance." Only one "Japanese" practice is widespread among these plants: most are devoted, in principle, to avoiding layoffs. However, even this is tempered by the fact that the plants typically have very high turnover rates, so that workforce reductions can often be accomplished without layoffs. In short, these plants conform to the human resource patterns of conventional American manufacturing and especially nonunion manufacturing, rather than to the Japanese model.[14]

QUALITY CIRCLES AND PARTICIPATION

A widely discussed feature of the Japanese model is its emphasis on worker participation, and especially the use of "quality circles" (QCs) or similar small group activities, to improve efficiency and to promote harmony between labor and management. The QC concept originated in the United States, but the practice became far more widely institutionalized in Japan, starting in the early 1960s. By 1984, 60 percent of all business establishments in Japan with over 100 employees had QCs or the equivalent, and the proportion rose to 84 percent for establishments with over 5,000 employees. Small group programs are especially pervasive in Japan's manufacturing sector. Regardless of sector, where such programs exist, typically more than 90 percent of employees participate (Cole, 1989: 30, 94–99).

In the United States, QCs and similar small groups were institutionalized to a much lesser extent, and later, than in Japan—and largely in response to the success of Japanese industry. The best recent data on the use of QCs and small groups in the United States come from a 1987 survey of large firms in the United States conducted for the General Accounting Office (GAO). Seventy percent of the companies surveyed reported using either QCs or some other type of participation, but in most cases the programs included a relatively small portion of the workforce (Lawler et al., 1989: 26, 62). This survey found that, as in Japan, the use of QCs and other small groups is more common in manufacturing than in service industry firms. At 32 percent of the manufacturing firms surveyed, 20 percent or more of employees participated in QCs, but only 13 percent of the manufacturing firms reported that more than 40 percent of their employees were in QCs. The figures were slightly higher for employee participation groups other than QCs: 37 percent of the manufacturing firms reported that 20 percent or more of their workers were in such groups, and at 17 percent of the manufacturing firms, more than 40 percent of employees participated.[15]

My survey of Japanese-owned manufacturing firms in California with over 100 employees (with a median size of 275 employees) found that about 35 percent had QCs for at least some of their hourly workers.[16] Only two of the twenty plants I visited had QCs, but seven others had some other type of small group participation for at least some of their blue-collar employees. These programs were typically quite limited, however. For example, in one plant, a few department managers (but not others) hold occasional meetings with workers to discuss production problems and quality issues. At another plant, all blue-collar workers are required to attend quarterly meetings, for about an hour, where issues are identified for subsequent management attention. A third plant forms problem-solving project teams on an *ad hoc* basis; each such team includes two hourly workers but is made up mainly of engineers and managers. Another plant holds short (10–15 minutes) morning meetings in each department to discuss problems from the previous day and plans for the day, with all meetings led by the supervisor.

I observed a QC meeting in progress at one plant at the time of my visit. Like most Japanese-owned plants in Southern California, the workforce here was made up almost entirely of immigrants. The plant cafeteria, where the QC meeting I attended took place, was decorated with some twenty flags—one for each of the countries represented in the workforce. Although the national diversity of the workforce was celebrated in the wall decorations, it presented serious problems in the QC meeting, since many workers had a limited command of English and no single language was shared by the entire group. The meeting I witnessed was facilitated by a woman manager who frequently prompted the workers who spoke, and there was almost no unsolicited participation in the discussion. Furthermore, supervisors at the plant, according to another manager there, view the immigrant workers in their charge as "simple people—even though the QC process reveals how smart they really are." Despite the existence of QCs at this plant, then, it is a far cry from the participatory model that strives to maximize the involvement of blue-collar workers in streamlining the production process.

The second plant that had QCs also had many other trappings of the Japanese model. This was the only plant visited where workers actually participated in organized calisthenic programs (a standard practice in Japan), although the program has recently been scaled back from a daily to a biweekly ritual. Currently the calisthenics are part of a shift-wide meeting where managers give informational speeches to the assembled workforce. In the past, this plant had also held informal gatherings of employees at the end of the workday to discuss production problems; these meetings have now been supplanted by the QCs. This plant also organizes all of its production employees into "profit and loss" centers, or mini-enterprise units, with regular meetings to keep everyone informed about each unit's progress.

This plant is exceptional, however. While the sample size is too small to permit drawing any definitive conclusions, the Japanese-owned manufacturing firms generally appear to resemble American-owned manufacturing firms more than their parent companies in Japan with regard to the extent to which QCs and similar participatory small group programs are used. There is some employee involvement or participation in these firms, but the typical goal is to promote communication and harmonious relations between workers and management (often as part of a union avoidance strategy) rather than to engage workers intellectually in the micro-management of production, as in NUMMI's *kaizen* process.

THE TEAM CONCEPT AND LABOR FLEXIBILITY

Another characteristic feature of the Japanese management model, closely related to QC and small group participation, is the organization of workers into self-managed, flexible teams, sometimes labeled the "team concept." At NUMMI, for example, production workers are organized into teams of six to eight people, each with a team leader. Team members rotate jobs and make collective decisions about how to manage the parts of the production process for which they are responsible (for details, see Brown and Reich, 1989; Holden, 1986; Parker and Slaughter, 1988). Even where team organization is absent, under the Japanese system workers are cross-trained to perform a variety of tasks, and job classifications are vague and few in number. This maximizes management's flexibility in deploying workers as needed and also reduces the boredom and monotony inherent in traditional manufacturing production jobs.

The team system is more characteristic of the Japanese auto transplants (both union and nonunion) than of Japanese-owned plants in other industries. In fact, most of the managers I interviewed were unfamiliar with the team concept as used at NUMMI. (Some had never even heard of NUMMI itself.) When asked if any production work in their plant was organized in teams, these managers frequently answered affirmatively at first, but further probing revealed that they were referring to a general emphasis on cooperation or the use of rhetoric about the importance of teamwork, rather than flexible, self-managed work teams like those at NUMMI. One plant actually had "team leader" and "group leader" among its regular job titles, but these turned out to be ordinary lead workers and supervisors. Another plant had a program whose title included the word "team" and the manager I interviewed said that the plant eventually hoped to move toward the team concept, but it had not yet done so. Self-managing work teams are quite rare in U.S. manufacturing as a whole; according to the GAO survey, only 9 percent of large manufacturing firms have such teams for more than 20 percent of their workforce, and none of those surveyed has them for more than 40 percent of their workforce.[17] The Japanese-owned plants I visited conformed to this pattern; in fact not one had work teams of the NUMMI type for their hourly workers.

The one that came closest was an electronics plant that organizes its workers into mini-enterprise units. These range from small units of 3 to 4 workers to large ones of 80 to 120. Each unit operates as an autonomous "profit and loss center," buying and selling from other units within the firm (or from outside in some cases) and trying to minimize costs and maximize prices. For production work, the units coincide with the departments of the plant, and department managers keep track of the accounting details, informing workers (90 percent of whom are female) on a monthly basis of the unit's profits and losses. While this reportedly promotes cost-consciousness among workers, it is a more top-down system than the self-managed teams that exist at NUMMI. In addition, this plant has no regular system of job rotation, although it is the most "Japanese" of the plants I visited in other respects (it is the one mentioned earlier with a calisthenics program and QCs).

Most of the plants I visited in Japan did not have a full-fledged team system either—it seems to be more common in the auto industry there as well as in the United States. But all but one of the Japanese plants did have some sort of job rotation system. In contrast, only three plants among the twenty I visited in California had regular job rotation for production workers. In all three, managers reported that the intent was to offer relief from especially heavy or fatiguing jobs. In one case, the plant had experienced high rates of repetitive-motion injuries, according to a union organizer who had tried (unsuccessfully) to recruit its workers. In another plant, where assemblers rotate jobs every two hours, a manager reported that this system had been introduced some ten years ago in response to a union organizing drive, not as part of an effort to use Japanese management methods.

Closely related to flexibility is the question of job classifications. Whereas U.S. manufacturing, especially in unionized plants, traditionally involved relatively large numbers of job classifications with clear boundaries between them, the Japanese model is generally associated with a minimal number of broad classifications. Among the 49 plants that answered our survey question about this matter, the number of job classifications for production workers ranged from 2 to 120, with a median of eight classifications. In interviews several managers indicated that they hoped to merge classifications in the future, however. At NUMMI, there are only three classifications, and all the semiskilled production workers are in a single classification.

The team concept, job rotation, and cross-training function much more smoothly if wage rates are determined on a predictable basis. At NUMMI, where virtually all production workers earn the same pay (except team leaders, who get a small premium), cooperation among team members is never undercut by resentments over differential pay rates. The same is true under the *nenkō* wage payment system that prevails at large manufacturing plants in Japan (but rarely at small firms in this dual economy), where wages are based mainly on age and seniority in the context of a lifetime employment system. Here, too, pay differences do not impede teamwork or flexibility, since all workers are treated similarly over the course of their life cycle (Cole, 1971: 75–88). Even the Japanese auto transplants in the United States have not tried to emulate the *nenkō* wage system; instead they conform to the pattern set long ago by the unionized Big Three domestic auto firms, where wages are tied to job classifications and where pay differentials among production workers are minimal.

The Japanese-owned plants in Southern California that I visited are all owned by large firms in Japan, but their wage and promotion systems bear no resemblance to either the *nenkō* system or the domestic auto industry pattern. Instead, at these plants, starting pay rates are directly linked to job classifications, and within classifications individual wages are shaped by some combination of seniority and ability, with ability usually playing the dominant role. Most plants have substantial wage spread among their hourly workforce, with the best-paid individuals typically earning two or three times as much as the worst-paid. Except in the few unionized plants, each worker is evaluated biannually, and promotions and raises are awarded on this basis. In some of these plants, seniority has an influence on wages, but in most ability or "merit" is more important—at least officially.[18]

In the case of the low-wage, low-skill production workers who make up the bulk of the hourly workforce at most of these plants, however, merit is defined in narrow terms: attendance (the most frequently mentioned item), punctuality, quality and quantity of work, and "attitude" are the usual criteria, not creativity or initiative. As one manager at a plastics plant put it, "we're not looking for the MBA type." An employee handbook summarized the typical notion of merit: "Your job has been awarded to you based upon your previous experience, education, training, ability, attendance, safety record, and attitude. Future job assignments and promotions will be made in the same manner." Many plants had instituted additional incentives for good attendance, tying it not only to raises and promotions but also to special rewards (cash bonuses, gifts, and/or public commendation) for perfect or near-perfect attendance, or for not using sick days. Most plants also had progressive discipline systems to punish excessive absenteeism.

In short, both the absence of teams or regular job rotation in most of these plants, and the highly individualized, merit-based wage systems used, like other aspects of their work organization, are generally typical of nonunion manufacturing firms in the United States, contrasting sharply to the practices of the parent companies in Japan.

NO-LAYOFF POLICIES AND WORKER ATTACHMENT TO THE FIRM

The one area in which many of the Japanese-owned plants in California do appear to conform to Japanese management practices involves employment security. The majority of these plants are committed to avoiding layoffs of hourly workers whenever possible, and many have *de facto* "no layoff" policies that have yet to be violated. Among forty-nine plants that responded to a survey question on this issue, about two-thirds (64 percent) reported that they had had no layoffs over the previous five years. Similarly, among the twenty plants I visited, eleven had never laid off hourly workers, and a twelfth had not done so since 1974. The layoffs that did take place in the other eight plants usually affected small numbers of people and were often brief. It might be objected that many of these plants were opened or acquired since the last recession, so that their no-layoff policies have yet to be seriously tested. However, six of the eleven firms that reported no layoffs in their entire history had opened or been acquired before 1980.

Some of the American managers interviewed stated that they would prefer to be able to lay workers off, but that "the Japanese are against this." In one large metals plant, the manager reported disapprovingly, when parts of the plant are shut down due to lack of business, workers are not laid off but instead moved to other areas, and are still paid for the highest job they are qualified for. "The Japanese fear layoffs, which they think invite unionism." In another case, a manager in a health care products plant complained that the *de facto* no-layoff policy protected "bad workers." A third manager, at a Japanese-owned plastics plant which has never laid anyone off, reported with apparent amazement that when things are slow, people are put to work cleaning up the plant. He compared this to his previous experience in American industry, where "people would be laid off at the drop of a hat." Indeed, while some U.S.-owned firms do have no-layoff policies (especially in the nonunion sector), they have never been in the majority, and their numbers have dwindled recently under competitive pressures (Foulkes, 1980: Chapter 6; *Business Week,* 1990: 86).

Among the plants with no history of layoffs was one that opened in 1972. When faced with a business downturn in the early 1980s, this plant introduced a work-sharing program to avoid layoffs, with all employees working three days a week instead of five. Another plant that opened in 1976 and that has had several layoffs in the past recently introduced work-sharing as well, and at the time of my visit was operating with a four-day work week for all employees. The manager interviewed at this plant claimed that this schedule was popular with the immigrant workers employed there, since many of them did odd jobs "off the books" on the fifth day of the week to supplement their incomes. The work-sharing policy also was highly effective for the company in retaining labor, he reported. Another manager who had tried to establish a QC program at his plant indicated that the one layoff that workers there had experienced undermined the program to such a degree that the firm was now determined to avoid future layoffs of the regular workforce, limiting any dismissals to temporary workers.

Indeed, this is standard practice in Japan, where the permanent workforce in large firms enjoys "lifetime employment" at the expense of temporary or part-time workers (often women) working directly for the firm or for its subcontractors. The no-layoff policies at Japanese-owned plants in this country are not fully equivalent to "lifetime employment," but both forms of employment security are often predicated on the existence of an expendable temporary workforce. Many nonunion plants in the United States with no-layoff policies also rely on temporaries as a cushion. All of the plants that reported no history of layoffs used temporary workers, as did most of the others. (The only exceptions were two unionized plants where the union contract prohibited or restricted the use of temporaries.) One manager was explicit about the link between the no-layoff policy and the use of temporary workers. "We don't use the L-word here," he said. "Instead we use leased employees."

Most of these plants recruit temporary workers through outside agencies, though a few hire them directly "off the street." One plant reported that it interviews prospective workers directly but then sends those it plans to hire to an agency; another suggests to all workers who inquire about jobs that they apply via the agency. Temporary workers are typically paid less than other hourly workers and receive no fringe benefits (though some receive limited benefits from the agency). At one plant that makes extensive use of temporaries, the manager told me that they are excluded from the QC program and do not receive the uniforms issued to other hourly workers. In some plants, workers reportedly remain "temporary" workers for years, but in other plants the pool of temporaries is used to recruit permanent workers, so that temporary status is equivalent to a probationary period.

While their no-layoff policies set the Japanese-owned firms apart from their U.S.-owned counterparts, this is less true of the use of temporary workers. A recent survey of U.S. firms conducted by the Bureau of National Affairs (BNA) (1986: 7–12) found that 74 percent of the manufacturing firms responding used agency temporaries, and 56 percent used "short-term hires." However, the BNA survey found that in most cases temporaries accounted for less than 1 percent of the regular workforce, and rarely more than 6 percent.[19] At the Japanese firms I visited, however, temporaries often comprised a more substantial proportion of hourly workers—as many as a third in some cases, typically 5 percent or less.

The no-layoff policies of these firms rest on another cushion as well: high turnover, especially in the electronics plants and others where wages are relatively low. One electronics plant manager attributed the high turnover in entry-level jobs, which had climbed to 4.5 percent in the most recent month on record at the time of my visit, to the fact that "workers care about cents per hour and will leave for 50 cents more per hour down the street at K-Mart." (There is in fact a K-Mart warehouse next door to this plant.) While this was the highest turnover figure reported in my interviews, at about half the plants turnover was characterized as "high," with those managers who reported actual figures citing rates from 17 to 28 percent annually.[20] These rates compare with a national average for manufacturing of about 13 percent (although rates were slightly higher on the West Coast).[21] Also contributing to high turnover rates were strict absenteeism policies; some managers indicated that poor attendance was a major cause of firings, though others were more lenient.

In many plants, both firings and quits (the major components of turnover) were largely confined to the lowest-paying jobs; workers who rose into better-paid positions, in contrast, sometimes had turnover rates that were *lower* than management desired. "We would like to have more turnover in the assembly group," one manger of a food products plant said, "because these are hustle-bustle jobs and it's hard for the older workers to keep up." Another manager in a large electronics plant that opened nearly twenty years ago also was concerned that turnover was not *higher*. "While many of our employees are young men who move on to other things after a few years, some of the people here have been around for a long time, and we're having some problems of motivation with them," he complained. A third manager suggested that the auto accessories plant he worked for "would actually be happier to have a bit more turnover, to help keep the wage bill down." It appears that the high turnover rates characteristic of these plants are not entirely unwelcome. For some firms, they even may be the functional equivalent of layoffs, in that as business slows, the workforce can be reduced substantially by attrition.

The existence of *de facto* no-layoff policies at the majority of these plants (albeit mitigated by high turnover rates and made possible by extensive use of temporaries), and the infrequency with which layoffs occur at the rest, are their most "Japanese" features. Even this is part of the human resources apparatus that has long been used in large domestic nonunion firms, after which California's Japanese-owned firms seem to model their policies.

MANAGEMENT ATTITUDES TOWARD UNIONISM

Only five of the sixty-six Japanese-owned plants in California with more than 100 workers are unionized, and all but one was effectively unionized prior to being bought by the Japanese. Several managers emphasized the link between their firms' human resource practices and their desire to operate on a nonunion basis. When asked if he was concerned about the prospect of unionization, one manager at an electronics plant replied, "Everything I do and breathe is designed to prevent a union from coming in here!" He added that if workers were unhappy enough to turn to a union, it would mean he had failed as a human resources manager. "I want to make unions superfluous," he said. This remark was echoed by many other managers. Several suggested that workers only turn to unions when management is abusive. "We treat our workers fairly," a metal products plant manager said, "so they don't need a union to speak for them." Another manager at a steel plant expressed great concern about how his first-line supervisors treat workers, and reported that he had even suspended some supervisors temporarily for "attitude adjustment." "If they're too hard [on workers]," he said, "we may be buying a union. We keep track of this very closely."

Several managers emphasized that their human resource policies were designed to forestall any interest in unionization. One electronics plant manager explained that union avoidance was a key reason for his efforts to promote frequent communications between workers and management. "This helps keep our finger on the pulse," he told us. "Without this you end up with an adversarial relationship, with unions fighting companies." Another manager at a metal products plant attributed a union drive that took place there the year before our visit to "poor communications," adding that prior to the union election "we established better communications, and so the union lost." A manager at a plastics products plant said that the participatory programs he was setting up were important "to avoid a union situation." Others noted the role of no-layoff policies in union avoidance. "The Japanese avoid unions by treating people right," one manager said regarding the no-layoff policy.

Virtually all the managers interviewed at the seventeen nonunion plants I visited spoke frankly about their desire to avoid unionization. None pretended to have a neutral stance toward organized labor, and several stated that keeping unions out was among their highest priorities. "I don't want a union here—ever!" one manager at an electronics plant exclaimed. A manager at a plastic products plant told me that workers "realize that it's kind of anti-union around here," adding that "the company would probably move away if a union came in." Another manager, when I asked if there had ever been any efforts to unionize at his auto accessories plant, replied "No, knock on wood." He went on to mention rumors that after the UAW's defeat at the Nissan plant in Tennessee, the union might try organizing suppliers instead, adding, "We're always alert—we don't want a union organization here."

At nine of the seventeen nonunion plants, management was aware of at least one effort to unionize, although in all but three cases the effort had been dropped before it reached the point of an election. At one electronics plant where there had been two separate unionization efforts, the manager told me that the Japanese are very fearful of American unions, and that they would probably shut down the plant if it ever were unionized. "That's the first file folder in my desk drawer," he added, pulling out a red file folder labeled "Union Activities" to show me. He recalled that the two previous efforts to unionize there had been "nipped in the bud" thanks to his "anti-union campaign" in the plant. "Once it starts, we get all the supervisors together and tell them what they can and can't do. We tell the workers what to expect, what the union will do, and what the consequences of unionization would be." At another electronics plant, among the largest in the state, a union campaign was under way at the time of my visit, and the firm had engaged three different labor consultants (one local, one national, and one in another city where the firm was setting up a new plant) to help them resist the effort. The manager I interviewed mentioned that he saw Nissan's successful anti-union campaign at Smyrna as a good model, a comment echoed by several other managers.

At another electronics plant where a unionization drive had been defeated in a close election a few years before my visit, the company had hired a labor consultant to orchestrate such a campaign. "We spent a lot of money educating people," a manager there recalled. "The consultant told workers that it would be a mistake on their part to unionize, because they now have a voice in the plant and they would lose that." At this plant, even though the union was ultimately defeated, the Japanese company president felt personally responsible for the fact that unionization was even attempted. "He saw it as a sign of his own failure," the American manager recalled. "He carried it to such an extreme that he didn't even go back to Japan for the funeral when his mother died in the middle of the campaign."

I visited two steel plants that had been closed for a period prior to being acquired by the Japanese, both of which had been unionized before and had then made a "transition to a nonunion operation." Both plants rehired some hourly workers they had employed before the closures, but on a highly selective basis. "Many of the former workers were pro-union, and we don't hire them," a manager at one of these plants said. "Remember, we're trying to run it nonunion. We hire a lot of out-of-towners." At this plant, there had been a union drive right after the plant reopened, and "management brought out the big guns," he recalled. "We had a meeting with all the employees in a big room. It was staged so that at one point a worker asked if the managers would mind leaving, and then they passed around a petition which almost everyone signed, saying they didn't want a union."

These firms did not hesitate to express their anti-union views directly to their employees. One manager of a food products plant told me that his firm wants to be "up front" about the issue. "We tell our workers, 'If you want a union, don't join us.' " Some firms published official statements to this effect in their employee handbooks. One such handbook included a section entitled, "Company X—A Non-Union Company," which stated:

> At Company X, employees have chosen not to have a union. . . . In today's uncertain world, with all the pressures of our modern society, we want to keep Company X free from the artificially created tensions which could be brought on by an outside party, such as a union. We feel that a union would be of no advantage to any of us—*it could hurt the business which we all depend on for our bread and butter.* Furthermore, we have enthusiastically accepted our responsibility to provide you good working conditions, good wages, good benefits, fair treatment, and the personal respect which is rightfully yours. All this is part of your job with Company X and cannot be "purchased" by anyone having you pay union dues. We know that you want and are able to express your problems, suggestions and comments to us so that we can understand each other better. This can be done without having a union jammed between you and your supervisor. We want you to speak up for yourself—directly to us. We will do our best to listen and respond. [emphasis added]

Another employee handbook's "Statement on Unions" was more menacing:

> Company Y does not have a union, and you are not required to be a member of a union to work here. *Further, we will do all in our power legally to see that no employee ever has to pay union dues to work here.* Our employees seem to be satisfied with this arrangement. . . . Unions have not provided any of the wages and benefits we enjoy, and we do not expect them to help us improve upon these benefits in the future. . . . If any person attempts to pressure you into joining or signing a card in support of a union you should consider the matter carefully, and if there are any questions, feel free to go to your supervisor. . . . *Company Y will resist any efforts to bring a union into this plant by all legal means at our disposal.* [emphasis added]

The fact that most of these plants have parent firms whose workers are represented by unions in Japan did not prevent them from resisting efforts to unionize their plants in the United States. One manager I interviewed at a food products plant in Japan, a former union president himself, spoke at length about how good the union-management relationship was at the plant in Kawasaki that I visited. But he added that the firm had located one of its plants in North Carolina in part because, "honestly speaking, they have no big, strong labor unions there." I asked why, given how positively he characterized the union's role in Kawasaki, the firm was so eager to avoid unionization in the United States. "If we could find the same kind of labor union there, we would welcome it," he replied. "But in the United States, the unions tend to make trouble, they have a class struggle concept. It's very harmful." Other Japanese managers used a different logic to reconcile the contradiction between their acceptance of unionism at home and their resistance to it in the United States. At a unionized electronics plant in Japan, a manager told me that the union was a useful vehicle for communication between managers and workers. But in the same firm's

California plant, "where there are American people working, with cultural values that we don't fully understand, we'd rather not have a union."

In the postwar period, and especially during the American occupation, Japanese unions were modeled directly after those in the United States. However, Japan's more radical unions were crushed in the 1950s, and the nation's labor movement developed its own distinctive character. Organized on an enterprise basis, Japanese unions today are generally viewed as less militant and as more management-oriented than their counterparts in the United States (see Gordon, 1985; Cook, 1966; Shirai, 1983; and Cusumano, 1985: Chapter 3). While the differences are sometimes overstated, the Japanese managers who pointed out that unions in the United States are unlike those in Japan are correct.

These plants, then, do not conform to the "Japanese" human resource practices that characterize both NUMMI and other Japanese auto transplants in the United States as well as many large manufacturing facilities in Japan itself. The reasons for this are complex, but include the fact that most of these plants perform highly routinized production tasks in their role as export-substitution branches of their parent firms, which continue to carry out the more complex phases of the production process in Japan. Another reason California's Japanese-owned plants are not very "Japanese" is that most of them rely on a highly "localized" management staff. Although my survey is too crude and the number of cases too small to be definitive on this point, the data do suggest a positive relationship between the extent to which Japanese nationals are represented in management and the use of QCs and teams.

NUMMI shows that Japanese firms *could* replicate a high-trust, unionized model of industrial relations in their U.S. plants, incorporating many of the elements that brought them success at home. But it appears that most are bypassing that option and instead conforming to American management ideology and practice, choosing to avoid unions wherever possible and relying on the human resource practices developed by U.S.-owned nonunion firms rather than on those used by their parent firms' plants in Japan. Those who look to JDI as a source of improvement in the U.S. labor relations system are likely to be deeply disappointed.

NOTES

1. Direct investment involves foreign ownership of a controlling interest in a domestically based firm or in a parcel of real estate. In contrast, indirect or portfolio investment (not considered in detail here), involves foreign ownership of bank accounts, securities, or bonds of firms or governments.

2. The most recent figures available are for 1990, when the total value of U.S. direct investment abroad was reported at $422 billion, compared with a total of $404 billion in foreign direct investment in the United States (U.S. Department of Commerce, August 1991: 54).

3. These data differ in some respects from those published by the U.S. Department of Commerce that are the basis of the previous discussion, because of different reporting requirements and data collection methods. The Japanese data are based on investment levels notified to and approved by the government (which are often higher than actual JDI), and they do not include disinvestment or reinvested earnings. Both countries count investments of more than 10 percent equity as FDI (see Fujita, 1990: 32). The U.S. data offer more detail about the composition of JDI inside the United States; however, only the Japanese data allow a comparison of patterns of JDI in the United States with JDI elsewhere in the world. The Japanese data cited in this paragraph are cumulative figures from fiscal year (FY) 1951 to the FY cited. Each FY runs from April 1 to March 31; for example, FY 1988 is from April 1, 1988 to March 31, 1989.

4. This includes the United States and Canada; data are not published at this level of detail for the United States separately. However, for all years shown, the vast bulk of JDI in North America was in the United States.

5. The 1990 figure is from U.S. Department

of Labor (1991: 229). For discussion of recent trends in unionization, see Freeman (1988).

6. U.S. Dept. of Commerce (July 1991: 77, 85); Glickman and Woodward (1989: 34). All these data exclude employment by foreign-affiliated banks.

7. There is now a large literature on NUMMI. A good overview comparing it to a GM plant which has unsuccessfully sought to imitate the team system is Brown and Reich (1989). See also Holden (1986) and Parker and Slaughter (1988).

8. Parker and Slaughter (1988: 111). For an analysis of the Ford-Mazda joint venture in Michigan from a similar point of view, see Fucini and Fucini (1990). This point of view is also common in literature on Japan. See, for example, Ichiyō (1986) and Dohse et al. (1985).

9. This figure includes only plants where Japanese companies held a majority ownership share. There were 245 such factories in California at the end of 1989, 18 percent of the national total. See Japan Economic Institute (1991: 4).

10. Questionnaires were sent to the seventy-two Japanese-owned firms in the state listed as having more than 100 employees in the Japan Economic Institute's national listing of U.S. manufacturing affiliates of Japanese companies published in late 1988 (Japan Economic Institute, 1988). Six of these firms were found to have been sold (and thus were no longer Japanese-owned) or not to be engaged in manufacturing activity. Of the other sixty-six, twenty-six responded to the survey by mail, and responses were obtained from an additional twenty-four by telephone. Sixteen plants refused or failed to respond, for a total response rate of 76 percent. The firms were promised that they would not be identified directly or indirectly in published reports of the research results.

11. No attempt was made to select a random sample for the factory visits in California or in Japan, but plants in a wide variety of industries, acquired and new, unionized and nonunion, were included. The fact that only one firm in California turned down a request for an interview suggests that the twenty cases are reasonably representative. The firms themselves designated the management interviewees, usually human resource managers. The interviews lasted between forty-five minutes and three hours; most were between sixty and ninety minutes. They were not tape-recorded (to encourage frankness); instead I and my research assistant took notes and wrote them up later the same day, together with our impressions from the factory tours that most visits included. As with the survey, the firms were promised that they would not be identified directly or indirectly in published reports of the research results.

No attempt at representativeness was made in the Japanese factory visits, due to difficulties of access and time and language constraints, but I did attempt to visit plants in the same range of industries I had seen in California. Two of these visits

were arranged through my contacts with managers I previously interviewed in California; the other three were arranged by the Japan Institute of Labor.

12. For discussion of the tendency of Japanese-owned auto firms to avoid locating in areas where blacks make up a large proportion of the labor supply, see Cole and Deskins (1988).

13. For Japanese-owned plants, these averages are weighted and are average wages for *employees* in the plants (not the average of each plant's average wage). The statewide data are for June 1989 and are computed from California Employment Development Department (1990: 42–43).

14. Most conform to the pattern described in the classic account by Foulkes (1980). See also the discussion in Kochan et al. (1986: Chapter 4).

15. The response rate on this survey was 51 percent, with 476 responding firms. The data for manufacturing firms specifically are not included in this publication, but were kindly provided in unpublished form by the Center for Effective Organizations at the University of Southern California.

16. The questions were formulated differently; my survey did not ask about the proportion of employees involved in QCs; and the average firm size in the two samples is quite different. The firms surveyed by the GAO had a median size of 9,000 employees, compared with a median of 275 for the firms I surveyed. Although one can only speculate about the effects of these differences, they might cancel each other out. On the one hand, the larger average firm size in the GAO study should make the frequencies of QCs higher than they would be otherwise, since large firms are more likely to have QCs than small ones. On the other hand, the fact that some firms have QCs and other small groups for only a small portion of their employees may lead to an exaggeration of the frequency of QCs in the results of our survey of California's Japanese-owned large manufacturing firms. The GAO survey found that 70 percent of the manufacturing firms surveyed had QCs for 1 percent or more of their employees, and 75 percent had employee participation groups other than QCs for 1 percent or more of their employees. These levels are far higher than those found in my survey, which did not inquire about the proportion of employees involved in QCs but simply asked, "Are there quality circles for hourly workers?"

17. Unpublished data supplied by the Center for Effective Organization at USC (see note 15).

18. See Foulkes (1980: Chapter 9) for discussion of the "mythical" aspect of the merit principle.

19. The response rate on the BNA survey was 55 percent. The figures on the proportion of regular employees made up by temporaries are for all respondents, not only for manufacturing.

20. This conflicts with the claim made many years ago by Johnson and Ouchi that Japanese

plants in San Diego and elsewhere had lower than average turnover rates. See Johnson and Ouchi (1974: 63).

21. These figures are from a 1986 survey conducted by the Administrative Management Society. For details, see Norback (1988: 13.23–13.24).

REFERENCES

Barnet, R., and R. Müller. 1974. *Global Reach: The Power of the Multinational Corporations.* New York: Simon and Schuster.

Brown, C., and M. Reich. 1989. "When Does Cooperation Work? A Look at NUMMI and Van Nuys." *California Management Review* 31 (Summer): 26–44.

Bureau of National Affairs. 1986. *The Changing Workplace: New Directions in Staffing and Scheduling.* Washington, D.C.: Bureau of National Affairs.

Business Week. 1990. "A Japanese Import That's Not Selling: Job Security Still Hasn't Gained Much Currency in the U.S." February 26, pp. 86–87.

California Employment Development Department, Economic Information Group, Labor Market Information Division. 1990. *California Labor Market Bulletin: Statistical Supplement,* June. Sacramento: California Employment Development Department.

Cole, R. 1971. *Japanese Blue Collar: The Changing Tradition.* Berkeley: University of California Press.

Cole, R. 1989. *Strategies for Learning: Small Group Activities in American, Japanese and Swedish Industry.* Berkeley: University of California Press.

Cole, R., and D. Deskins. 1988. "Racial Factors in Site Location and Employment Practices of Japanese Auto Firms in America." *California Management Review* 31 (Fall): 9–22.

Cook, A. 1966. *An Introduction to Japanese Trade Unionism.* Ithaca: New York State School of Industrial and Labor Relations, Cornell University.

Cusumano, M. 1985. *The Japanese Automobile Industry.* Cambridge: Harvard University Press.

Dohse, K., U. Jürgens, and T. Malsch. 1985. "From 'Fordism' to 'Toyotism'? The Social Organization of the Labor Process in the Japanese Automobile Industry." *Politics and Society* 14 (2): 115–46.

Economist. 1988. "Love and Hate in America." March 19.

Foulkes, F. 1980. *Personnel Policies in Large Nonunion Companies.* Englewood Cliffs, N.J.: Prentice-Hall.

Freeman, R. 1988. "Contraction and Expansion: The Divergence of Private Sector and Public Sector Unionism in the United States." *Journal of Economic Perspectives* 2 (Spring): 63–88.

Froebel, F., J. Heinrichs, and O. Kreye. 1980. *The New International Division of Labour: Structural Unemployment in Industrialised Countries and Industrialisation in Developing Countries.* Cambridge: Cambridge University Press.

Fucini, J., and S. Fucini. 1990. *Working for the Japanese: Inside Mazda's American Auto Plant.* New York: Free Press.

Fujita, M. 1990. "FDI Between Japan and the United States." *The Centre on Transnational Corporations Reporter.* United Nations, no. 29 (Spring): 31–34, 42.

Glickman, N., and D. Woodward. 1989. *The New Competitors: How Foreign Investors Are Changing the U.S. Economy.* New York, Basic Books.

Gordon, A. 1985. *The Evolution of Labor Relations in Japan.* Cambridge: Harvard University Press.

Holden, C. 1986. "New Toyota-GM Plant is U.S. Model for Japanese Management." *Science* 233 (July 18): 273–77.

Ichiyō, M. 1986. "Class Struggle in Postwar Japan." In G. McCormack and Y. Sugimoto, eds., *Democracy in Contemporary Japan.* Armonk, N.Y.: M.E. Sharpe.

Japan Economic Institute. 1988. *Japan's Expanding U.S. Manufacturing Presence: 1987 Update.* Washington, D.C.: Japan Economic Institute.

Japan Economic Institute. 1991. *Japan's Expanding U.S. Manufacturing Presence: 1989 Update.* JEI Report, no. 2A (January 18).

Japan Ministry of Finance, Institute of Fiscal and Monetary Policy. *Monthly Finance Review,* various issues.

Johnson, R.T., and W. Ouchi. 1974. "Made in America (Under Japanese Management)." *Harvard Business Review* 5 (September-October): 61–69.

Judis, J. 1991. "Citizen Kawasaki: Race, Unions and the Japanese Employer in America." *The American Prospect* 5 (Spring): 47–60.

Kochan, T., H. Katz, and R. McKersie. 1986. *The Transformation of American Industrial Relations.* New York: Basic Books.

Landers, R. 1988. "America's Vacation Gap." *Editorial Research Reports* 1 (June 17): 314–22.

Lawler, E., G. Ledford, and S. Mohrman. 1989. *Employee Involvement in America: A Study of Contemporary Practice.* Houston: American Productivity and Quality Center.

Maruyama, M. 1988. "The Inverse Practice Principle in Multicultural Management." *The Academy of Management EXECUTIVE* 2 (1): 67–68.

Nasar, S. 1991. "Boom in Manufactured Exports Provides Hope for U.S. Economy." *New York Times.* April 21.

Norback, C., ed. 1988. *The Human Resources*

Yearbook, 1988 Edition. Englewood Cliffs, N.J.: Prentice-Hall.

Parker, M., and J. Slaughter. 1988. *Choosing Sides: Unions and the Team Concept.* Boston: South End Press.

Sebestyen, C. 1972. *The Outward Urge: Japanese Investment World-Wide.* London: The Economist Intelligence Unit Ltd.

Shaiken, H., and H. Browne. 1991. "Japanese Work Organization in Mexico." In G. Szekely, ed., *Manufacturing Across Borders and Oceans: Japan, the United States, and Mexico.* San Diego: Center for U.S.-Mexican Studies, University of California at San Diego.

Shirai, T. 1983. *Contemporary Industrial Relations in Japan.* Madison: University of Wisconsin Press.

United Nations. 1990. *Monthly Bulletin of Statistics.* 44 (May).

U.S. Department of Commerce. *Survey of Current Business.* Various issues.

U.S. Department of Labor, Bureau of Labor Statistics. 1989. *Handbook of Labor Statistics,* Bulletin 2340 (August).

U.S. Department of Labor, Bureau of Labor Statistics. 1991. *Employment and Earnings* 38 (January).

Womack, J., D. Jones, and D. Roos. 1990. *The Machine That Changed the World.* New York: Rawson Associates.

II

POLICY ISSUES

The essays in this section focus on the policy choices facing business, labor, and government in the advanced societies. Are social cooperation and industrial policy the keys to comparative advantage? Which industrial relations practices are the most admirable and imitable? What stance should organized labor adopt with respect to economic integration?

In Chapter 7, Michael Storper argues that the key to high-wage production in the advanced nations is what he calls "product-based technological learning" (PBTL). PBTL industries can turn out a stream of continuously changing products, unlike mass production industries with their long runs of standardized goods. Whereas mass production is based on dedicated machinery and economies of scale, PBTL is based on human and organizational skills that permit firms to redeploy resources flexibly and continuously. Successful PBTL sectors create and retain industry-specific human and physical capital without becoming locked into a particular product or technique. In the United States, PBTL industries are centered on high technology (e.g., electronics and aerospace); in Germany and Italy, PBTL industries manufacture a wide array of precision mechanical products and style-sensitive consumer goods.

Precisely how PBTL industries balance specificity with flexibility varies from nation to nation. American firms rely heavily on layoffs to sustain flexibility; in corporatist countries such as Germany and Sweden, strong unions have closed off this option and have forced employers to rely instead on extensive training and peak-level cooperation to promote flexibility. Common to both approaches are national and industrial "rules" governing the market and institutional arrangements.

The regionalist systems found in France and Italy are another approach to PBTL. Storper analyzes several regional production complexes in those countries, including mechanical engineering in the Haute Savoie, aerospace in Toulouse, and machinery in Emilia-Romagna. The firms involved are small, much smaller than the average export-oriented PBTL firm in the

United States, Japan, or even Sweden. Significantly, each region contains a ready supply of highly skilled workers attached to the area and to the industry rather than to a specific firm. Unions, governments, and firms cooperate to provide high-quality vocational training and to facilitate labor mobility within the region. Storper concludes his essay by considering the implications of the French and Italian systems for organizational theory and public policy.

Regionalism and macrocorporatism are forms of industrial policy; under each system, government becomes deeply involved in the operation of labor, product, and credit markets. Probably the most highly touted examples of industrial policy are found in Asia, where the Japanese and South Korean governments played an important part in the postwar industrialization process and maintain a strong presence in their respective economies to this day. Japan's MITI (Ministry of International Trade and Industry) is praised as a model for other advanced nations; South Korea's industrial policies are held up as an exemplar for newly industrializing countries (NICs).

In Chapter 8, Kenneth L. Sokoloff takes issue with the conventional wisdom on industrial policy in NICs such as South Korea and Mexico. Both countries have shown impressively high growth rates in recent years. Both relied on industrial policies that entailed government targeting of particular industries for investment subsidies and import protection. Yet Sokoloff doubts whether these government policies were responsible for the high growth rates of the South Korean and Mexican economies.

Sokoloff finds that in South Korea, productivity growth was roughly the same in targeted as in nontargeted industries in the 1960s and 1970s. In fact, targeting appears to have led to excessive capital intensity in favored industries such as steel. In Mexico, where the industrialization process was somewhat different than in Korea, many of the worst performing industries were those with the greatest amounts of government involvement and protection. Thus industrial policy in South Korea did not contribute to prosperity, while Mexico's industrial policies actually hindered growth.

For students of economic development, Sokoloff's study is a warning that governments should not become heavily involved in subsidizing and channeling the growth of particular industries. It also offers a cautionary tale for the advanced nations. Sokoloff's analysis suggests that it is easy to over-sell the virtues of the institutional links associated with macrocorporatism; micro-organizational factors and market forces are equally, if not more, important. The implication is clear: we must specify more precisely what types of government actions contribute to growth, as under PBTL systems, and when government would be best advised to leave economic decisions to other actors. Additional research is needed, however, before we can apportion the contributions of macro and micro factors.

Regardless of how the industrial policy debate is resolved, labor faces difficult choices in the years ahead. Ongoing economic integration is closing off the possibility of Keynesian stimulation of the type historically associated with strong labor movements. In an open economy, any attempt by prolabor governments to push interest rates below market levels will lead to detrimental capital outflows. A commonly cited example is the Mitterrand government of the early 1980s, whose attempts to stimulate the French economy resulted in capital flight and the battering of the franc. Jeffry A. Frieden, however, says in Chapter 9, that even nations with an open economy can manipulate their exchange rate to bolster domestic industries. Devaluations are particularly helpful to export-oriented and import-competitive sectors. Thus government still can be used to stimulate the economy as before.

Yet this route to macroeconomic stimulus is closed under the European Monetary System, whose exchange rate mechanism does not allow for independent exchange rate policies (except within a very narrow range, recently expanded a bit). Why, then, have some European labor leaders spoken out in favor of monetary integration? The reality, says Frieden, is that European labor movements are deeply divided on this issue. Unions (and employers) in export-oriented industries generally favor stable exchange rates and monetary integration, while those in nontradables and import-competitive industries tend to prefer a flexible regime because they have little to gain from integration. Another point of division is the level of the exchange rate: export- and import-competitive industries generally prefer a lower rate than those in nontradables. As this analysis suggests, unions in export industries have conflicting desires: they want external stability but also wish to retain the option of periodic devaluations.

Frieden demonstrates the validity of these assertions by examining divisions over exchange rate policy in the French and Italian labor movements. The CGT, one of the main French labor federations, has a heavily blue-collar membership based in export-oriented and import-competitive manufacturing industries. In recent years it has favored devaluation and has been wary of monetary integration. By contrast, the CFDT, a federation with many white-collar members in services and the public sector, is inclined to support monetary integration and a strong franc. The same dynamics exist in Italy and elsewhere.

Thus exchange rate policies—and other issues raised by economic integration—segment the labor movement and align union members with their employers rather than with their fellow workers. This segmentation is more pronounced in countries with multiple union federations, such as France and Italy. Countries that have a single labor federation, however, may appear superficially to be more unified on matters of international economic policy than is actually the case. For example, the national unions constituting the DGB (Germany) and the AFL-CIO (the United States) do not agree with one another on many details of the EC and of NAFTA.

7

Boundaries, Compartments, and Markets: Paradoxes of Industrial Relations in Growth Pole Regions of France, Italy, and the United States

MICHAEL STORPER

DYNAMICALLY EFFICIENT INDUSTRIAL RELATIONS AND COMPETITIVENESS: LOCK-IN AND ADAPTABILITY

For much of the twentieth century, the impact of industrial relations on economic efficiency has been associated, whether implicitly or explicitly, with those who criticize unions in particular and worker protections in general as fetters on the optimal level of ongoing adjustment in the economy. Yet in recent years there has been a growing awareness that certain forms of institutionalized worker protections and unionism are associated with superior competitiveness, with examples frequently drawn from success stories in countries such as Germany or Japan, and even occasionally the United States (Freeman and Medoff, 1984; Sorge and Streeck, 1988; Dore, 1987; Koike, 1984). There is a sense that in certain countries the existence of highly institutionalized labor markets has something to do with a dynamic of self-selection into high-value-added, highly competitive economic activities, and that industrial relations are a central element of the institutional structure.

The nature of what constitutes highly competitive economic activity has undergone significant redefinition over the past twenty years. The social science literatures are replete with tales of the restructuring of the Chandlerian-Galbraithian firm, the spread of programmable technologies, the shortening of product cycles, the deepening of contracting and subcontracting relations, the revival of the role of small- and medium-sized units of production, and the emphasis on quality as much as on price competition (Best, 1990; Piore and Sabel, 1984).

There is an emerging consensus that these changes indicate a revolution in the conditions under which advanced (i.e., high-wage) economies can be competitive.

155

The story may be told in abbreviated form as follows. It used to be the case that a country could develop a superior technology (one which lowered the cost of production by economizing on total factor costs or by generating scale economies) and enjoy the fruits of such efficiency for a reasonable period of time, even where product and process technology were rather stable. Even stable technologies were not easily imitated, because raw technological differentials between countries were considerable.[1] Thus, even in mass production of standardized goods, it was possible for the advanced industrial countries to generate high-wage jobs in the context of international trade.[2]

This system of mass production began to become less viable for the high-wage economies around the end of the 1960s, for many reasons, but among them we can cite the increasingly easy technological imitation for standardized products and processes, and the increasingly rapid catch-up for new, but standardized products and processes. The result was that there was no longer a technological solution for mass production in the high-wage economies, because the low-wage economies could now compete technologically, and had the added advantage of low labor costs. Prices and costs for such standardized goods must converge more rapidly on a global scale now. In the advanced economies, economic adjustment to these new realities has involved severe reductions in mass production, as well as severe real-wage compression, accelerated substitution of labor by capital, and "third worldization" or feminization of the labor force for that which remains. The quantity of output accounted for by mass production, and the developmental returns to a given increment of mass production, are declining for these countries (Storper and Scott, 1992).

In this new context, by contrast, growing activities that generate high-wage or high-skill jobs seem to be based on different principles of competition, where the technological catch-up effect is avoided or outrun. The products or processes in question are based on a technology or skill advantage which is not subject to immediate imitation, such that a price-cost gap (quasi-rent) can open up and provide for, among other things, good jobs through growth in the real-wage rate (Dosi, Pavitt and Soete, 1990). In a world where catch-up tendencies are very strong, this kind of competition is necessarily rooted in dynamic advantages, i.e., the ability to turn out a stream of products which is in continuous evolution. These dynamic economies of variety involve competition on the basis of *product-based technological learning* (PBTL)(Storper, 1992b).

The organizational paradigms which fit with such PBTL are quite different from those of successful Chandlerian mass production systems in the postwar period. Much recent work in evolutionary economics has shown that "normal" technological change (i.e., not revolutionary technological breaks, but development within a basic technological paradigm) is subject to positive feedbacks and increasing returns (Nelson and Winter, 1982; Foray, 1990; Dosi, 1984). The number of adopters, the number of spillovers and interconnections between a product and other end-use goods and inputs, as well as learning associated with continued production, generate such increasing returns and its counterpart, a tendency to "lock in" on certain product and process configurations. The problem is that when competition centers on the configuration and quality of the product, producers must not only maximize such returns (and especially those that come from learning and experience), but they must also maintain a high degree of openness to developments which cannot be anticipated; in other words, uncertainty requires that they avoid lock-in to a given technology (Foray, 1990). The latter requires that they have a significant degree of organizational flexibility or adaptability. One empirically important form of flexibility which has been widely observed in recent years is that of production systems involving elaborate and shifting inter- and intrafirm divisions of labor or, more simply, production *networks* (Powell, 1990). These network production systems assume many forms, with great variation in the role played by big firms and the degree of hierarchy between big and small (Storper and Harrison, 1991). All such networks, however, are based around a complex and shifting web of contracts, subcontracts, strategic alliances, and supplier relations, sometimes complemented by financial cross-holdings *(chaebol, keiretsu)* or informal equivalents. The counterpart to this generally higher degree of externalization of the production system (as opposed to the high degree of functional vertical integration in postwar mass production),[3] is that the successful firms and production units caught up in these webs tend to be more specialized, and within their domain of specialization they often manifest significant internal adaptability: the ability to redeploy resources on a more or less continuous basis (Piore and Sabel, 1984; Cohendet and Llerena, 1989). This combination of features reduces risk of lock-in, within the context of a production system which enjoys economies of scale and scope and the benefits that specialization can bring to the learning process (Foray, 1990). Such production systems may be found in certain segments of many industries, typically those which are located in advanced countries and which perform well on world markets, while other segments of the same industries represent laggard versions. Among these PBTL industries we might cite, for example, the design-intensive or craft-based industries in Italy (shoes, furniture, fabrics and clothing, eyeglasses, lamps) and small industrial machinery (ISTAT, 1986); certain design-intensive industries in France, including women's clothing and certain mechanical engineering and precision instruments industries there (especially mechanical engineering in the Jura and the Haute Savoie), as well as large-scale electronic systems construction and civilian aircraft in French high-technology industries; in Germany, a wide range of mechanical engineering and consumer durable sectors; and in the United States, mainly high-technology industries such as electronics, computers, and aerospace. In all these cases, the high degree of competitiveness of the country in question is suggested by the fact that its export share for the industry is much higher than its total share of world trade (Storper, 1992a). Though it is obviously not sufficient to base an economy only on such PBTL sectors, it can be argued that every national economy needs to have a certain number of such industries within its borders, so that it can reap the quasi-rents associated with technology- and skill-based production.

Existing theory would suggest two dimensions of labor demand in PBTL industries. On the one hand, many of the skills associated with PBTL must be quite specialized, as technological knowledge is by definition non- or imperfectly standardized. Processes of interpretation and use of judgment are critical in such cases, and much of this interpretation and judgment are firm-, industry-, or technology-specific. According to theory, external labor markets are of limited use in the presence of such asset specificity (Marsden, 1990). Yet the increase in uncertainty (avoidance of lock-in) we alluded to above should lead to a demand for quantitative and qualitative labor flexibility arrangements. Quantitative, or numerical flexibility should make possible rapid responses to changing production costs and demand levels, while qualitative flexibility, often in the form of specialization supplying and contracting is an "indirect" way of acceding to qualitatively diverse and specific labor skills with low fixed costs and investment risks for the acquirer. Satisfying labor demand for PBTL, in other words, apparently involves a delicate interplay of internalization for specificity and externalization for flexibility-adaptation of the labor supply. We may then ask what kinds of labor relations are likely to be "dynamically efficient" under such conditions.

Some theorists have suggested that the ideal form of employment arrangement under such circumstances is the division alluded to above: a core, internal labor force possessing firm-specific skills, and outsourcing or less secure employment for the rest (Atkinson, 1985). On the other hand, a transactions costs perspective would suggest that pure arms-length outsourcing is inadequate, if skills of externalized workers are highly specialized (i.e., sectorally or technologically specific), yet itself offers no solution, for the forms of contracts required for such situations are likely to be overwhelmed by contingent claims (Williamson, 1985).

Empirical observation often suggests that particular sets of labor market rules (institutional "environments," rather than "institutional arrangements," as Williamson [1985] would say) can generate outcomes quite different from this new labor market dualism, and that some of these outcomes might be more efficient over time than the new dualism. In particular, the comparative case study literature suggests that there are at least three solutions which are superior to the new dualism. One places a high degree of reliance on internal labor markets in core firms, where labor is trained more to industry- and firm-specific, but less to occupation-specific, skills, and firms develop effective mechanisms for internal redeployment over time (Koike, 1984; Mincer and Higuchi, 1987). In another, internal labor markets are as just described, but are combined with relational subcontracting, where the subcontracting firms in turn have flexible internal labor markets (Dore, 1987): we may call this the case of "quasi-externalization" of internal labor markets. To illustrate the third, I identify a set of cases consisting of bounded and relational external labor markets characterized by high levels of industry-specific skills, with low levels of exit for workers and firms. We may call this the case of "quasi-internalization" of external labor markets. In all of these cases, the predictions of standard skills-as-investments/capital theory about supposed tradeoffs or incompatibilities between specificity and adaptability seem to be strongly attenuated. Moreover, it appears that it is labor market rules and practices (institutional environments) that push firms and workers to generate these outcomes (institutional arrangements). It therefore behooves us to see if we can draw some lessons from the industrial relations that lead to these arrangements.

In this chapter we shall discuss the cases of quasi-internalization and quasi-externalization, and concentrate the bulk of our attention on the latter. The empirical universe I discuss in the pages that follow is a group of PBTL industries in France, Italy, and the United States, which I am studying in depth, and another group of industries in Germany and Japan whose characterizations I draw from secondary literature. All of these industries are strong points of their respective national economies in the sense that they are export specializations of that country. We can thus be reasonably sure that they are highly competitive versions of the sector at hand and that, to the extent that labor market rules and industrial relations contribute to their competitiveness, they may be examples of dynamic efficiency in industrial relations.[4]

COMPARING LABOR ALLOCATION IN PBTL INDUSTRIES ACROSS COUNTRIES

There are very different ways of allocating labor in PBTL industries, with different consequences for technological learning and for their technological trajectories in general. We will review some of the different ways in which labor is allocated internally, and the intersection between PBTL firms and external labor markets, to get a sense of these differences. Three basic approaches, which amount to different ideal types for combining specificity, specialization, and flexibility, may be identified.

The "German-Japanese" formula involves high levels of internal task flexibility and high levels of ongoing labor training in the context of the well-developed, internal labor markets of big firms in the German precision metalworking, mechanical engineering, and complex consumer durables industries, and in the Japanese assembly industries (Marsden, 1990). These big firms, in turn, stand at the center of elaborate networks of suppliers and subcontractors, with whom they have relatively stable and durable relations. As a result, their internal labor flexibility is combined with the benefits of quasi-externalization of labor markets, principally in the indirect form of relational contracting between firms. The big firm is the center of the PBTL industry, but the production system as a whole is structured around coordination of a host of firms in the effort to maintain skilled, internally deployable workforces. This set of arrangements has been extensively studied in recent years (Hyman and Streeck, 1988; Sabel, Kern, and Herrigel, 1990; Buttler, 1990).

At the opposite end of the spectrum, we might characterize an "American way" in technologically innovative industry. In American high-technology industries, big firms offer limited internal labor market security for scientific-engineering-technical (SET) workers. There are surprisingly high rates of labor turnover for SET workers (both voluntary and involuntary), who are partially absorbed by well-developed occupational labor markets (Angel, 1987). Big firms have arms-length subcontracting and supplier relationships for advanced technology inputs; some of the possible insecurity this creates is counteracted by those firms' diversity of market relationships, in turn dependent on their technological mastery, but volatility in employment relationships is nonetheless a common feature of life in these firms. For routine production tasks, they rely on their own facilities, some located in Silicon Valley or Orange County and other core areas, many located well outside of the core areas of California or the Northeast, where routine production workers enjoy little job security and are rarely unionized. The same is true of subcontracting firms for routine inputs, who transmit the insecurity they face from arms-length subcontracting agreeements and their lack of technological uniqueness to their workers in terms of low levels of job security and minimal levels of training (Carnoy, 1985). In sum, the whole system is permeated by high levels of external flexibility, whose effects are dampened by the existence of well-developed occupational labor markets for SET workers and, indirectly, by the innovative activities of firms, which enable them to counteract the effects of arms-length interfirm relationships. I will return to the American case later on in this chapter.

The French and Italian PBTL cases have a great deal in common. The Italian cases are, by now, quite well known, as the phenomenon of the "Third Italian" industrial renaissance, known in the English-speaking world as the prototype of "flexible specialization" (Bagnasco, 1977; Piore and Sabel, 1984). Little attention has been paid to the French cases in the non-French literature. Just to give an idea of the magnitude of these cases, we may note that, of the top fifty exports of Italy (in terms of world market share), according to our criteria, fully thirty-two are PBTL sectors, and they account for 82 percent of the value of the top fifty exports. Italian specializations include a dozen sectors in which it has more than 25 percent of all world exports. Broad groups of Italian mastery, largely located in the Third Italian provinces of Emilia-Romagna, Tuscany, Friuli-Venezia-Giulia, Veneto, and the Lombardy (excluding Milan) include textiles and apparel, furniture, lamps, glass, ceramic tiles, jewelry, eyeglasses, small industrial machinery, metalworking machinery, and woodworking machinery. The role of PBTL sectors in France is weaker, but there is greater range. Of the top fifty French exports, fourteen are PBTL sectors, but they account for almost 46 percent of the value of output of the top fifty. They include some fashion-intensive industries as in the Italian case (women's clothing, perfumes, cotton fabrics), but also a number of high-technology sectors such as aircraft and engines, data processing equipment, and radioactive elements (Storper, 1992b). These industries are found scattered in selected pockets around France, generally avoiding the area of mass production which begins about 150 km from Paris and cuts a wide circle around it in central and northern France. In both countries, the modal PBTL industry is composed largely of small- and medium-sized firms (but not exclusively, especially in France), highly clustered at the regional level.

In their PBTL industries, large firms play a smaller role, on average, than in the German and Japanese cases and, as a result, the possibilities for constructing internal labor markets are more limited. External labor markets composed of specialized workers are, however, "quasi-internalized" through relational interfirm linkages (contractual and informal), giving structure and continuity to the external labor market. This is made possible by the high degree of regionalization of the production system and the dense network of overlapping contact networks which permeate the labor market, combined with exit and entry barriers for workers. The labor exchange process and the ongoing formation of labor skills are effectively bounded, encouraging worker and employer investment in skills and repeated, though not continuous, employment relationships. In both countries, these local systems are buttressed by national labor law, with a strong dose of sectoral regulation (in France), or occupational regulation (Italy). Some examples of this particular solution to the specialization-specificity-flexibility problem include the following.

Mechanical Engineering in the Haute Savoie[5]

In the French department of the Haute Savoie in an intermediate Alpine valley by the name of Arve, situated about 25 km from downtown Geneva, there are about 550 highly specialized firms, employing about 10,000 workers, in specialized metalcutting (known in French as *décolletage*). There are also related activities in machining, accounting for another 100 firms and about 2,000 workers; this activity accounts for 75 percent of local manufacturing employment and 70 percent of French national output in specialized metalcutting, including 63 percent of national exports (Courlet, 1991). The history of this activity is a long one, dating back to the early 1700s, when German and Swiss watchmakers set up subcontract shops in the Valley. Since then, specialized mechanical work has had its ups and downs, depending largely on whether the border to Switzerland was open or not (Guichonnet, 1961; Gravier et al., 1969).

Today, median firm size is twenty employees, with 57 percent having fewer than ten workers and only forty-six firms having more than fifty employees. The local firms' output is directed largely to the automobile, electrical products for industry, electronics, electrical appliance, and armaments industries. The industry is set up as an interlocking network of firms, from prime contractors down to artisanal workshops in homes. While the very largest firms in the Valley are generally capable of supporting their workers over the long run, virtually all the rest have significant recourse to external labor flexibility (Courlet, 1991). The Valley constitutes a highly localized, yet highly specialized labor market. Since the mid-nineteenth century, it has steadily developed a series of labor training institutions, beginning with the Royal Watchmakers School in 1848, and continuing today with the *Centre Technique du Décolletage*. These institutions work in extremely close cooperation with the Valley's firms, and any graduate is immediately known to the key local employers (Courlet, 1987). This is underpinned by the dense family relationships between groups of firms and, by extension, groups of workers. The dense family and community-based relationships between employers are key not only to the nurturing of repeated, long-term interfirm supplier relationships, but also to the circulation of highly specialized but externalized workers. In essence, skill specificity is developed at the level of the Valley's production complex as a whole, not at the level of any particular firm; and training institutions are set up not only to socialize the costs of training, but to insure that specificity is defined at this, the labor market, level. Yet it is not an impermeable entry barrier; the training institutions allow entrants (both in the sense of youth and migrants from France and abroad) and they socialize them both to skills and to sector- and community-specific norms (Preault, 1991). The latter are "enforced" by local firms, banks, governments, and Chambers of Commerce (Boichard, 1986). Thus, community reciprocity is key to the functioning of this market, a strong case of "embeddedness" (Granovetter, 1986; Mingione, 1990).

Aerospace in Toulouse

Outside of Paris, the French aircraft industry is located largely in the regions surrounding Bordeaux and Toulouse, with Bordeaux a relatively old center of military aircraft production and Toulouse a relatively recent, and growing, center of civilian aircraft production as the key site of the European Airbus Industrie consortium, which currently holds 30 percent of world passenger aircraft markets.

It is a very different case from that of the Haute Savoie, since the Toulousain complex is a part of a production system that includes major firms and their subcontractors in Britain, Germany, and Spain. Aerospatiale, the major French contractor, Airbus Industrie, the prime contractor, and other major subcontractors, such as Matra, Dassault, Latecoere, Microturbo, Rockwell-Collins, Bendix, Thomson, SNPE, and Motorola are all found here, with a total employment of about 18,000. These big firms account for the lion's share of employment in the regional complex, although much smaller firms dominate electronic systems engineering and specialized software (Salais and Storper, 1993).

In the Toulousain aircraft industry, there are two major groups of workers, as in the aircraft industry elsewhere: the SET workers, and skilled production workers. The skilled production workers are strongly attached to firms through internal labor markets, and this-arrangement is formalized in the collective agreements between employers and unions (mostly the *Confédération Générale du Travail* [CGT], the union most closely allied with the French Communist Party, most prone to strike, and whose leaders are generally composed of former skilled workers, although there is a certain amount of competition between the CGT and the CFDT which is allied to the Socialist Party). The Toulousain region is, in turn, governed by a Socialist majority with very strong sympathies toward these skilled industrial workers. As we shall see later on, there are very high fixed costs (and thus disincentives) to hiring and firing such industrial workers in France. This reinforces the role of internal labor markets in an industry such as aircraft; but internal labor flexibility is somewhat limited by the craft consciousness of the unions and the structure of national branch agreements, or what are known as *conventions collectives* (Didry and Salais, 1991). The fact that the state plays a strong role in the aircraft industry presumably would reinforce the position of workers and make them more disposed to accept internal flexibility; but the CGT, as a union strongly marked by craft tradition and as a Communist-allied union, has opposed such flexibility as an incursion on worker rights (Chapman, 1990; Terrail and Tripier, 1986). Layoffs are thus initially very costly to aerospace firms, but after a period ranging from six months to one year, the state typically takes over the support of the workers, and the costs of external flexibility are shifted. Where the state comes back in is in negotiating the rehiring of laid-off workers with these firms when major new construction programs are launched; and the regional government usually participates with added incentives, whether direct or indirect. Workers, even when laid off, rarely leave the area. As a result, there is a—not entirely satisfactory—hybrid system consisting of internal rigidities, use of the external labor market, and, difficult but not impossible, recirculation of workers among the big firms of the area. Underpinning the whole system is the direct mediation of the state and indirect mediation via connections between labor unions, the local political structure, and national political parties (much less so than direct contractual relations between companies and unions).

More interesting is the SET worker labor market. A counterpart to the location of Aerospatiale and Airbus in Toulouse—both decisions of the powerful Parisian technocracy—has been the implantation of numerous major training institutions for SET workers, beginning in 1968 with the *Centre National d'Etudes Spatiales,* and continuing with the ENSICA *(Ecole Normale Supérieure d'Ingénieurie et de Construction Aéronautique),* the ENAC *(Ecole Nationale de l'Aviation Civile),* the Sup-Aero *(Ecole Nationale Supérieure de l'Aéronautique et de l'Espace),* and two major research laboratories in aerodynamics and automation. The powerful central state, in other words, complemented its locational decisions for production with a strong commitment to localizing technical-engineering training in the same area (Bauchet, 1986).

The local government has also played a major role in attracting and clustering university campuses, firms, and the training and research institutions noted above; and the rapidly growing ranks of SET workers (known as the *cadres*) have heavily influenced local government, with the mayor of the major technology-based suburb having come from their ranks, formerly worked in the aerospace industry, and been part of the local socialist-educated workers governing coalition (Gilly, 1990).

I noted above that production workers rarely leave the area. In part, this is because Toulouse—as part of southern France—has a very strong family structure, with the percentage of extended families quite high with respect to the national average, and a relatively hierarchical family structure holding these families together (known in France as the *famille de souche,* the strong family tree) (Todd, 1990). Surprisingly, this dynamic of strong localism is true of the SET workers as well as the production workers. Recent studies show that of the engineers at Matra, Aerospatiale, and CNES, 40 percent, 70 percent, and 50 percent, respectively, were trained in Toulouse. Overall, almost 90 percent of Toulousain engineers have been educated in the region. And, most of those who have their diplomas from elsewhere in France are natives of the region who return after their education (Grossetti and Mas, 1990). Thus, even though training, research, and production are dominated by outposts of national firms, and their products are destined to principally national-scale or even international-scale clients, the market for technical labor is highly localized. Moreover, internal and external labor markets are bound together at the local level through cooperative apprenticeship programs between local research and training institutions and the large technology contractors. At the *Institut National Supérieur d'Aéronautique* (INSA), for example, fifty of seventy-nine internships are filled by locals.

Given the deep roots of these SET workers in the local society, the local bases of their training, and the tight relationships between production firms and training institutions, it should not be suprising that the local external labor market functions quite efficiently. Though we do not have precise data on levels of interfirm exchange of SET workers, all the interviews I conducted in Toulouse suggested that this is a central dynamic of the local economy. Moreover, it would appear that there is a critical local external flexibility mechanism: when large firms do have to lay off SET workers and the latter cannot find reemployment in the large firms, they start up their own firms, which are then almost always swept into subcontracting relationships with larger firms, where their former colleagues are working. Of the 155 such firms which started up between 1971 and 1988, the majority were producing information services for the aerospace firms.

Precision Machinery Production in Emilia-Romagna

Emilia-Romagna is the heart of the postwar Italian industrial "miracle." Centered on the major cities of Bologna, Modena, Reggio Emilia, and Parma, it is responsible for about 10 percent of Italy's exports (with only 6% of population). For a population of 3.95 million, there are 325,000 businesses, or one for every twelve residents; 58

percent of the population works in businesses with nineteen or fewer employees, and there are 139,000 firms with fewer than twenty-two workers and an owner-operator. Of the region's 600,000 manufacturing workers, about 241,000 are in mechanical engineering, and about 200,000 in design-intensive production (clothing, textiles, shoes, ceramic tiles).

In mechanical engineering in Emilia, 32.7 percent of workers are in firms with fewer than nine workers, 27.4 percent are in firms having 10–49 employees, 28.6 percent in firms having 50–499 employees, and 11.3 percent of the workforce is employed in firms that have more than 500 *addetti* (employees). This masks some differences within the region, as the capital city's engineering industry is overwhelmingly composed of the firms with fewer than forty-nine workers, and almost all the big firms are located in Modena, Parma, or Reggio Emilia. While the Emilian mechanical engineering industry has tripled its employment since 1960, the size distribution of employment has remained constant.

The roots of Bolognese machine production are most likely in the system of technical schools which has characterized the city since the physicist Giovanni Aldini and the economist Luigi Valeriani, who had studied systems of technical education in Britain and France, bequeathed their estates to the city of Bologna for the establishment of schools in the mechanical arts. The Technical Schools of Bologna opened in 1839. These schools, which became the Istituto Aldini-Valeriani (IAV) in 1878 and later specialized in electrotechnical research and education had, from the beginning, a dual mission: training which was both practical and theoretical, reflecting Aldini's own orientation as a physicist and Valeriani's concern with applications (Cappecchi, 1990a). Throughout its long history, it has trained people to design and conceptualize machines, not merely to make them; in a development that was to become typical of the Bolognese technical schooling system, the IAV was like a training center for working group leaders *(capoperai)* rather than for line workers (Cappecchi, 1990a and b). Others followed, with variations on this theme, including the *Istituto Alberghetto* in Imola (1881), the Women's Design School in 1894 (started by the rural socialist-feminist organizer Argentina Altobelli) and, elsewhere in the region, the *Istituto Tecnico* in Reggio Emilia, originated by the physicist Augusto Righi, and the Corno Institute in Modena (1921). Of course, the mingling of theoretical scientists with the applied mechanical arts was consequent on the existence of these theoreticians in the first place, owing to the presence of Italy's oldest university, in Bologna; but the fact that they mingled with the community probably had to do with the commitment of socialist intellectuals to spreading scientific knowledge to the working class. One example of the latter was the establishment, in 1901, of the *Università Popolare Giuseppe Garibaldi.*

Bologna thus created for itself a specific set of potential innovative agents: skilled workers imbued with theoretical (or, at least, quasi-theoretical, i.e., conceptual) capabilities. It is in this respect that we can speak of Bolognese industrialization as depending on key forms of "local knowledge" in the art of constructing semi-customized machinery, and not principally on the availability of production capacity for commands which issue from outside the system.

Industrialization did get one of its early pushes from the subcontracting activities of state-owned companies, in railroads and other infrastructure sectors, but rapidly assumed its own endogenous dynamic. In the early part of the twentieth century, the list of start-ups is astounding, including De Morsier and Calzoni in agricultural machinery, Barbiere and Minganti in machine tools, Acma in food packaging, Sasib in cigarette making and packaging, Weber in carburetors, Ducati in cinema and radio equipment, Rizzoli and Lollini in medical and dental devices, Maserati in high performance automobiles, and others.

The fascist and postwar periods decimated the region's economy, and there were massive layoffs in the early 1950s. Combined with rapid out-migration from agriculture, there was a strong need to create employment, especially as there was virtually no out-migration from the region: population closure held the local social system together and created pressures for local actors to develop the economy.

The postwar period reinforced the political subculture of the area, and this played a role in the ways local labor markets were structured in that period. While the Fascists had successfully divided peasants from workers and skilled from unskilled workers, the wartime resistance movements cut across such divisions. By the end of the war, Emilia was "Red." A very solidaristic local movement for success in the face of a hostile national government (Christian Democrat) and an indifferent Marshall Plan (virtually none of whose resources made it to Emilia) developed. The Italian Communist Party (PCI) which, in the Milan region devoted its energies to organizing big factories, found itself dominant in Emilia, but with no big factories to organize (Trigilia, 1986, 1990). Providentially, it had the sense to support worker-based entrepreneurship as a way to survive in the face of Rome's hostility. The PCI made its workers the key actors in a regional strategy of economic development, and these workers benefited from political reciprocity from bankers, other workers, and local government, as well as the traditionally very strong family structure of the region (statistically, Emilia is the center of a family structure almost unique in Europe, with a high proportion of extended families but equal inheritance among siblings, thus pushing people to maximize family wealth; see Todd, 1990).

As a result, Bologna went through an explosion of spinoffs in the mechanical engineering industry from the 1950s on. Clusters of firms making packaging machines, precision instruments, electronic measuring devices, and so on, were created (names such as Acma, Scagnoli, Peci, Ima, Wrapmatic, Arcotronix, Sinudyne, Eurosonic, Canducci, Marposs). The quality that links all these companies is that they make semi-customized or high-quality machines. There are two subgroups: those who make more standardized "catalog" products, and those who make genuinely semi-customized machines. The firms tend to be smaller in the latter case and larger in the former, with labor processes there taking on a more rationalized industrial character. But in all cases, the work process involves significant levels of worker responsibility, and local subcontracting and supplier relationships are the rule, many of these between larger firms and their former workers who started up their own firms. Thus, workers are "trained" both by training institutions and in firms, *but with the expectation* that they may leave and start up their own firms, which will retain a relationship with the firms they left, now as suppliers (Brusco, 1982). High levels of industry-specific technical skills are diffused downward and outward, in an ever-widening circle, and because this takes place in a context of high levels of trust and reciprocity (underpinned by long-standing family relationships and mediated by local political structures), it generates not competition for existing firms, but precisely the organizational flexibility they require in markets for semi-customized machinery.

In all of these French and Italian cases (and there could be many more), the local production system is underpinned by "rules of participation" of a host of actors (a variable mix of employers, local governments, families, workers, training institutions, and so on). These actors mobilize particular industry-specific skills in an external local labor market, where the latter is highly structured so that its externalities are sufficiently specific to be useful to a wide range of firms, and where local bounding of labor supply reduces the risk of loss of the positive externalities, as well as the risk of free-rider or adversely competitive effects from exercise of the skills which are created. Specificity and flexibility are, to some degree, combined.

All of this has been posed in descriptive terms. I wish now to argue that a number of these success stories of what appear to be dynamically efficient systems for labor allocation do not fit comfortably into existing literature on industrial relations, particularly that which is concerned with union density and the degree of centralization of bargaining. These "paradoxical" dimensions of labor relations in PBTL industries suggest some conceptual and practical problems that call for further debate and research.

FIRST PROBLEM: FUNCTIONAL FLEXIBILITY IN GERMANY AND JAPAN

The literature has suggested a strong relationship between levels of union density and the level of bargaining centralization (low = enterprise or workplace, high = nation, medium = industry or region), leading to two groups of countries: the high-density centralized cases (HDCC) and low-density decentralized cases (LDDC) (Rogers, 1990; Buttler, 1990; Lange, 1988). Theoretically, this would seem to be the case because centralization permits the overcoming of free-rider tendencies, on one hand, and lowers transactions costs of organizing and maintaining organization, on the other, leading to high density, with the reverse holding for decentralized systems (Wallerstein, 1987; Rogers, 1990).

Another set of relationships has also been suggested, although there is much less careful research to confirm it. HDCC economies are characterized, *ceteris paribus,* by a tendency toward greater internal "functional" flexibility of labor and relatively little external "numerical" flexibility, while in the LDDC economies firms appear to rely more heavily on numerical flexibility (hiring, firing) than on redeployment and polyvalent skilling within the firm (Campbell and Vickery, 1988; Sorge and Streeck, 1988). The mechanism which generates these effects is simple: in HDCCs, there are almost always greater penalties for firing workers and greater costs to hiring new ones (Piore, 1986).

A third line of research takes the phenomena of density and centralization and links them to country size (Wallerstein, 1987). Small countries, with inclusive interest group structures and high degrees of openness, develop centralized structures, because broad cooperative coalitions can be founded, and this underpins high density; whereas large countries cannot overcome dispersion of interests, and typically cannot identify common purposes enough to develop inclusive coalitions. Their resulting decentralized structures impose excessive transactions costs and other burdens on any organizing effort, and low density is the result. It follows, then, that small countries should have high levels of functional flexibility and low levels of numerical flexibility due to the power of unions; and big countries should have high levels of external, numerical flexibility, and a tendency away from functional flexibility due to union weakness. And this thesis is tempting if one thinks of the United States on one hand, and small European countries such as Sweden, Belgium, or Austria, on the other (see Figures 7.1 and 7.2).

The problems emerge when we consider medium-sized countries such as Germany, France, Italy, or Japan. Germany is a country with a medium level of union density (about 40%), and bargaining at the "meso" levels of industry and region (Visser, 1989). All this is perfectly consistent with the size hypothesis. Nonetheless, the German system affords disincentives to external labor flexibility which are every bit as strong as those found in small, much more unionized countries with more centralized bargaining, and the resulting functional flexibility is reputed to be more effective in the German case than, say, the Belgian or even the Swedish (Maurice et al., 1986; Piore, 1986). How can this be so? Perhaps because they combine bargaining and hence, training and redeployment coordination, at both *lander* (region) and sectoral level, providing certain inter-sectoral efficiencies; but this should be the case in a small country as well, where negotiation at the economywide (hence intersectoral) level takes place (Swenson, 1989). Another possibility is that firms and their supplier networks are apt to be bigger in Germany, affording them more play with indirect forms of labor flexibility, through interfirm relations (Sabel, Kern, and

Figure 7.1. Relation of centralization of structure to level of bargaining. *Source:* C. A. Blyth, "The interaction between collective bargaining and government policies in selected member countries." *Collective Bargaining and Government Policies* (OECD, Paris, 1979), 92–93.

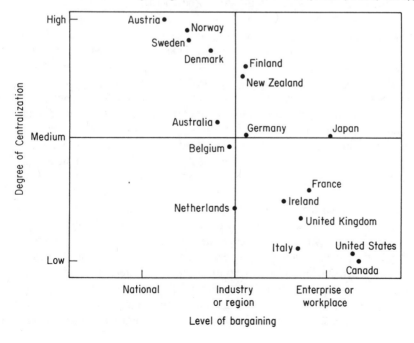

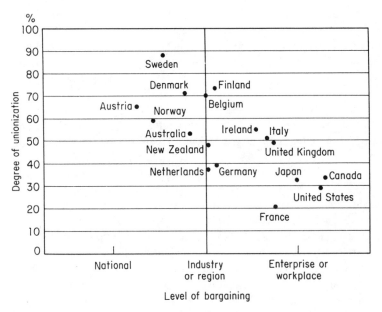

Figure 7.2. Relation of unionization to level of bargaining. *Source:* C. A. Blyth, "The interaction between collective bargaining and government policies in selected member countries." *Collective Bargaining and Government Policies* (OECD, Paris, 1979), 92–93.

Herrigel, 1990). But if this is true, how is the supposed "disadvantage" of size, with its dispersion of interests and tendency to free-rider effects, overcome?

Japan is another curious case. Often taken to be an LDDC economy, in fact its formal enterprise-level bargaining is informally centralized at the sectoral level through the "spring offensive," where unions and employers line up their demands and resolve them in common; at the very least, Japan is an LDMC (moderately centralized). Further, it is difficult to say whether Japan's economy leans toward functional flexibility or numerical flexibility; viewed from the standpoint of big firms and their collaborators in the big *keiretsu,* Japan is a case par excellence of the privileging of internal functional flexibility and a definite aversion to numerical flexibility, and the same is true of first- (and sometimes second-) tier subcontractors in, say, the Toyota system. But then there are the third-tier subcontractors, which are the equivalents of overseas arms-length subcontractors to German mechanical engineering industries, which fall outside the bargaining system (Dore, 1987; Koike, 1984).

The successes of both these economies in combining high levels of functional flexibility and employment security, and in dynamic adjustment of their industrial systems through ongoing technological change, are undeniable. The predictions about these flexibility and dynamic efficiency properties that we would make from country size, national union density levels, and centralization levels, are not entirely consistent with these configurations of flexibility and security, however.

It appears that in both cases there are functional equivalents of high density and centralization which enhance the cohesion that characterize the (very large) "insider" groups in these countries' economies (skilled workers in German mechanical engineering; workers inside the *keiretsu* firms and first-tier subcontractors in Japan) and permit them to act as involved participants in the process of industrial adjustment which underlies PBTL. The functional equivalents of high density and centralization draw boundaries around organized interests. In the German case, these are largely regional boundaries, where regional negotiations within and across sectors, complemented by relational subcontracting between firms at a regional level, make possible high levels of internal flexibility. It is, from this perspective, not entirely accurate to think of the German economy as only medium density and moderately centralized.[6] In Japan, the functional equivalents are, obviously, the *keiretsu* in first place, and the sector in second. The *keiretsu* functions like the equivalent of small, cohesive community in the Japanese economy, within which a successful combination of specialization-specificity-flexibility can be generated, without excessive negative externalities, or what I termed earlier "quasi-externalization" (and others, such as Dore [1987], have called "flexible rigidities").

QUASI-INTERNALIZATION AND QUASI-EXTERNALIZATION IN FRANCE AND ITALY

It has been observed, from time to time, that labor economics in general, and the industrial relations literature in particular, suffer from an Anglo-Saxon bias (Perulli, 1992). France and Italy have been described by a number of prominent thinkers as "Catholic capitalist" societies, partaking of a southern European social formation which is not easily understandable from an Anglo-Saxon viewpoint (Carboni, 1990; d'Iribarne, 1989). Barrington Moore (1966) attempted to capture this difference by suggesting that in southern Europe, the claims of organized groups ("solidarity") has always existed in a strong tension with the pursuit of economic growth.[7] Students of industrial relations have also noted key, consistent differences between Latin Europe and northern Europe (and, by extension, the United States): the coexistence of low density with extremely high levels of militancy and anarcho-syndicalism, for example, a combination not observed elsewhere.

France is a low union density (20%), decentralized bargaining case; Italy is a medium union density (50%), decentralized bargaining system. Yet in both of these countries, the price of hiring and firing is quite high (as compared with, say, the United States). Notwithstanding much debate (and in the case of France, heavy employer pressure) to reduce the penalties to external labor market flexibility, and even some legal moves in that direction, there has actually been very little change. The French and Italian economies, in this regard, have remained much more similar to the German than to the American or British.

The anomalies abound. How can Italy, a decentralized bargaining country, have a medium level of union density, and strong disincentives to external flexibility? How can France, a country with lower union density than the United States (in spite of much smaller size), and decentralization, keep such disincentives to external flexibility? What explanations can we offer for the cases of quasi-internalization of external labor markets in the Haute Savoie and in Emilia, or quasi-externalization in the case of Toulouse?

These anomalies, I want to argue, have not been recognized in much of existing systematic industrial relations research, and if they were, they would open up some new possibilities. In essence, the labels "low density," "medium density," and "decentralized" are misleading for these countries. They result from what an ethnographer might call the "blind spots" in the field of vision of the social scientist, which prevent us from seeing that the successful PBTL complexes of Germany, France, and Italy (but not their economies as a whole), have *conventions of labor participation* and labor market organization which are functionally equivalent to high-density, centralized bargaining. Conventions are practices, routines, agreements, and their associated informal or institutional forms which bind actors together through mutual behavior expectations which coordinate their actions under conditions of uncertainty (*Révue Economique,* 1989).

As the German case is well known, let us just briefly refer to the conventions that stand in for high density and centralization in the French and Italian regions discussed above. In France, the participation of labor is more structured at the national level than the label low density suggests. Labor union members are really *activists (les "militants");* and sympathizers—those who are ready to follow union actions—are several times this hard core. While France has no legal closed shop, minimum working conditions and wages in the whole economy have been established, since the 1930s, by industry-level agreements *(accords de branche),* which are in turn criss-crossed by other, occupation- or industry-level agreements *(conventions collectives)* (Didry and Salais, 1991; Lyon-Caen, 1991). Virtually all industries and all categories of workers are covered by these agreements which, in most cases, establish legal minima rather than actual wages, but which serve as real guides to working conditions, including industry- and occupation-specific customs concerning skills, job definitions, hiring, layoff and rehiring conditions, and sometimes, training. Unions are frequently signatories to the agreements, as are employer groups; and even without the closed shop, the agreements cover all workers in the industry, and have a strong impact on the nonwage dimensions of employment.[8]

The significance of these branch and occupational agreements is frequently underestimated, because they do not have the same formal content as those found typically in Germany or Scandinavia. But they are the tip of the iceberg. They express the importance of belonging to a *category,* which is a pervasive feature of French economic life. Labor sociologists call this *la logique d'honneur,* meaning the deeply held principle that membership in a defined group is essential to one's identity, and that there is a certain set of duties and rights that pertain to that group. D'Iribarne (1989) notes, for example, that employers have much more difficulty intervening in the task structure of the labor process in France than in the United States, with or without unions, because it is considered the obligation of the worker to get the job done, but by his or her own procedures, not those of the employer; it is duty, or honor, to get the job done, but it is also the right of the worker to get it done in his or her own way. Likewise, each group (category, usually legally defined) has historically established privileges, and the state—through the system of total coverage of the economy by branch agreements—has codified these expectations, which are extremely resistant to change (we could cite thousands of specific, codified privileges) (Maurice, et al., 1986; Marsden, 1986; Sellier, 1991). The aggregate result is that France is a high mandated benefit, high indirect wage country, but this is built up, category by category. Some have called this a system of "categorical rents," *les rentes de situation.*

Unions, and their broader circles of nonmilitant sympathizers in France, are also linked to political parties, so that their influence goes well beyond the various agreements, and well beyond the workplace. With France's highly centralized political system, it should be remembered that *local* governments (especially until the decentralization reforms of the 1980s) were very highly dependent on administrative powers of the central government (through the prefectural system). This works to labor's favor when Left parties are in power, of course, since unions that have only moderate power in a locality or in a particular firm have the means to apply pressure on Paris and back to firms and localities through the prefect, who controls all manner of potential favors to firms and localities (Bleitrach and Chenu, 1974; Hayward, 1985). But even when labor parties are not in the Matignon and the Elysée (the palaces of the prime minister and president, respectively), in localities where labor is powerful, they will have strong influence on what are known as *notables,* the local system of power brokers who bargain for the locality with the prefects who represent Paris (Ganne, 1985).

It can be seen that, at least in those regions where the right combinations of firms and workers, and the right constellations of political power exist, so also do the means to quasi-internalize some of the externalities of regional, industry-specific labor markets. There are many overlapping social constraints and possibilities for interest aggregation between the horizontal categories I have described in this chapter; this vertical interest aggregation brings them together for a common project. The key dimensions of this vertical solidarity which overcomes horizontal compartmentalization (but respects its coherences) are sectoral-regional: in all the cases I examined, it involves strong regional concentrations in a given, innovation-dependent product market.

France, however, is not Germany—as the French industrial record shows. Why, in the face of these structures, are French examples of PBTL-based production less frequent than German ones? This is a subject of much (anguished) reflection in France today. Most analyses center on: (1) the dramatic differences in education and training systems between the two countries, with France's system somewhat paralyzed by the same categorical structures noted above, i.e., categorical training and credentialing rather than sectoral training (Maurice et al., 1986); (2) the long history of ambivalence with respect to the role of markets in France, with intermittent protectionist tendencies and a large role for family capital which is not subject to much domestic competition either (Saglio, 1988); and (3) a vicious circle of extreme employer hostility to unions and to negotiation in general, which pushes them into Taylorization in order to defeat workers (this is most pronounced in the mass production sectors), and workers into defense of categorical rights (d'Iribarne, 1989). So the successes of the French system are sectorally-regionally fortuitous, not systematic, and there has been a failure to invent rules which push for dynamic efficiency across the economy. Instead, French industries are subjected to periodic shocks from the powerful, technocratic state, which modernizes them and then lets them go back into categorical stasis (in some cases paralysis) until the next crisis (Hall, 1986; cf. Labaube, 1988; Petit, 1988).

The Bolognese case is typical of the industrial communities of north-east-central

Italy in that it envelops the process of "industrial" relations in strong community-based voice mechanisms; *citizenship* is the critical support mechanism for dynamically efficient industrial relations (Pye and Verba, 1965; Carboni, 1990; Mingione, 1990; Cappecchi, 1990a, 1990b; Becattini, 1987; Trigilia, 1986). The borders between industry and community, between work and other roles are quite fluid (Berger, 1980; Cappecchi, 1990b; Brusco, 1983; Paci, 1988). These industries are all characterized by a high number of entrepreneur-artisans, people who work as well as own, and they are often former workers (Barbagli et al., 1988). Their current workers are potential future colleagues and most of them are connected, directly or indirectly, by family or friendship ties. Identities and roles are quite blurred, with a high percentage changing economic roles, but staying within the same industry and region, over their lifetimes. One of the most important consequences of this lifetime pathway is that there are high levels of voluntary worker mobility: workers who leave to start up their own firms—some of which fail—and reenter as workers (but with even higher skills and contacts which might then benefit their new employer), as well as combinations and recombinations of small firms, especially within the network of extended family relations—which is also a system for extending "apprenticeship" favors to the sons or daughters of other members (who will later on become cooperative competitors) (Brusco, 1983).

As in the French case, particular "horizontal" groups are highly organized. Small firm owners (the artisans, *artigiani*) are typically members of local branches of the *Confederazione Nazionale d'Artigianato* (CNA), which then federates them at province, regional, and national levels. CNA coverage of eligible small firms is about 85 percent in Emilia, and the key effect of this on the labor market is that firms have a high level of information about labor availability. The CNA is one of the means by which the supply of industry-specific labor is effectively circulated among firms, whether directly (transfer through firing and rehiring) or indirectly (through reciprocal work sharing, an informal type of subcontracting to smooth production cycles). Unionization rates are high among skilled workers in the large firms, and in these cases, unions negotiate directly with employer groups; they account for about one-third of the workforce in the industry, with unions having a much lesser presence in the artisanal firms (de Luca, 1989; Brutti, 1990). But, as in France, unions are linked to political parties: the former Communist Party (now rebaptised the *Partito Democratico della Sinistra*) in Emilia and Tuscany; the Christian Democrats in Friuli-Venezia-Giulia and the Veneto. In both cases, the parties extend the influence of unions well beyond the workplaces that are organized, because these parties control the powerful local and regional governments with which the local branches of the CNA must negotiate for all manner of favors and aids (such as the extensive series of all-equipped industrial parks that they provide to local firms, giving them great leverage over the latter) (Brusco and Rizio, 1985). Developmentalist local governments, whether "red" as in Emilia or "white" as in Udine or Verona, act as brokers between artisans, workers, and, in Bologna, the educational system to which we referred earlier (Cappecchi, 1990b; Trigilia, 1986; Scarpitti, 1989; Lassini, 1985).

The system facilitates training and circulation of workers with industry-specific skills at the local or provincial (subregional) level where, censuses have demonstrated, there are relatively low levels of regional population entry and exit. Reputation effects are extremely high for both employer-artisans and workers. Crises do come about, but in general the multiple and overlapping networks which bind the actors together push them to lobby for regulated adjustments. When major layoffs in big local firms hit Emilia, and the PBTL industries could not immediately absorb them, lobbying in Rome for the transitional unemployment payment system (the *Cassa Integrazione Guadagni*) came from all sectors, not just unions, in whose narrow interest the *Cassa* lay. Likewise, when homeworkers (who form an important element, about 15%, of the workforce in fashion-production in Emilia and elsewhere) wanted regularization of their conditions, they were not only unopposed by the CNA (which subcontracts to them), they were actively supported, leading to a national law regulating the conditions, hours, and minimum wages for homeworkers (Ritaine, 1987). The striking weakness of centralized structures for bargaining in Italy is, in other words, belied by the regional conventions which underlie economic citizenship there. In the context of extremely decentralized, hence flexible, production systems, these conventions bound the stock of labor market externalities, preventing both extra-regional leakage and excessive free-rider effects within the region. The external labor market is "quasi-internalized" in the short run, and in the long run, adjustments of the whole structure to new realities are struggled with through the economic citizenship system.

Obviously, conflict and the tendency to not want to concert or to free-ride do exist in all of these places; none is a world of cultural consensus and absence of conflict (Regini, 1988). Indeed, the French cases we have cited are, in a sense, exceptions to much of recent French industrialization and labor relations. In industry after industry (shoes, parts of clothing, much metalworking) and region after region (especially in former craft regions of the Rhône-Alpes, and in the recently industrialized areas of the Vendée), big corporate actors have broken the old system by reorganizing the production process (Courault and Rerat, 1987). But the consequence, in all these places, has been a change in product, so that the system is no longer organized for PBTL, but for traditional cost control and economies of scale. As this occurs, the regional skill pools have tended to dry up, and the result, after several years, is relocation of production, usually outside France. In the process, France's share of world trade in these sectors has been shrinking. In other words, these systems are vulnerable to attack under some conditions, but the price is PBTL competitiveness.

QUESTIONS FOR THEORY

The constant in the experiences recounted here is some kind of bounding and compartmentalization of the external labor market, on one hand, and geographical concentration of the employers in a specific sector, on the other. Within these spaces, conventions operate which make it possible for skill specificities to be generated and externalized without leaking or falling prey to free-rider effects. I have argued that geographical bounding of the labor exchange process promotes effective bundling of interests through multiple and overlapping connections among members of groups and between groups. In Germany, there is an advanced, highly formalized version of such a system in effect throughout the national territory, consisting of *lander*- and sector-level binding negotiations and contracts, combined with *lander*-, sector- and firm-specific training mechanisms. In France and Italy, regionally distinctive conventions permit externalities to be generated, recaptured and recirculated, allowing specificities to flourish, and dynamic adjustment in the context of innovation to take place.

One can interpret these phenomena almost as one wishes, depending on the theoretical approach adopted. From one standpoint, the existence of industry- and region-specific human capital leads to the efficiencies of labor markets in these industrial complexes. For example, the "skills" of certain suppliers may be called "relation specific skills," and it can then be shown that they have a strong motivation to engage in repeated, faithful interactions with core, client firms because they earn "relational quasi-rents" on their (unstandardized) products, which compensate them for the risks of attachment (Asanuma, 1989). But this appears not as explanation, but as retrospective functionalism. Moreover, since the same theoretical perspective suggests that core firms will always try to extract themselves from dependency on relation-specificity by standardization or integration, it is not clear what the glue is that would hold the relationship together over the course of more than one technological cycle.

Turning from the logic of industrial organization to that of institutions, many other questions arise. For the Chicago School, these interest groups must be spontaneous bundles, who transform economic impulses into political action with no transactions costs (Moe, 1987). But these are not once and for all systems, with no crises and conflicts. What we observe is that there are mechanisms for holding exit tendencies in check. In France, we can trace many of them to the construction of the Paris-dominated administrative system from Colbert through Napoleon, and its counterpart, which is local administration and local resistance (Ganne, 1985). Much of the local "resistance," moreover, rests on a bedrock of nonmarket relations, and on other transformed historical institutions, like old artisanal groups; they seem to be decidedly unspontaneous, and they seem to survive many rounds of technological change. The conventions, in other words, are repeatedly reembodied in new institutions, like the industry agreements.[9]

From the standpoint of newer, more "positive" theories of institutions, based explicitly on the existence of principal-agent problems and transactions costs, we might account for the happy outcomes described in the cases at hand as "repeated games with learning," minimal principal-agent problems and low transactions costs, leading to cooperative games (Lange, 1988; Pratt and Zeckhauser, 1985; cf. Jacoby, 1989; Rogers, 1990; Weiler, 1990; Granovetter, 1986). Descriptively, this apparatus is appealing; but it says little about how such conventions arise and how they evolve, i.e., the key aspects of systemic behavior (Moe, 1987).

In other words, while these examples may be described as functional equivalents of small countries within big countries, we do not know, from such an analysis, why they arise and survive in big countries. I am tempted to believe, on the basis of my "thick" field research in France and Italy, that these practices have become embedded in local cultures and expectations, interpretative frameworks for what is good and bad, acceptable and nonacceptable: examples include the logic of honor in France, trajectories of worker-entrepreneurs in Italy, or consensus, economic nationalism, and strategic conceptions of the firm in Japan. The fact that they seem to be competitive should not make us think there is a single standard of efficiency which then drives the configuration of economic activity and its institutions.

INDUSTRIAL RELATIONS, ADJUSTMENT, AND
ECONOMIC SPECIALIZATION

The latter point needs to be made in more economistic terms, for economics always has a response: the long-run forces of competition will drive out the less efficient or reduce its income, and vice-versa. But we now know that to be, at best, an oversimplification. For economies are characterized by a very high level of inter- and intra-sectoral diversity in what they make and how they make it. The latter point ("diachronic specificity"; Jacoby, 1989) refers in part to a force rarely recognized in economic thinking: that there are different sources of profit, and that rents and quasi-rents play an important role in competition, especially when technological innovation and change, or scarce skills, are involved; the advantage is absolute, not comparative (Dosi, Pavitt, and Soete, 1990; Amendola and Gaffard, 1990). Moreover, as recent advances in evolutionary economics and the theory of increasing returns have shown us, small and localized events, if they take markets and shape technological choices and consumer preferences, may have very big, durable outcomes (Nelson and Winter, 1982). All of this means that localized means of resolving the essential problem of uncertainty that underlies all economic activity in capitalism are not necessarily washed away by some long-run competitive convergence to a putative best practice. So long as they are competitively viable, according to the locally accepted definition of viability, they can indeed have a long life.

In the context of an increasingly global system of production and exchange, localized systems of industrial relations may be among the factors that push economies into particular patterns of specialization, as Streeck has suggested for the case of German "diversified, quality-oriented" output systems (Hyman and Streeck, 1988). Do these conventions provide tactical space to different interests, i.e., employers in their deployment of human and physical capital and the narrow set of matches between resulting cost structures and products? This would certainly seem to be the case when the export specialization patterns of three countries are compared. Italy, for example, is extremely strong in the high end of fashion-oriented or craft- and design-based manufacturing; the United States has almost none of the latter among its strong exports but is highly specialized in high technology, of which there is virtually none among Italian specializations. This "noncompetition" due to selection obviously stems from much more than different labor relations systems; but it is also quite likely that the latter make an important contribution to diversity and selection by creating some options (mobilizing skills and positive externalities) and blocking others (akin to Mokyr's [1990] point that technical progress is due as much to a lack of resistance as to anything positive).

LESSONS FOR THE AMERICAN CASE?

American PBTL specializations are overwhelmingly concentrated in the high-technology industries centering on aviation and electronics. I draw on what I understand to be the reality in Northern California electronics and Southern California electronics and aerospace, to tell the following stylized story about their labor markets and the conventions that organize them.

In electronics, the two critical segments of the workforce are scientific-engineering-technical (SET) workers, and nonunionized production workers. SET workers in large firms are caught up in internal labor markets, but these, and their colleagues in smaller firms or in their own entrepreneurial start-ups, are most heavily linked by external occupational labor markets (OLMs) whose basic structure is defined by professional credentials which rest on the rules of scientific procedure (Angel, 1987).

In aerospace, the role of internal labor markets for SET workers appears stronger than in electronics, with lower turnover levels and longer tenure as the principal evidence of this. Professional networks in occupational labor markets (and connections between engineers who have worked for Department of Defense contractors) play important roles, but less so than in electronics. The industry sports a high percentage of skilled, unionized production workers as well (principally the International Association of Machinists).

Do these systems facilitate PBTL adjustments? Are they dynamically efficient? Some have speculated that the American success in product innovation in electronics may be related to the sheer size of its OLMs for SET workers, and the fact that they are not concentrated within one or a small number of business organizations. Experimental behavior and entrepreneurial spinoff have been key to the exploration of alternative technological pathways.[10]

If we accept this as plausible, it is not clear that it works for certain other kinds of technological learning. The United States has, in recent years, all but lost the merchant semiconductor industry to Japan. It may well be that this was in part due to Japanese dumping of chips in the early 1980s, or to the superior conditions of finance and investment in Japan. But I suspect that these are, at best, incomplete accounts. For the fact that U.S. semiconductor companies *can* lay off skilled SET workers, and that this is considered to be an acceptable social practice in the United States, is very likely a disincentive to stay in those markets. I would guess, in other words, that were such factor mobility not possible, those companies would have redoubled their strategies not to lose the merchant semiconductor market, either by trying harder on quality control, or by pressuring the government to do something about Japanese dumping and U.S. overproduction.

I suspect as well that the relatively high levels of turnover and job-hopping by talented engineers in American microelectronics contributed to the semiconductor equipment manufacturing disaster. In the late 1970s, the United States held 90 percent of the world market for such equipment; in 1987, the share was down to 30 percent and slipping. Detailed case studies have shown that this was due, in part, to pervasive distrust between chip makers and equipment makers; the former, fearing that the latter would reveal their new designs to competitors, did not keep the latter posted on the new kinds of equipment they needed. When new chips were made, the Japanese were the only ones who could readily supply the equipment, because their equipment and chip makers had communicated well (Stowsky, 1987).

In aerospace, the huge "success story" of the United States has been predicated on growth, albeit with occasional business cycles involving a certain amount of temporary layoff for both SET workers and production workers. One wonders how such a system will function if, indeed, we have entered into a sustained period of military build-down, and heightened international competition in civilian aviation. Already,

Los Angeles-based firms have decentralized production facilities to places such as Georgia (Lockheed) (while the French are busy centralizing in Toulouse). Does the practice of easy layoff and the notion that mobility—interfirm and interregional—will take care of the problem, act as a perverse signaling device to American technology companies? If they were stuck with much higher costs of layoff of both SET workers and skilled production workers, would there be more rapid and more concerted mobilization for learning new technologies such as electric vehicles, mass transit, and new civilian aerospace applications?

Some may reply that this is, in any case, idle speculation. The existing low-density, low-centralization, low-concertation system is, to be sure, strongly self-reproducing in the United States: you cannot get noncoalescent interests to coalesce, because they are noncoalescent.[11] Yet both France and Italy are countries where the national systems are not so completely different from that of the United States. These European examples of, albeit fortuitous, quasi-internalization or quasi-externalization in the context of low-density decentralized systems in relatively large, diversified economies, may suggest a practical approach for us. I mean something like labor-industrial "sectionalism," regional coalitions of capital and labor which would begin to build toward islands of quasi-internalization/externalization in a sea of dispersed interests. In Southern California, the very fact that there is a debate about converting the military industries to production of electric vehicles and mass transit equipment, using the existing SET and skilled production labor from the aerospace industry, suggests that the region-industry level may be more appropriate for the bounding and bundling of interests than the nation or industry levels (not to mention craft or class). Indeed, one is tempted to think that the structure of county federations of labor, in its heyday, could have performed such a role.[12] We need research into the rise and performance of county federations to determine whether they were, or still might be, capable of bounding and bundling labor interests, i.e., forming cooperative coalitions that could participate actively in the process of economic adjustment in American regions. What are the possibilities and obstacles?

I do not want to sound utopian. Such a project of creating functional equivalents of bounded bargaining processes in a country as large and diverse as the United States, with its particular ideological heritage, would be extraordinarily difficult. It might be impossible in the absence of national reforms that would prevent free-rider effects (such as company relocation). But the French, German, and Italian examples do suggest that in a world economy dominated by technological competition, where dynamically efficient production systems require dynamically efficient industrial relations, building such communities of interest as the basis of specificity and flexibility is one possible strategy for more attractive employment and production futures.[13]

NOTES

I wish to acknowledge the support of the UCLA Institute of Industrial Relations, the French Ministry of Research and Technology, the research group "Institutions, Emploi et Politique Economique" (Paris), the International Studies and Overseas Programs of UCLA and the Center for International Business Education Research (CIBER) at UCLA, and the German Marshall Fund of the United States.

1. As was implied in Leontief's (1953) interpretation of the contrary factor intensities paradox.

2. As was implied in Vernon's (1966) early versions of the product cycle.

3. This refers to functional vertical integration versus financial/ownership vertical integration.

4. According to Dosi, Pavitt, and Soete (1990), all export specialization sectors, measured

as those sectors in which a country's share of world exports is greater than its share of world exports and imports combined, should be those in which the country has an "absolute" and not merely a "comparative" advantage (i.e., location is not sensitive to the wage-profit frontier); and absolute advantage is, in the great majority of cases, rooted in technological advantage. In turn, a subset of these absolute advantage sectors should be based on PBTL and not on process-based technological advantage.

5. Cases cited are very abbreviated versions of longer studies which form part of a forthcoming book. Somewhat more detailed versions can also be found in my paper "Regional Worlds of Production" (1992b).

6. But notice the implication of this reasoning: If functional equivalents exist and function as if the economy were centralized, small, and highly organized, then the role of size *per se* can be questioned, and so can the theoretical agenda which underlies a size-oriented analysis, i.e., that it is calculation based on "natural" cohesion, "common" external threat, and transaction costs that matters. We would be back, as I shall suggest later on in this chapter, to a more purely historical analysis of institutions, not a New Institutional Analysis. By admitting that institutions have this *ex post* function of pushing cohesion forward, it does not follow that we must subscribe to that as a causal analysis.

7. Prefiguring North's (1990) claims about institutionalized sclerosis, but with neither the same analytical apparatus nor predictive purposes.

8. Bargaining between employers and workers at the firm level has been mandatory since 1983, but there is no legal obligation to complete an agreement; as a result, enterprise-level bargaining has not replaced branch-level agreements. There is a long history to this attempt to push bargaining down to the firm level, which essentially has to do with the Socialist Party's view that French employers *(patronat)* have traditionally failed to be sufficiently interactive with unions.

9. Lange (1988) draws our attention to such an "institutionalization of concertation" through repeated interactions, learning, and the formation of mutual expectations. Under these circumstances, we might say that "conventions" have been formed.

10. Note that this explanation is radically different from the "Pentagon stimulates innovation" story; I am aware of this debate, but this is not the place to go into it.

11. A theme that runs through much of the literature, at least implicitly. See, for example, Kochan, Katz, and McKersie (1986); see Lange (1988) for a formalization, and Rogers (1990) for an analysis rooted in the law.

12. I am grateful to Phil Ansell for suggesting this point.

13. The term is adapted from Osterman (1988).

REFERENCES

Amendola, M., and J. L. Gaffard. 1990. *La Dynamique Economique de l'Innovation*. Paris: Economica.

Angel, D. 1987. "The Local Labor Market for Engineers in Silicon Valley." Los Angeles: UCLA Department of Geography, Ph.D. dissertation.

Asanuma, B. 1989. "Manufacturer-Supplier Relationships in Japan and Concept of Relation-Specific Skill." *Journal of the Japanese and International Economies* 3: 1–30.

Atkinson, John. 1985. "Flexibility, Uncertainty, and Manpower Management." Brighton: Institute of Manpower Studies, Report no. 89.

Bagnasco, A. 1977. *Tre Italie*. Bologna: Il Mulino.

Bamber, Greg J., and Russell D. Lansbury, eds. 1987. *International and Comparative Industrial Relations*. London: Allen and Unwin.

Barbagli, M., V. Cappecchi, and A. Cobalti. 1988. *La Mobilitá Sociale in Emilia Romagna*. Bologna: Il Mulino.

Bauchet, P. 1986. *Le Plan dans l'Economie Française*. Paris: Presses de la Fondation Nationale des Sciences Politiques.

Becattini, G., ed. 1987. *Mercato e Forze Locali: il Distretto Industriale*. Bologna: Il Mulino.

Berger, S. 1980. "Reflections on Industrial Society: the Survival of the Traditional Sectors in France and Italy." In S. Berger and M. Piore, eds., *Dualism and Discontinuity in Industrial Societies*. New York: Cambridge University Press.

Best, M. 1990. *The New Competition: Institutions of Industrial Restructuring*. Cambridge: Polity Press.

Bleitrach, D., and A. Chenu. 1974. "Les notables locaux et les technocrates." *Cahiers Internationaux de Sociologie* 28: 35–57.

Boichard, J., ed. 1986. *Le Jura: de la Montagne a l'Homme*. Toulouse: Privat.

Brusco, S. 1982. "The Emilian Model: Productive Decentralization and Social Integration." *Cambridge Journal of Economics* 6: 167–84.

Brusco, S. 1983. "Flessibilita e solidita del sistema: l'esperienza emiliana." In G. Fua and C. Zacchia, eds., *Industrializzazione senza Fratture*. Bologna: Il Mulino.

Brusco, S., and E. Rizio. 1985. "Local Government, Industrial Policy, and Social Consensus: The Experience of Modena." Paris: paper delivered to OECD Italy Seminar, "Opportunities for Urban Economic Development."

Brutti, Paolo. 1990. "Industrial Districts: The Point of View of the Unions." Geneva: International Conference on Industrial Districts and Local Economic Generation, October 18–19.

Buttler, Friedrich. 1990. "Why and Under What Circumstances do Firms Prefer Internal Flexibility of the Labour Force to External Flexibility?" Ferrara, Italy: paper delivered to European Association for Industrial Economics, annual conference.

Campbell, Duncan, and Graham Vickery. 1988. "New Technologies and Organizational Responses." Milan: International Meeting on Industrial Automation, New Occupations and Training Strategies, October 3.

Cappecchi, V. 1990a. "L'industrializzazione a Bologna nel Novecento: dagli inizio dec secolo alla fine della seconda guerra mondiale." *Storia Illustrata di Bologna* 18/IV: 341–60.

Cappecchi, V. 1990b. "L'industrializzazione a Bologna nel Novecento dal secondo dopoguerra ad oggi." *Storia Illustrata di Bologna* 9/V: 161–80.

Carboni, C. 1990. *Lavoro Informale ed Economia Diffusa; Costanti e Trasformazioni Recenti.* Roma: Edizioni Lavoro.

Carnoy, Martin. 1985. "The Labor Market in Silicon Valley and Its Implications for Education." Stanford, Calif.: Stanford Education Policy Institute, Project Report No. 85–A8.

Chapman, H. 1990. *State Capitalism and Working Class Radicalism in the French Aircraft Industry.* Berkeley: University of California Press.

Cohendet, P., and P. Llerena. 1989. *Flexibilité, Information et Décision.* Paris: Economica.

Courault, B., and M.F. Rerat. 1987. "Un modèle de production régionale en transition: Le cas de la chaussure dans le Choletais." *Cahiers du Centre d'Etudes de l'Emploi* 30: 91–112.

Courlet, C. 1991. "Le district industriel de la Vallée de l'Arve: origines, fonctionnement, et évolution récente." Grenoble: IREP/Développement, Université des Sciences Sociales de Grenoble.

Courlet, C. 1987. "Cooperation industrielle, PME et développement local: L'exemple Savoyard." In ADEFI-GRECO, *Industries et Régions.* Paris: Economica: 191–204.

de Luca, Loretta. 1989. "Unemployment and Labour Segmentation: The Growing Challenges of the Italian Model." Geneva: ILO, Labor Market Analysis and Employment Planning, Working Paper No. 34.

Didry, Claude, and Robert Salais. 1991. "L'écriture des Conventions du Travail: Entre le Métier et l'Industrie, un Moment Critique; les Conventions Collectives de 1936–37." Paris: Groupement de Recherche, "Institutions, Emploi et Politique Economique," paper.

d'Iribarne, Philippe. 1989. *La Logique de l'Honneur; Gestion des Entreprises et Traditions Nationales.* Paris: Seuil.

Dore, R. 1987. *Flexible Rigidities.* Stanford: Stanford University Press.

Dosi, G. 1984. *Technical Change and Industrial Transformation.* New York: St. Martin's.

Dosi, G., K. Pavitt, and L. Soete. 1990. *The Economics of Technological Change and International Trade.* New York: New York University Press.

Foray, D. 1990. "The Secrets of Industry Are in the Air: Elements pour un Cadre d'Analyse du Phenomène de Réseau d'Innovateurs." Montreal: Paper presented at the International Workshop on Networks of Innovators, May.

Freeman, Richard, and James L. Medoff. 1984. *What Do Unions Do?* New York: Basic Books.

Ganne, B. 1985. "Du notable au local: transformations d'un modèle politique." *Annales de la Recherche Urbaine* 28: 23–32.

Gilly, J.P. 1990. "Groupes et Nouveaux Espaces Productifs." Toulouse: Université de Toulouse, Laboratoire d'Etudes et de Recherches en Economie de la Production.

Gravier, J.F., G. Armand, and J. Joly. 1969. *Le Décolletage Savoyard.* Paris: Conservatoire National des Arts et Métiers.

Guichonnet, P. 1961. "Une originale concentration industrielle: le décolletage et l'horlogerie en Haute Savoie." *Le Globe* 101: 23–63.

Granovetter, Mark. 1986. "The Sociological and Economic Approaches to Labor Market Analysis: A Social Structural View." In George Farkas and Paula England, eds., *Industries, Firms, and Jobs: Sociological and Economic Approaches.* New York: Plenum.

Grossetti, Michel, and Pierre Mas. 1990. "Un Marche Local du Travail: Les Ingénieurs à Toulouse." In F. Michon and D. Segrestin, eds., *L'Emploi, l'Entreprise, et la Société: Débats Economie-Sociologie.* Paris: Economica, 127–38.

Hall, P. 1986. *Governing the Economy: The Politics of State Intervention in Britain and France.* New York: Oxford University Press.

Hayward, J. 1985. *The State and the Market Economy: Industrial Patriotism and Economic Intervention in France.* Brighton: Wheatsheaf.

Hyman, R., and W. Streeck, 1988. *New Technologies and Industrial Relations.* Oxford: Basil Blackwell.

ISTAT. 1986. "Indagine sulle diffusione dell'innovazione tecnologica nell'industria manifatturiera italiana." *Notiziario* 4: 41-45.

Jacoby, Sanford. 1989. "The New Institutionalism: What Can It Learn from the Old?" *Industrial Relations* 29: 316–40.

Kochan, Thomas A., Harry C. Katz, and Robert McKersie, 1986. *The Transformation of American Industrial Relations.* New York: Basic Books.

Koike, K. 1984. "Skill Formation Systems in the U.S. and Japan: A Comparative Study." In M. Aoki, ed., *The Economic Analysis of the Japanese Firm.* Amsterdam: North Holland.

Labaube, Alain. 1988. "Flexibilité, flexibilités: La lutte contre le chômage." *Le Monde,* December 13, p. 21.

Lange, Peter. 1988. "The Institutionalization of

Concertation." Chicago: Conference on the Micro-Foundations of Democracy, April 29–May 1.

Lassini, A. 1985. *Gli Interventi Regionali per i Servizi alle Imprese.* Milan: Franco Angeli.

Leontief, W. 1953. *Studies in the Structure of the American Economy.* New York: Oxford University Press.

Lyon-Caen, Antoine. 1991. "Grandeur et Décadence de la Loi Professionnelle." Paris: Colloquium on Collective Conventions, May 23–24.

Marsden, David. 1990. "Training Systems, Labour Market Structures, and Competitiveness." Paris: OCED Conference on "Technology and Competitiveness," June 24–27.

Marsden, David. 1986. *The End of Economic Man? Custom and Competition in Labor Markets.* New York: St. Martin's Press.

Maurice, Marc, Francois Sellier, and Jean-Jacques Silvestre. 1986. *The Social Foundations of Industrial Power: A Comparison of France and Germany.* Cambridge, Mass.: MIT Press.

Mincer, Jacob, and Yoshio Higuchi. 1987. "Wage Structures and Labor Turnover in the U.S. and Japan." Cambridge, Mass.: National Bureau of Economic Research, Working Paper no. 2306.

Mingione, E. 1990. *Fragmented Worlds.* Oxford: Basil Blackwell.

Moe, Terry M. 1987. "Interests, Institutions, and Positive Theory: The Politics of the NLRB." *Studies in American Political Development* 2: 236–99.

Mokyr, J. 1990. *The Lever of Riches.* New York: Oxford University Press.

Moore, B. 1966. *Social Origins of Dictatorship and Democracy.* Boston: Beacon Press.

Nelson, R., and S. Winter. 1982. *An Evolutionary Theory of Economic Change.* Cambridge, Mass.: Harvard University Press.

North, D. 1990. *Institutions, Institutional Change, and Economic Performance.* New York: Cambridge University Press.

Osterman, Paul. 1988. *Employment Futures.* New York: Oxford University Press.

Paci, M. 1988. *La Struttura Sociale Italiana; Costanti Storiche e Trasformazione Recenti.* Bologna: Il Mulino.

Perulli, Paolo. 1992. "The Role of the Region in Capital/Labor Relations Studies." *International Journal of Urban and Regional Research.*

Petit, Pascal. 1988. "Problems of the State in Dealing with the System of Wage/Labour Relations: The Case of France." In R. Boyer, ed., *The Search for Labour Market Flexibility: The European Economies in Transition.* Oxford: Clarendon Press, 26–57.

Piore, Michael. 1986. "Perspectives on Labor Market Flexibility." *Industrial Relations* 25 (2): 146–66.

Piore, M., and C. Sabel. 1984. *The Second Industrial Divide.* New York: Basic Books.

Powell, W.W. 1990. "Neither Market nor Hierar-

chy: Network Forms of Organization." *Research in Organizational Behavior* 12: 295–336.

Pratt, J.W., and R.J. Zeckhauser, eds., 1985. *Principal and Agents.* Boston: Harvard Business School Press.

Preault, P. 1991. Comments of Professor Preault of the University of Grenoble on a visit to the Valley of the Arve, June.

Pye, W., and S. Verba. 1965. *Political Culture and Political Development.* Princeton: Princeton University Press.

Regini, M., ed. 1988. *La Sfida della Flessibilita: Impresa, Lavoro, e Sindacati nella Fase 'Post-Fordista.'* Milan: Franco Angeli.

Révue Economique. 1989. Special Issue on "L'Economie des Conventions" 40 (September).

Ritaine, E. 1987. "La modernité localisée? Leçons italiennes sur le developpement regional." *Révue Française de Science Politique* 39 (2): 155–77.

Rogers, Joel. 1990. "Divide and Conquer: Further 'Reflections on the Distinctive Character of American Labor Laws.' " *Wisconsin Law Review* 1: 1–147.

Sabel, C., H. Kern, and G. Herrigel. 1990. "Collaborative Manufacturing: New Supplier Relations in the Automobile Industry and the Redefinition of the Industrial Corporation." Cambridge, Mass.: MIT Department of Political Science, unpublished manuscript.

Saglio, Jean. 1988. "La Concurrence: Une Règle du Jeu Economique Parmi d'Autres." Lyon: Maison Rhône-Alpes des Sciences de L'Homme, paper.

Salais, R., and M. Storper. 1993. *Les Mondes de Production.* Paris.

Scarpitti, L. 1989. "Ambiti e mete di interventi di politica industriale a livello locale." Rome: ENEA, Direzione Centrale Studi, Studi-Techn. 89–3.

Sellier, F. 1991. "Articulation des Niveaux de Négotiation et Construction des Acteurs." Paris: Colloquium on Collective Conventions, May 23–24.

Sorge, Arndt, and Wolfgang Streeck. 1988. "Industrial Relations and Technical Change: the Case for an Extended Perspective." In R. Hyman and W. Streeck, eds., op. cit.

Storper, M. 1992a. "The Limits to Globalization: Technology Districts and International Trade." *Economic Geography.*

Storper, M. 1992b. "Regional Worlds of Production: Conventions of Learning and Innovation in the Flexible Production Systems of France, Italy and the USA." *Regional.Studies.*

Storper, M., and A. J. Scott. 1992. "Regional Development Reconsidered." In H. Ernste and G. Meier, eds., *Regional Policies and Contemporary Responses: Expanding Flexible Specialization.* London: Frances Pinter.

Storper, M., and B. Harrison. 1991. "Flexibility, Hierarchy, and Regional Development: the Changing Structure of Production Systems and their Forms of Governance in the 1990s." *Research Policy* 20: 407–22.

Stowsky, J. 1987. "The Weakest Link: Semiconductor Production Equipment, Linkages and the Limits to International Trade." Berkeley: BRIE Working Paper no. 27.

Swenson, Peter. 1989. *Fair Shares: Unions, Pay, and Politics and Sweden and West Germany.* Ithaca: Cornell University Press.

Terrail, J.-P., and M. Tripier. 1986. *Destins Ouvriers, Cultures d'Entreprise, Pratiques Syndicales.* Paris: Centre de Recherches et d'Etudes sur la Societé Française.

Todd, E. 1990. *L'Invention de l'Europe.* Paris: Seuil.

Trigilia, Carlo. 1986. *Grandi Partiti e Piccole Imprese.* Bologna: Il Mulino.

Trigilia, Carlo. 1990. "Small Firm Development and Political Subcultures in Italy." In F. Pyke, W. Sengenberger, and G. Becattini, eds., *Small Firms and Industrial Development in Italy,* Geneva: ILO.

Vernon, R. 1966. "International Investment and International Trade in the Product Cycle." *Quarterly Journal of Economics* (May): 190–207.

Visser, Jelle. 1989. "Syndicats européens: La grande mutation." *Problèmes Economiques* 2132: 17–28.

Wallerstein, Michael. 1987. "Union Growth from the Unions' Perspective: Why Smaller Countries Are More Highly Organized." UCLA, Department of Political Science, paper.

Weiler, Paul C. 1990. *Governing the Workplace: the Future of Labor and Employment Law.* Cambridge, Mass.: Harvard University Press.

Williamson, Oliver. 1985. *The Economic Institutions of Capitalism.* New York: The Free Press.

8

Some Thoughts and Evidence on Industrial Policy: Industrialization in South Korea and Mexico

KENNETH L. SOKOLOFF

With the growing concern about the recent slow growth of the U.S. economy, it is perhaps no surprise that whether or not to have an "industrial policy" has become a hotly debated and familiar issue over the last decade. For better or worse, the American instinct has always been to take action when events are not to taste. Influenced by the economic successes of Japan and other countries, who have both undercut American dominance in previous industry strongholds like consumer electronics, automobiles, and steel and narrowed its lead in per capita income, many observers suspect that our economy is being placed in jeopardy by the aid targeted by the foreign governments to such industries—support of a level and nature that the United States has traditionally been reluctant to provide. So dramatic has the contrast in economic performance been, that the political coalition in favor of resisting government intrusions into the economy has developed cracks and threatened to crumble completely. Indeed, some academic economists, the most devout believers in free trade, have questioned the faith and flirted with the endorsement of various forms of industrial policy.[1]

Although the participants in the debate over industrial policy may differ about the precise details, there is general agreement about the sorts of programs involved: trade protection, direct subsidies on capital costs and investment in research and development, or a relaxation of anti-trust enforcement. These measures, or combinations thereof, support the growth or economic vitality of industries considered strategic—in one or another respect. The economic logic for this approach depends on the existence of technological or other positive externalities, scale economies at the industry level, or of some sort of market failure in the private allocation of capital. Any of these conditions might warrant government intervention to encourage a larger industry, closer to the optimum size, than market forces would otherwise generate, and some economists have recently joined representatives of the potential beneficiaries in suggesting that a number of industries may fit one of these criteria. Many others, however, are skeptical about these claims, and express the view that offering such protection to any industry would invite a costly orgy of rent-seeking political activities by all. In addition, they point out that shielding domestic producers from foreign competition may have the undesirable effect of lowering the incentives they face to invent, innovate, and generally reduce costs.[2]

An economic historian of the United States, like myself, is both amused and concerned by the debate. Amused, because it tends to resemble a ritual in which politics and emotion elevate symbols and emblems above substance, and concerned because of what it implies about the basis for decisions about national policy. Indeed, despite the enormous amount of resources at stake in considering whether to undertake an industrial policy or not, as well as the intellectual importance of the underlying question, there have been remarkably few, if any, systematic studies of the prevalence or quantitative significance of external economies or of the overall effects of industrial policy. Most of the scholarly support has come from either theoretical work demonstrating the possibility and mechanisms of beneficial impacts, from case studies of Japan and South Korea—two countries which are commonly cited as among the most successful practitioners of interventionist industrial policies—or from selected examples of successful research programs conducted with extensive government assistance or involvement.[3] Although a full-blown investigation of the issue is beyond its scope, this chapter will put this evidence in a larger perspective, and examine the patterns of manufacturing productivity growth in South Korea and Mexico, two newly industrializing countries that embraced and then distanced themselves from policies which channeled assistance to targeted industries. It will conclude with some observations on the general sources of technical progress and the consistency of the empirical record with the claims being made on behalf of an industrial policy.

INDUSTRIAL POLICY AND NATIONAL ECONOMIC PERFORMANCE

National Performance

There is no doubt that one of the major elements behind the recent interest in industrial policy has been the strong record of economic growth by countries like Japan and South Korea since World War II, and the belief that their enviable performances were largely due to the active role of their governments in allocating resources between industries. Few dispute the well-documented characterizations of Japan and South Korea as being more oriented toward the attempted management of free markets and toward industrial policy than other industrialized or industrializing countries.[4] Similarly, no one is surprised that Japanese and Korean government officials claim responsibility for positive developments when they can do so with a modicum of plausibility; after all, why should they be different from everyone else? What should be asked, however, is whether the industrial policies they carried out actually had much of an impact in boosting the growth rates of these nations or whether their effect was primarily redistributive in nature.

Answering this seemingly straightforward question by estimating what would have happened in a hypothetical Japanese or South Korean economy if a completely different set of policies had been pursued is of course a highly ambitious, if not impossible, exercise. There are too many conceivable effects, both positive and negative, of the government actions at issue to ever be assured of having properly accounted for them all. Another means of obtaining at least a qualitative resolution, however, is to compare the performances of these economies to those of appropriate peer groups. As is indicated in Table 8.1, Japan and South Korea have exhibited unusually, if not exceptionally, high growth rates over the last quarter-century by the standards of reasonable sets of peers. To begin, South Korean per capita income grew at 7.0 percent per annum from 1965 to 1989, whereas all low- and middle-income countries in the world grew at 2.5 percent per annum over the period. Despite this impressive record, however, it cannot be said that South Korea was an extraordinary outlier, or that industrial policy had a demonstrable effect, because the great

Table 8.1. Growth Of Per Capita Income In Selected Countries, 1965–1989

Low- and middle-income countries	
South Korea	7.0%
Indonesia	4.4
Thailand	4.3
Malaysia	4.0
Taiwan	7.3
Hong Kong	6.3
Singapore	7.0
Average in East Asia	5.2
Upper-income countries	
Japan	4.3%
Italy	3.0
France	2.3
Canada	4.0
West Germany	2.4
United States	1.6
Sweden	1.8
Norway	3.4
Switzerland	4.6

Notes and sources: Other than South Korea and Japan, the countries are arranged according to their per capita income level as of 1987. The growth rates are from World Bank, *World Development Report* (New York: Oxford University Press, 1991) or computed from the GNP estimates in the Council for Economic Planning and Development, *Taiwan Statistical Data Book* (1990).

majority of East Asian economies did remarkably well over the period. Indeed, the average East Asian low- and middle-income country grew at 5.2 percent per annum over the period.

The strong record of East Asian nations overall reflects the relatively general spread of industrialization throughout the region beginning roughly in the 1960s and leads one to question whether South Korea's success should be credited to its industrial policy. Most of Korea's advantage over the regional average appears due to sustained economic growth having gotten under way there earlier. The other "Four Tigers," Hong Kong, Singapore, and Taiwan, which also began to industrialize during the early 1960s, have realized very similar growth performances. Indeed, despite their recognized lack of targeted industrial policies, their rates of advance in per capita income were 6.3 percent, 7.0 percent, and 7.3 percent, respectively. Over a more recent period, say the 1980s, when sustained industrialization diffused to other East Asian countries like Malaysia, Thailand, Indonesia, and China, the region averaged growth of 6.3 percent per annum, or just slightly below the rate of South Korea. The clear implication, especially since these other societies have typically not opted for targeted policies, is that East Asia nations have all done well once they achieved sustained economic growth, as most of them have now done. Overall, although there is certainly no evidence that South Korea was hampered by its industrial policy, the basis for concluding that such programs were an important contributor to the prosperity of the country seems weak.

The record of growth in Japan is perhaps more consistent with advocacy of a targeted industrial policy. As reported in Table 8.1, per capita income in Japan rose at 4.3 percent per annum over the period 1965 to 1989, as compared with a 2.5 percent per annum average among the OECD (Organization for Economic Cooperation and Development) countries. Among the Western industrialized economies, only Switzerland did better—at 4.6 percent per annum—and very few were above a 3.0 percent rate. There is no doubt, accordingly, that over this period, or over the twentieth century as a whole, Japan has realized an extraordinary rate of economic growth. Even the recent difficulties of 1992–93 cannot obscure or reverse this fact. What is controversial, however, is whether Japan's greater reliance on government intervention into the economy to support particular industries is responsible for its superior performance. A number of alternative hypotheses could be offered to explain this one exceptional case, and have been—prior to the recent preoccupation with industrial policy.

Even if these *ad hoc* methods of assessing the impact of industrial policies by gauging the experiences of hand-picked examples like Japan and Korea relative to those of other economies yielded stronger quantitative results, one would be hard pressed to draw qualitative conclusions in which one had confidence. After all, the entire procedure is biased, as is the selectivity shown by advocates of industrial policy, by the focus on only successful examples. For example, few proponents of industrial policy mention that despite being much more inclined toward such programs, European countries are not typically recognized as harboring either the world's technological leaders or its strongest national economies. A more systematic evaluation would examine a random sample or a comprehensive set of countries employing activist targeted policies—including the many whose economic performances have not been quite as stellar as those of Japan and Korea. The problem with this latter approach, however, is the uncertainty involved in categorizing various countries by the existence or character of their economic program—in other words, placing them in the appropriate reference group. Since nearly all countries provide some *de facto* targeted or focused assistance to one or more industries, it is no easy task to make unambiguous classifications.

Variation Across Industries Within Countries

Another research strategy is to examine the variation across industries within national economies. The advantage here is that the available information normally permits, or is more likely to permit, reliable distinctions between industries as to which are the intended beneficiaries of industrial policies. One can then proceed to compare the performance of the targeted industries with that of those neglected. This chapter makes a modest contribution in this direction by using a conventional growth accounting framework to evaluate the patterns of productivity change in two countries noted for interventionist industrial policies—South Korea and Mexico. Due to the lack of firm-level data, this study relies on evidence at the industry level. The data on South Korea encompass 1963 to 1979, while those on Mexico refer to 1970 to 1980—boom periods in both cases. It would be preferable to examine the record over longer spans, but the intervals are constrained by the availability of data, as well as the desire to abstract from events like the debt crisis (beginning in 1982) and the movement by the Korean government away from a policy of targeting selected industries for support (abandoning the so-called HCI [heavy and chemical industries] program in the early 1980s) which likely had substantial effects on the Mexican and South Korean economies, respectively.

There are a number of features of the South Korean and Mexican economies that render them quite appropriate, if not apt, for such an assessment of industrial policy. First, the two countries were at similar levels of development in the early 1980s, just after the end of the period under consideration. Not only were their per capita income levels roughly the same and the allocations of their labor force much alike—with 29 percent of South Korea's workers employed in manufacturing in 1981 as opposed to 26 percent in Mexico—but both countries experienced rapid economic growth over the designated years.[5] Second, and obviously of much relevance, both countries were undertaking activist industrial policies, with governments subsidizing investment in selected industries with the expressed hope that such actions would speed the progress of their economies overall.

Although a variety of rationales, and thus standards for evaluation, might be offered for a study of the impact of an activist industrial policy, a productivity gauge is adopted here. This choice is based upon the view that the most compelling argument for government assistance to particular industries is that support will help them realize more rapid improvements in technology or competitiveness than would otherwise be the case—and hence spur more rapid economic growth over time and be long term in nature. After all, there is a general consensus that slow technical change or productivity growth has been responsible for most of the deficiencies of U.S. economic performance over the last two decades. Moreover, an investigation of industrial policy should include a test of the criticism that government assistance to an industry encourages less than efficient use of inputs and slower rates of technical change by protecting it from the full rigors of market competition. Since industrial policy typically concerns only manufacturing industries, the empirical analysis presented below is confined to that sector.

South Korea. Industry-level data on the twenty-five manufacturing industries have been assembled from several sources for the years 1963 to 1979. They contain information on the total number of employees, the net capital stock, and on the net value added as deflated by industry-specific price indexes.[6] Basic descriptive statistics are reported in Table 8.2 for each of the industries, four classes of industries, and all of manufacturing. After separating out the natural-resource-based industries, whose data manifest some anomalies owing to the existence of state-run monopolies, the composition of the remaining three categories ("heavy," "medium," and "light") was determined on the basis of the capital-to-labor ratio in 1979. Although the precise division of industries is perhaps somewhat arbitrary, the classifications facilitate analysis and exposition. The relative performance of the heavy industries is of particular interest here, because they were all targets of the so-called HCI policy during the 1970s, when massive amounts of investment funds were made available to heavy and chemical industries through loans on preferential terms.[7] The only other industries that were significant beneficiaries of the program were transport equipment and electrical goods (in the medium and light categories, respectively).

It is immediately apparent from the index of capital intensity that there is enormous variation across manufacturing industries in the net value of capital stock per worker. Iron and steel, one of the principal targets of the HCI program, was by 1979 nearly six times as capital intensive as the manufacturing sector average, and nearly thirty-three times as much as clothing and footwear. Overall, the capital intensity of the heavy industries exceeded the manufacturing average by 250 percent, whereas the light fell 40 percent short.

It is not at all surprising that labor productivity, as measured by value added per worker, was positively correlated with capital intensity and varied less across industries than the latter ratio. It is interesting, however, that the index of capital intensity divided by the labor productivity (equivalent to an index of the capital-output ratio) was much higher for the heavy industries than in the other subgroups. Production theory implies that the capital-output ratio will increase with the capital intensity of an industry, but the dispersion in Korea was unusually great. When combined with any plausible estimates for the elasticities of output with respect to capital in individual industries, the capital-output ratios suggest that the marginal revenue product of capital was much lower in the heavy industries, especially iron and steel, than in the medium and light industries. This follows from the observation that the marginal product of capital equals the output elasticity of capital divided by the capital-output ratio. A second implication is that in 1979 the level of total factor productivity was significantly lower among the industries classified as heavy (and again especially in iron and steel) than in Korean manufacturing overall.

Industry shares of the total value added and employment in manufacturing are reported in Table 8.3. They suggest that at least in quantitative terms, the light and medium industries dominated the manufacturing sector in the Republic of Korea during this period. Both of these classes of industries surpassed the heavy category in

Table 8.2. Characteristics of South Korean Manufacturing Industries

	Index of capital intensity, 1979 (Mfg = 100)	Index of value added per worker, 1979 (Mfg = 100)	Index of capital stock per *won* of value added, 1979 (Mfg = 100)
Heavy industries[a]	342	185	182
Iron and steel	590	198	298
Industrial chemicals	245	219	112
Nonferrous metals	210	129	163
Nonmetal products, n.e.c.	169	140	121
Medium industries[a]	106	122	97
Transport equipment	139	105	132
Machinery	127	97	131
Glass products	107	109	98
Paper products	96	94	102
Other chemicals	88	203	43
Metal products, n.e.c.	79	81	98
Printing	78	106	74
Light industries[a]	57	69	81
Textiles	76	72	106
Wood products	69	65	106
Electrical goods	53	75	71
Rubber products	51	72	71
Leather products	50	73	68
Plastic products	48	91	53
Pottery	43	60	72
Furniture	40	72	56
Manufactures, n.e.c.	33	58	57
Clothing and footwear	18	50	36
Natural resource industries[a]	197	419	68
Petroleum & coal products	324	361	90
Tobacco products	204	991	21
Beverages	200	247	81
Food Products	88	106	83
All manufacturing	100	100	100

[a]Weighted average, using value-added shares from Table 8.3, column 2.
Sources: The information on value added, gross output, wages, and employment were drawn from the relevant years of the *United Nations Yearbook of Industrial Statistics*. The estimates of the net value of the capital stock were prepared by the Economic Planning Board, and appear in *Preliminary Data on Korean Capital Stock by Industry, 1960-1979* (Seoul: KDI, 1987).

Table 8.3. Characteristics of South Korean Manufacturing Industries

	Exports as a share of gross output 1963–79 (%)	Value-added share, 1963–79 (%)	Employment share, 1963–79 (%)
Heavy industries	14.4[a]	15.2	9.2
Iron and steel	23.1	5.3	2.9
Industrial chemicals[b]	7.1	4.9	2.4
Nonferrous metals	8.6	0.8	0.7
Nonmetal products, n.e.c.[c]	13.1	4.2	3.2
Medium industries	16.9[a]	21.7	20.9
Transport equipment	23.2	5.7	4.6
Machinery	18.2	3.0	3.5
Glass products[c]	13.1	0.9	0.9
Paper products[d]	7.2	2.3	2.2
Other chemicals[b]	7.1	4.8	2.8
Metal products, n.e.c.	36.1	2.8	4.1
Printing	7.2	2.2	2.7
Light industries	43.5[a]	37.4	57.8
Textiles[e]	53.8	14.8	22.5
Wood products	44.4	2.6	3.2
Electrical goods	36.7	7.4	8.4
Rubber products	16.0	2.6	4.4
Leather products	6.5	0.7	1.0
Plastic Products[b]	7.1	1.3	1.5
Pottery[c]	13.1	0.3	0.7
Furniture	22.3	0.4	0.8
Manufactures, n.e.c.	47.7	2.7	5.5
Clothing and footwear[e]	53.8	4.6	9.7
Natural resource industries	1.4[a]	25.4	12.1
Petroleum & coal products	2.7	5.8	1.3
Tobacco products	0.0	6.4	1.1
Beverages	0.5	5.8	2.1
Food products	2.4	7.4	7.5
All manufacturing	22.5[a]	100.0	100.0

[a]Weighted average, using value-added shares from column 2.
[b]In the trade statistics, industrial chemicals, other chemicals, and plastic products are aggregated together.
[c]In the trade statistics, nonmetal products, glass products, and pottery are aggregated together.
[d]In the trade statistics, paper products and printing are aggregated together.
[e]In the trade statistics, textiles, clothing, and footwear are aggregated together.
Sources: See the note in Table 8.1. The sectoral price indices and estimates of exports were drawn from various issues of Bank of Korea, *Monthly Economic Statistics* and Bank of Korea, *Economic Statistics Yearbook,* respectively.

shares of value added and employment. Together, they accounted for nearly 60 percent of manufacturing value added between 1963 and 1979, and nearly 79 percent of employment; in contrast, the highly capital-intensive industries captured shares of only 15.2 and 9.2 percent, respectively. Even at the individual industry level, many of those classified as light, such as textiles and clothing and footwear, exceeded the largest of the heavy industries—iron and steel. The light industries not only registered the largest shares of value added and employment, but they were even more disproportionately represented among exports of manufactures. Whereas the manufacturing average shipped 22.5 percent of its output abroad, with the medium and heavy subsectors recording shares of 16.9 and 14.4, respectively, the light industries exported 43.5 percent of their output. This light subsector alone accounted for roughly three-quarters of all exports of Korean manufactures. Although textiles were most responsible for the predominance of light goods among manufactured exports, other industries of this class, such as electrical goods and clothing and footwear, also surpassed iron and steel and transport equipment, which led the heavy and medium categories, respectively, in the share of output exported.

The rates of growth of real value added for each industry are reported in Table 8.4. It is clear that this initial phase of economic growth from 1963 to 1979 was marked by an extremely rapid expansion of manufacturing production, with output increasing at an extraordinary pace of about 22 percent per annum. Furthermore, the advance was quite balanced across the four classes of industries identified, though the natural resources subsector did lag somewhat behind the others. The extensive government support of the heavy industries might have led one to expect that their share of the manufacturing sector would rise over the period. But, on the contrary, the opposite tendency is evident, with the light or less-capital-intensive industries growing slightly more rapidly than the other categories on average.

Table 8.4 also presents estimates of the annual rates of growth of labor productivity and of capital intensity. It is immediately apparent that the HCI industrial policy, whose principal instrument was the provision of subsidized capital, was effective at raising the capital intensity of the heavy industries; their ratio of capital to labor rose at an astonishing rate of 11.7 percent per annum—or nearly double the rates for the medium and light subsectors (6.5 and 6.1 percent per annum, respectively). Given this sharp discrepancy in the extent of capital deepening over time, however, it is curious how balanced the rates of labor productivity growth were across the subsectors. They all experienced rates of advance in the 11.7 to 12.4 percent per annum range. Using a conventional growth accounting framework, these data allow for the decomposition of the increase in labor productivity over the period into the component that can be ascribed to capital deepening, and the remainder, which is attributed to a residual commonly considered to be a proxy for total factor productivity (TFP).[8] The precise division of responsibility, if not the qualitative conclusions, can sometimes be sensitive to the estimate of the output elasticity of capital employed in the calculations, but it is clear from the figures reported in Table 8.4 that the finding that total factor productivity growth accounts for the bulk of the advance in labor productivity in the light, medium, and heavy subsectors is robust. No reasonable output elasticity of capital can reverse this implication. It is also apparent that the accumulation of capital per worker is much more important, and total factor

Table 8.4. Rates of Growth of Labor Productivity, Capital Intensity, and Real Value Added in 25 South Korean Manufacturing Industries, 1963–1979

	Annual rates of growth, 1963–1979		
	Value added per worker	Net capital per worker	Real value added
Heavy industries	12.0	11.7	21.9
Iron and steel	14.1	15.4	25.7
Industrial chemicals	12.1	14.7	23.4
Nonferrous metals	14.9	9.3	25.6
Nonmetal products, n.e.c.	10.0	13.4	17.7
Medium industries	12.0	6.5	21.8
Transport equipment	14.5	7.9	25.6
Machinery	13.6	10.2	25.3
Glass products	8.7	17.8	19.4
Paper products	7.5	9.2	16.9
Other chemicals	12.6	0	20.2
Metal products, n.e.c.	15.3	6.9	26.4
Printing	9.6	5.0	15.6
Light industries	11.7	6.1	24.2
Textiles	10.4	8.3	19.2
Wood products	6.6	5.1	15.9
Electrical goods	14.7	6.1	36.1
Rubber products	11.2	4.2	23.7
Leather products	12.6	− .1	34.6
Plastic products	9.4	− 1.1	31.6
Pottery	14.5	15.8	19.4
Furniture	10.4	1.7	15.9
Manufactures, n.e.c.	13.9	8.6	27.6
Clothing and footwear	9.9	.9	26.9
Natural resource industries	12.4	6.6	18.8
Petroleum & coal products	22.0	14.9	23.2
Tobacco products	14.2	8.5	18.9
Beverages	12.7	8.6	15.2
Food products	10.1	4.1	19.0
All manufacturing	11.0	6.8	21.9

Sources: See the notes to Tables 8.1 and 8.2.

productivity correspondingly less so, in the heavy industries than in the rest of the manufacturing sector.

Estimates of the amount of labor productivity growth attributable to capital deepening and total factor productivity growth are reported in Table 8.5. They were derived from a conventional growth accounting framework, and computed with the estimated values of the output elasticities. These figures indicate a markedly different pattern in the heavy subsector than in the other classes of manufacturing industries. In the former case, over 70 percent of the labor productivity growth of 12.0 percent per annum between 1963 and 1979 can be explained by capital deepening. Total factor productivity advance appears to have been relatively insignificant in all of the individual industries in this subsector except nonferrous metals, and was especially so in iron and steel and industrial chemicals—which were two major targets of South Korea's industrial policy during the 1970s.

In contrast, although they realized labor productivity growth at a similar rate of 11.7 percent per annum overall, the light industries increased total factor productivity at a much faster pace, 7.4 percent per annum versus 3.3 percent for the heavy indus-

Table 8.5. Sources of Labor Productivity Growth in 25 South Korean Manufacturing Industries, 1963–1979

	Contribution of capital deepening	Rate of TFP growth (Residual)	Output elasticity of capital
Heavy industries	8.7	3.3	.74
Iron and steel	11.6	2.5	.76
Industrial chemicals	10.9	1.2	.74
Nonferrous metals	6.8	8.1	.74
Nonmetal products, n.e.c.	9.9	0.1	.74
Medium industries	4.7	7.3	.72
Transport equipment	5.8	8.7	.73
Machinery	7.4	6.2	.72
Glass products	12.8	−4.1	.72
Paper products	6.6	0.9	.72
Other chemicals	0	12.6	.72
Metal products, n.e.c.	4.9	10.4	.71
Printing	3.6	6.0	.71
Light industries	4.3	7.4	.70
Textiles	5.9	4.5	.71
Wood products	3.6	3.0	.71
Electrical goods	4.3	10.4	.70
Rubber products	2.9	8.3	.70
Leather products	−0.1	12.7	.72
Plastic products	−0.8	10.2	.71
Pottery	10.9	3.6	.69

Furniture	1.2	9.2	.69
Manufactures, n.e.c.	5.9	8.0	.68
Clothing and footwear	.6	9.3	.68
Natural resource industries	4.8	7.6	.73
Petroleum & coal products	11.2	10.8	.75
Tobacco products	6.2	8.0	.73
Beverages	6.2	6.5	.72
Food products	2.9	7.2	.72
All manufacturing	4.9	6.1	.72

Notes and sources: See the notes to Tables 8.2 and 8.3. The decomposition of the growth in labor productivity between the amounts attributable to changes in the capital-to-labor ratio and in total factor productivity, respectively, was based on the standard growth accounting framework. For a more complete discussion, see Dollar and Sokoloff, "Patterns of Productivity Growth." The estimated growth rates of value added per worker and net capital per worker employed in the calculations were reported in Table 8.4. The industry-specific estimates of the output elasticity of capital were computed from the parameters of a modified translog production function estimated over a pooled cross-section of the industry data over the years from 1963 to 1979. The production function was of the form:

$$\text{Ln}(Y/L)_{it} = \gamma_i d_i + \beta_j \text{Ln}(K/L)_{it} + \beta_2 \, [\text{Ln}(K/L)_{it}]^2$$

In this specification, there are individual intercept terms for each industry, but the estimated coefficients β_1 and β_2 hold for all. Since the function includes a quadratic term, however, the output elasticity of capital, or α, varies across industries with capital intensity. The estimates of α reported above and utilized in the decomposition were computed according to the expression $\alpha_i = \beta_1 + 2\beta_2 \, \text{Ln}(K/L)_i$, with the weighted average of each industry's capital-to-labor ratio over the entire period from 1963 to 1979. It is evident from examination that the estimated elasticities are generally high, relative to the standards of work on other countries, and increase with the capital intensity of the industry. These features are consistent with the implications of the evidence on distributional shares in Korea, as well as with estimates obtained from translog or Cobb-Douglas production functions estimated over data from single years. For example, the share of value added to capital, from our data, is 0.59 in clothing, 0.67 in textiles, and 0.78 in steel. As discussed in Dollar and Sokoloff, "Patterns of Productivity Growth," these figures are in line with the work of other investigators. See that article for further discussion.

The higher the capital coefficient employed in the growth accounting decomposition, and the smaller the differences between the α's applied to the heavy and other manufacturing industries, the stronger the quantitative results. Since the capital coefficients employed in the calculations are near the upper part of the feasible range, and vary only marginally across industries, the findings would seem robust to reasonable alternative estimates of α.

tries. Capital deepening played a more modest role in this subsector, accounting for less than 40 percent of the advance in labor productivity. Textiles did not quite conform to the average experience of this subsector, but most of the light industries, including electrical goods, rubber products, leather products, and clothing and footwear, did have their progress largely driven by total factor productivity growth. Of these, only electrical goods had been given special assistance by the HCI program.

The medium industries were much like the light in terms of the record of their sources of productivity growth. Total factor productivity grew virtually as fast, 7.3 versus 7.4 percent per annum, and accounted for over 60 percent of the labor productivity growth. Here, three of the seven industries in the class, paper products, glass products (whose figures seem implausible), and machinery do diverge from the general pattern, but they are outweighed by the remaining four. Again, there is one industry in this group, transport equipment, that was supported by the national industrial policy and does well by realizing rapid total factor productivity growth over the period. Although their data seem less reliable, the natural resource industries are similar to the light and medium, with total factor productivity increasing at 7.6 percent per annum and "explaining" more than 60 percent of the advance in labor productivity.

Two conclusions stand out from this industry-level examination of South Korean manufacturing between 1963 and 1979. They are that the record of industrial policy in that country is decidedly mixed and that there was a sort of dual manufacturing sector. Although there was a remarkable homogeneity in the rates of labor productivity growth achieved, the heavy industries aided by the activist industrial policy of those years differed from the less favored in realizing that progress primarily through capital deepening. Their rates of total factor productivity growth were significantly lower than the average for the rest of manufacturing. The impact of the subsidies to investment in industries like iron and steel and industrial chemicals, which were evidently the major beneficiaries of the program, appears therefore to have been primarily in encouraging extraordinary, if not extravagant, capital accumulation and deepening. In the case of steel, the remarkably rapid addition of capital per worker allowed Korea to obtain an internationally competitive industry, but through heavy subsidies to capital—not through attaining high productivity. Overall, both their lower rates of total factor productivity growth and their lower marginal productivity of capital suggest that South Korea had over-allocated capital in the direction of steel and other favored industries, and would have been better off without its HCI program. Indeed, South Korea seems to have come to this realization when it abandoned this targeted form of industrial policy in favor of general incentives early in the 1980s.[9]

Only two of the light, medium, and natural-resource industries, transport equipment and electrical goods, received support from the HCI industrial policy. Despite, or perhaps because of, this relative neglect by the government, these classes of industries registered much more rapid progress than their more capital-intensive counterparts. Moreover, the two former groups were also more successful in exporting their products. What accounts for the contrast in performance between the virtual dual manufacturing sectors is unclear. The extreme and likely excessive extent of capital deepening by steel and chemicals raises the possibility that the government subsidies encouraged industries along paths with slower total factor productivity growth. However, the relatively good records of transport equipment and electrical goods suggest a more ambiguous role—one in which there is no substantial or consistent net impact of government subsidies on the long run (i.e., productivity-based) competitiveness of the targeted industries; since the industrial policy involved a transfer of capital resources to a lower-value use, this would mean that it constituted a net drag on the Korean economy. Alternative explanations of the cross-industry pattern of productivity growth include the view that at early stages of development there is more potential for total factor productivity growth among labor-intensive industries and that Korea's international comparative advantage in relatively labor-intensive industries led to greater market-based incentives and mechanisms for technical change in those areas.

Mexico. The Mexican economy makes for a good comparison with South Korea. Both countries experienced rapid economic growth during the 1970s, but they pursued quite different industrial policies. The Mexican government was much more interventionist than the Korean, with long traditions in practices like subsidies on capital and other inputs for the targeted industries, ownership shares, and protection from domestic as well as foreign competition being common.[10] Significantly, whereas Korea maintained an undervalued currency which was conducive to the growth of exports, Mexico's was if anything overvalued.

The examination of Mexican manufacturing is based on production data extracted from reports of the World Bank (1986), and is confined to the period from 1970 to 1980. The information employed is not as extensive as that for South Korea, but includes the growth of net capital stock, the labor force, the raw materials consumed, and the value of gross output produced—all deflated to constant prices. Table 8.6 presents estimates of the annual rates of growth of labor productivity (as mea-

Table 8.6. Rates of Growth of Labor Productivity, Capital Intensity, and Real Gross Output in Mexican Manufacturing Industries, 1970–1980

	Annual rates of growth, 1970–1980			
	Gross output/labor	Capital/labor	R.Mat./labor	Gross output
Heavy industries	3.3	6.4	3.6	7.6
Basic industrial metals	2.0	8.0	1.9	5.0
Nonmetallic mix products	4.3	4.3	4.5	6.8
Basic chemical products	4.8	2.6	4.6	8.5
Other industrial chemicals	4.1	6.6	4.1	8.3
Petroleum and petrochemicals	6.8	9.6	6.1	10.5
Metal products	3.0	6.9	3.1	4.9
Transport equipment	0.4	8.0	0.4	5.0
Automobiles	3.2	1.2	3.4	10.3
Medium/light industries	4.2	3.1	4.0	7.5
Electrical machinery	4.4	2.5	4.2	9.6
Machinery	4.5	−0.8	4.6	9.9
Paper and products	4.7	1.5	4.7	7.2
Textiles and apparel	3.2	4.4	2.8	4.8
Pharmaceuticals	6.5	3.0	6.5	8.4
Synthetic fibers	4.0	−1.0	4.0	12.2
Rubber and plastic products	5.7	7.2	5.7	9.5
Wood products	2.2	4.8	2.1	6.5
Soaps, detergents, cosmetics	4.8	1.5	4.7	7.8
Food products	2.0	−0.5	1.9	5.3
Tobacco products	2.5	3.1	2.5	2.2
Beverages	2.5	−3.7	2.5	7.0
Other food products	1.9	−0.1	1.8	5.1
All manufacturing average	3.4	3.4	3.4	7.4

Sources: The estimates are computed from figures contained in World Bank, "Mexico: Trade Policy, Industrial Performance and Adjustment" (Washington, D.C.: World Bank unpublished manuscript, 1986). All of the sector averages are weighted by the industry-shares of gross output in 1975.

sured by the ratio of gross output to labor), the capital-to-labor ratio, the raw-materials-to-labor ratio, and of gross output for twenty manufacturing industries in Mexico over the decade under study. Since the actual levels of the capital-to-labor ratio cannot be computed from the World Bank data, the manufacturing industries are classified into two groups—heavy and medium/light—with the division based primarily on the South Korean ordering. A third category of three industries—food products—is also reported separately. After consulting the levels of capital intensity for these industries in other countries, it seems unlikely that the composition of the two principal classes would be much altered even if Mexican data were on hand. Moreover, the differences between the records of these two groups are so large that the robustness of the qualitative results appears assured.

The most immediate reaction to these figures is that they depict an industrial expansion that was very different from that experienced by South Korea. The Mexican rates of growth of labor productivity and of manufacturing output are of much smaller orders of magnitude. Whereas all of the Korean classes of manufacturing industries managed at least 11.7 percent per annum advance in labor productivity, no Mexican class did better than 4.2 percent. In general, the individual Korean industries realized rates of progress that were three to four times faster than did their Mexican counterparts. A similar pattern characterizes the growth of output. The gap is somewhat smaller in terms of the rates of capital deepening, but even here the manufacturing industries in Korea added capital per worker at roughly twice the pace that they did in Mexico. Perhaps a comparison with the extraordinary standard set by South Korea, and other East Asian countries more generally, leads to a loss of perspective, but it is clear that the industrial expansion of Mexico in the 1970s was not nearly as dynamic as that under way in South Korea.

As reported in Table 8.6, the medium/light industries realized more labor productivity growth over the decade than did the heavy industries (4.2 to 3.3 percent). This occurred despite rate of capital deepening by the latter that was more than twice the rate of the former (6.4 to 3.1 percent). These patterns are not unlike those of South Korea. Indeed, the evidence of excessive capital accumulation in, and misallocation of resources to, heavy industries is more dramatic in Mexico. In South Korea, their much more rapid capital deepening was at least sufficient to yield rates of increase in labor productivity equal to the manufacturing average. They failed to do so in Mexico, and their record was especially dismal in major industries which were highly favored by the government, such as basic industrial metals (largely iron and steel) and transport equipment. These industries made enormous additions to their stock of capital to labor, raising this ratio at rates of 8 percent per annum, but realized relatively small gains in labor productivity (3.0 and 0.4 percent per annum, respectively) and negative total factor productivity growth.

The decomposition of the sources of labor productivity growth for Mexico, including the estimates of total factor productivity advance, are presented in Table 8.7. The decomposition differs in form from that computed for South Korean manufacturing in that output is measured for the Mexican industries in terms of gross value—as opposed to value added. Hence, Mexican labor productivity growth is decomposed between the amounts attributable to capital deepening, raw materials deepening, and total factor productivity. The different formulation generates somewhat lower rates of productivity advance for Mexico than value-added-based measures would have,

Table 8.7. Sources of Labor Productivity Growth in Mexican Manufacturing Industries, 1970–1980

	Contribution of capital deepening	Contribution of raw material deepening	Rate of TFP growth (Residual)
	Percent per annum		
Heavy industries	1.6	2.0	−0.1
Basic industrial metals	1.7	1.3	−1.0
Nonmetallic mix products	1.5	2.0	0.8
Basic chemical products	0.8	2.5	1.6
Other industrial chemicals	1.7	2.5	−0.1
Petroleum and petrochemicals	4.0	2.9	−0.2
Metal products	1.7	1.7	−0.3
Transport equipment	1.9	0.2	−1.5
Automobiles	0.2	2.3	0.9
Medium/light industries	0.7	2.3	1.2
Electrical machinery	0.6	2.2	1.6
Machinery	−0.2	2.3	2.4
Paper and products	0.4	2.8	1.5
Textiles and apparel	0.7	1.8	0.7
Pharmaceuticals	0.8	3.3	2.5
Synthetic fibers	−0.3	2.4	1.8
Rubber and plastic products	1.9	3.0	0.8
Wood products	1.4	1.2	−0.3
Soaps, detergents, cosmetics	0.4	2.8	1.6
Food products	−0.1	1.1	1.1
Tobacco products	1.6	0.7	0.3
Beverages	−1.3	1.1	3.0
Other food products	0.0	1.1	0.8
All manufacturing average	0.7	1.8	0.8

Notes and Sources: See the note to Table 8.1.

but the qualitative results are unaffected. The figures confirm the impression from Table 8.6 that total factor productivity growth was very modest in Mexican manufacturing during the 1970s. There was no progress in the highly protected and supported heavy industries, which actually suffered a slight drop over the period. The medium/ light and food products subsectors did better, with advances of 1.2 and 1.1 percent per annum, but were also low relative to the standards of newly industrializing economies in general. The pace of total factor productivity growth in the manufacturing sector overall was far slower (at 0.8 percent per annum) than in South Korea, and only half that of manufacturing in the United States during that country's initial phase of industrialization in the nineteenth century.

Within the growth accounting framework, the increase in raw materials consumed per unit of labor accounts for nearly half of the increase in labor productivity in each of the three classes of manufacturing industries. Beyond this component, which was not observable for the South Korean industries, the relative significance of the alternative sources of labor productivity growth in Mexico resemble those in the East Asian nation. In the heavy industries, the increase in labor productivity was exclusively due to capital and raw materials deepening, as total factor productivity declined. It is remarkable that during a boom decade, these capital-intensive industries received a disproportionate amount of government support and yet failed to increase their operating efficiency. As in South Korea, it was the medium/light industries that managed the highest rates of total factor productivity increase in the economy despite their less favored status in the eyes of the government and their lower rates of capital deepening (3.1 percent per annum versus 6.4 percent in the heavy subsector).

The implication of this evidence on Mexican manufacturing is that its process of industrialization in recent decades has been much different from that of South Korea. Whereas the latter country has clearly been making major strides in raising the productivity of its industries, most of Mexico's economic growth seems to have derived from sectoral shifts in resources from the traditional (and low-productivity and predominantly agricultural) sector to the modern industrial (high-productivity) sector. Within industries, capital deepening and total factor productivity increase have made only modest contributions—by Korean standards—to raising output per worker within industries. Why Mexico was not able to attain higher rates of industrial productivity growth is a question beyond the scope of this paper, but perhaps the lack of competition plays some role. Many of the worst performing industries in Mexico were highly concentrated, often run with government involvement, and protected from foreign and even domestic competition. Moreover, the exchange rates between the peso and foreign currencies during the flush-with-oil-revenue 1970s generally worked against the development of extensive export markets and thus of incentives to compete with foreign companies. Another contributor to the disappointing performance of Mexican manufacturing may have been the extensive system of subsidies that distorted the costs of inputs to firms, and encouraged less than efficient technical decisions about the use of factors of production. Only with the fundamental changes in policy introduced by the Salinas administation in recent years has there been a meaningful movement away from the long Mexican tradition of an activist state intervening frequently and strongly to protect domestic industrial interests and to influence allocations of resources throughout the economy.

CONCLUSIONS

The evidence reviewed in this chapter provides no support for the view that industrial policies which target subsidies or other forms of government assistance to specific industries yield higher rates of economic growth. Not only is there no substantive basis for claims that the high rates of economic growth attained by countries like South Korea can be attributed to their industrial policies, but the cross-sectional examination of industry-level data for Korea and Mexico indicates that industries receiving help through such programs realized slower—not higher—rates of productivity growth over time. The clear implication is that industrial policies tended to shift resources away from, instead of toward, those industries which were making the greatest progress at increasing the productive capacity of their respective economy. They also failed to yield any demonstrable improvement in the rate at which industries increased their productivity. If there are any clues to promoting productivity growth here, they point to the empirical association between productivity growth and export orientation, and suggest that nations would do better encouraging private investment to flow to those industries in which they have a comparative advantage, and where, correspondingly, there are extensive markets and returns to invent, innovate, and compete for.[11]

Of course there remain some questions as to how directly relevant the evidence presented here is to the wisdom of implementing an industrial policy. The discussion here has focused on the implications for economic growth, but one might instead argue for a targeted assistance program to simply preserve a domestic industry or maintain a certain level of employment. Even if political or noneconomic interests are the principal concern, however, one should understand the economic consequences or costs of whatever policies are under consideration. Another caveat to straightforwardly applying the findings about South Korea and Mexico to construct a general assessment of the desirability of industrial policy is that the outcomes might reasonably vary with the level of economic or technological development. For example, the pattern observed in both countries of the less capital-intensive (and untargeted) industries realizing more rapid total factor productivity growth than the more capital-intensive (or targeted) ones might only hold for societies at an early stage of industrialization—where there are important one-time organizational improvements to be introduced or technology to be borrowed from abroad. At a later stage, where technological advances are more likely to be embodied in capital equipment or originate in major commitments of resources to inventive activity, it is plausible that the economic returns to industrial policy might be greater. All the same, the poor judgments made about the targeting of assistance in South Korea and Mexico reinforce skepticism about the efficacy at any time of determining the allocation of resources between industries through political processes.

NOTES

1. For example, see P. Krugman, *Rethinking International Trade* (Cambridge: MIT Press, 1991); and L. Tyson, *Who's Bashing Whom?: Trade Conflict in High-Technology Industries* (Washington, D.C.: Institute for International Economics, 1992).

2. See J. Bhagwati, *Protectionism* (Cambridge: MIT Press, 1988).

3. For Japan, see C. Johnson, ed., *The Industrial Policy Debate* (San Francisco: ICS Press, 1984); C. Johnson *MITI and the Japanese Miracle: The Growth of Industrial Policy, 1925–1975* (Stanford: Stanford University Press, 1982); and C. Johnson, L. Tyson, and J. Zysman, *Politics and Productivity: The Real Study of Why Japan Works* (Cambridge: Ballinger, 1989); and Tyson, *Who's Bashing Whom.* For South Korea, see A. Amsden, *Asia's Next Giant: South Korea and Late Industri-*alization (New York: Oxford University Press, 1989); L. Jones and I. Sakong, *Government Business and Entrepreneurship in Economic Development: The Korean Case. Studies in the Modernization of the Republic of Korea, 1945–1975* (Cambridge: Council on East Asian Studies, 1980); L. Westphal, "The Republic of Korea's Experience with Export-led Industrial Development," *World Development* 6 (1978):347–82; L. Westphal, Y. Rhee, and G. Pursell, "Korean Industrial Competence: Whence It Came From," *World Bank Staff Working Paper,* no. 469 (Washington, D.C.: World Bank, 1981); and World Bank, *Korea Managing the Industrial Transition: The Conduct of Industrial Policy,* Vol. I (Washington, D.C.: World Bank, 1987).

4. See Amsden, *Asia's Next Giant*; and Johnson, *MITI and the Japanese Miracle.*

5. For example, the Korean GDP grew at a per annum rate of 10.0 percent during 1965–73, and at 7.3 percent between 1973 and 1983, as opposed to 7.9 and 5.6 percent in Mexico for the respective periods. All rates were of course well above those for population growth. See World Bank, *World Development Report, 1985* (New York: Oxford University Press, 1985).

6. Value added and employment data come from United Nations, *Yearbook of Industrial Statistics* (New York: United Nations, various years). Industry capital stock data were provided by the Economic Planning Board of the Republic of Korea. For more details about the data and estimation procedures, see D. Dollar and K. Sokoloff, "Patterns of Productivity Growth in South Korean Manufacturing Industries, 1962–1979," *Journal of Development Economics* 33 (1990): 309–27.

7. The HCI program, and its mixed results, receive a detailed discussion in World Bank, *Korea Managing the Industrial Transition: The Conduct of Industrial Policy.* The financial data and further demonstrations of the poor results of the program are provided in A. Virmani, "Government Policy and the Development of Financial Markets: The Case of Korea," *World Bank Staff Working Paper,* no. 747 (Washington, D.C.: World Bank, 1984).

8. For a full discussion of the framework and methods used in the estimation, see Dollar and Sokoloff, "Patterns of Productivity Growth."

9. Indeed, Korean policy makers came to recognize that the best performances were coming from the industries oriented toward competition in the world market. See Amsden, *Asia's Next Giant*; World Bank, *Korea Managing the Industrial Transition;* and Virmani, "Government Policy and the

Development of Financial Markets" for further discussion and information on the relative support of different industries.

10. See R. Aubey, *Nacional Financiera and Mexican Industry: A Study of the Financial Relationship Between the Government and the Private Sector of Mexico* (Los Angeles: UCLA Latin America Center, 1966); T. King, *Mexico: Industrialization and Trade Policies Since 1940* (London: Oxford University Press, 1970); C. Reynolds, *The Mexican Economy: Twentieth-Century Structure and Growth* (New Haven: Yale University Press, 1970); and D. Story, *The Mexican Ruling Party: Stability and Authority* (New York: Praeger, 1986).

11. See Bhagwati, *Protectionism,* for a general discussion of the problems with a protectionist-oriented industrial policy. See Westphal, Rhee, and Pursell, "Korean Industrial Competence," for specific Korean examples of export-based technological advance in manufacturing. For treatments of the responsiveness of inventive activity and manufacturing productivity to the extent and size of markets during early American industrialization, see K.L. Sokoloff, "Inventive Activity in Early Industrial America: Evidence from Patent Records, 1790–1846," *Journal of Economic History* 48 (1988): 813–50; and "Invention, Innovation, and Manufacturing Productivity Growth in the Antebellum Northeast," in R. Gallman and J. Wallis, eds., *American Economic Growth and Standards of Living Before the Civil War* (Chicago: University of Chicago Press, 1992). It could easily be argued that access to international markets today is analogous to access to broad urban markets in the early nineteenth-century United States.

9

Labor and the Politics of Exchange Rates: The Case of the European Monetary System

JEFFRY A. FRIEDEN

It is widely believed that the great economic openness of modern industrial societies has fundamentally reduced the possibilities of successfully implementing labor-oriented or social democratic economic policies. This is especially the case in regard to the very high contemporary levels of financial-market integration. Analysts and activists from all sides of the political spectrum assert that the ability of investors to move financial assets from country to country at low cost and high speed has significantly increased the political power of the investing community, and significantly curtailed the ability of labor to prevail in economic policy debates.

This chapter outlines the effects of increased financial integration on the possibilities for labor-oriented macroeconomic policies. It argues that cross-border capital mobility alters, but does not eliminate, the scope of national monetary policy—primarily by shifting it away from interest rates and toward the exchange rate. This has been illustrated with great force in Europe over the past several years, especially in the ongoing process of European monetary integration.

In this context, I examine the role that European labor movements have played in the development of the European Monetary System (EMS) since 1979. I am especially interested in explaining the attitude of European labor, and different sectors within it, toward the EMS. Because of the importance of France and Italy in the evolution of the EMS, and of French and Italian labor in Europe, I focus on these two cases—especially on the years from 1979 to 1985, when the two countries changed course most dramatically. This leads to an evaluation of the extent to which developments in the 1980s should be taken to indicate that labor is incapable of affecting national macroeconomic policies.

MONETARY POLICY IN A FINANCIALLY INTEGRATED WORLD

It is common to see arguments that the great mobility of capital across national borders has weakened the political position of labor. Prominent among such assertions are that labor-oriented macroeconomic policies are increasingly difficult to sustain, as they lead to massive outflows of funds and attacks on the national currency. Examples given to support this position include that of the British Labour government in 1976, and the French Socialist government in 1981–1983. The argument is typically that labor-based governments find their hands tied by today's very high level of international capital mobility.

However, open economy macroeconomics has clear predictions about the implications of capital mobility for monetary policy—and they are not as argued by what might be called the "labor pessimists."[1] The basic insight is that if financial assets are freely traded across borders, so that interest rates cannot vary, monetary policy continues to affect domestic economic activity by way of exchange rate movements.[2]

In other words, national monetary authorities can only stimulate a financially open economy by allowing the currency to depreciate; if the exchange rate is fixed, increased money supply growth and temporarily lower interest rates will simply lead to an outflow of funds until domestic interest rates go back to world interest rates. This in turn implies that there is a tradeoff between national monetary policy independence and exchange-rate stability: either a financially integrated country allows its currency to fluctuate or it accepts the loss of monetary policy as an instrument. Allowing the exchange rate to move has costs for those heavily involved in world trade and payments; losing national monetary policy autonomy has costs for those heavily dependent upon domestic market conditions. In any event, it is *possible* for governments to pursue independent monetary policies, although the costs (in exchange rate volatility) may have increased. A labor-based government *could* stimulate the economy, if it were willing to allow the currency to depreciate.

All of this is to say that the common assertion that financial integration constrains all governments to the same policies is incorrect. Labor-based governments *could* implement policies that diverge from their neighbors despite high levels of financial integration. If they have not, it is because other factors have driven them toward convergent policies. Such factors might include evolution in labor's policy preferences, or considerations on other policy dimensions.

Another way to put this is that labor's macroeconomic policy preferences have changed as the world has become financially integrated. In a world without capital mobility, labor found little reason not to support monetary expansion, which tended to stimulate the economy.[3] With capital mobility, reflation implies devaluation, and not all workers have similar interests when it comes to the exchange rate.

A striking indication of this change is the fact that much of European labor has been favorably inclined to the surrender of national monetary independence in the interest of European monetary integration, today in the guise of a fixed-rate regime but eventually looking toward a single European currency. Even several non-EC (European Community) members (Finland, Norway, Sweden, and Austria, for example) and labor movements within them have moved in the direction of trying to tie their currencies to the fixed-rate system established by the EC. Especially inasmuch as commitment to the EMS implies accepting German monetary policy, which is extremely conservative, the trend calls out for explanation.

The starting point for any evaluation of these developments is that, while monetary expansion in a closed economy tends to be positive for labor, there is no reason to expect the exchange rate regime (fixed, managed, or floating) or exchange rate level (appreciated or depreciated) to have a uniform impact on labor.[4] These policy choices affect different groups of workers differently, depending on how the industries in which they are employed are affected.

Figure 9.1 summarizes my expectations of labor's exchange rate preferences. The horizontal axis refers to the currency's value. Workers in tradable sectors prefer a relatively low (depreciated) exchange rate, which makes their goods cheaper on world markets and raises the domestic price of imports with which their goods are competing. Those in the production of nontradable goods and services, and in large multinational enterprises less dependent on the domestic market, prefer a stronger exchange rate, although this policy preference will probably be less intense than that of workers in tradables industries.[5]

The vertical axis summarizes labor's policy preferences over the exchange rate *regime,* simplifying the choice to one between a fixed rate (such as the gold standard or the European Monetary System) and a floating rate. Workers in sectors heavily oriented toward external markets prefer exchange rate stability to domestic monetary independence, as they are concerned about their industries losing foreign markets and relatively unconcerned about the home market. Workers in domestically oriented sectors prefer a flexible exchange rate, as they are primarily concerned about domestic conditions and gain little by sacrificing national monetary autonomy in order to preserve a stable exchange rate.

If this typology is accurate, then, labor in tradables sectors will support a lower exchange rate than those in nontradables and globalized sectors; while labor in domestically oriented sectors will support a flexible exchange rate while those in internationally oriented sectors will support a fixed exchange rate. It should be noted that

Figure 9.1. Exchange rate policy preferences of different sectors of the labor movement in a financially integrated economy. As regards the level of the exchange rate, "high" refers to a more appreciated exchange rate and "low" to a more depreciated exchange rate. As regards the degree of exchange–rate flexibility, "low" implies a fixed rate such as is implied by the exchange rate mechanism of the European Monetary System, while "high" implies freely floating rates. Given capital mobility, this variation also implies variation from the absence of national monetary independence to effective and nationally autonomous monetary policy. These are, of course, only rough approximations, and variation is along a continuum rather than dichotomous.

Preferred level of the exchange rate

		High	Low
Preferred degree of exchange–rate flexibility/ national monetary independence	Low	Labor in sectors reliant upon global production	Labor in sectors reliant upon exports
	High	Labor in nontradables sectors	Labor in import-competing sectors producing for the domestic market

the two dimensions are linked; for example, a country on a fixed exchange rate regime cannot devalue without losing some of its international credibility. In this instance, labor (say in exporting sectors) will have to evaluate the relative importance to it of the two dimensions and choose accordingly.

Another fact that differentiates the politics of exchange rates from that of monetary policy *per se* is that the exchange rate is, almost by definition, implicated with a variety of other international issues. It is relatively easy to segregate a national monetary policy stance from other relationships with foreign countries, but exchange rates are harder to treat in isolation. One obvious linkage is trade policy: trade partners typically, and rightly, regard a deliberate attempt to hold the national currency's value down as tantamount to trade protection and may retaliate either with a competitive devaluation or with targeted protective barriers. In this instance the link between policy areas can alter domestic political lineups: if deliberate "undervaluation" causes retaliation against the country's export-oriented steel sector, for example, the sector may choose to support a realistic exchange rate (with no retaliation targeted at them) as the lesser of two evils. More generally, a labor movement might be willing to alter its exchange rate preferences in the interest of another international policy that it valued more—while this would be unlikely with monetary policy in and of itself. This sort of linkage politics is especially significant, as we shall see, in the case of European monetary unification.

LABOR AND EUROPEAN MONETARY INTEGRATION: AN OVERVIEW

The dominant characteristic of European macroeconomic policy for the past decade has been the gradual movement toward monetary unification within, and now beyond, the European Community. The European Monetary System was established in 1979 with an eye toward reducing exchange rate fluctuations among EC members. The principal component of the EMS for our purposes is the exchange rate mechanism (ERM), which restricts the prices of member currencies to a narrow band beyond which fluctuation is prohibited. Original members of the ERM included all then-members of the EC save the United Kingdom; Spain and Portugal joined later; the United Kingdom also joined later, only to leave in September 1992, while Greece remains outside the ERM. A number of non-EC members have also, and with varying degrees of success, moved to link their currencies to the ERM by way of pegging to the European Currency Unit (ECU), which is a basket of EMS currencies. These last include countries with powerful labor movements and labor-oriented policies— Sweden, Norway, Finland, and Austria.

The EMS is a fixed exchange rate regime similar to the postwar Bretton Woods system or the gold standard. (As is customary, we shall use membership in the EMS as equivalent to participation in the ERM, although in fact the two are not the same.) Members are expected to pursue monetary policies that keep their currencies within specified values relative to other member currencies. In effect, this means that the leading member of the EMS, Germany, sets monetary policy for the system as a whole. A national monetary policy different from Germany's would lead to an inflow or outflow of funds, put pressure on the currency, and force a change either in the currency's value or in the nation's monetary policy.

The history of the EMS has been checkered. For the first few years of the EMS, currency realignments were quite common, but between 1987 and 1992 there were no changes in parities within the system. After 1989 the pressures of German unification introduced substantial new strains into the EMS, which eventually led the British and Italians to leave the ERM in September 1992 and forced devaluations of the currencies of Ireland, Spain, and Portugal within the ERM.

Despite the difficulties of 1992–1993, the core of the ERM remains relatively solid: the currencies of Germany, France, Belgium, the Netherlands, Denmark, and Luxembourg have remained tied to each other, and Italy, Ireland, Spain, and Portugal remain firmly committed to rejoining this core. Some form of currency union appears likely to develop. The crucial turning point in the formation of a credible EMS is typically regarded as the period between 1982 and 1985, when the three high-inflation members of the system—France, Ireland, and Italy—brought their inflation down toward German levels and were thus able to sustain their exchange rates within the agreed-upon margins.

Binding their currencies to EMS values was not painless for the three high-inflation countries. Apart from the general loss of a policy instrument, there were more specific effects. Because currency values were fixed while the three countries' inflation rates were substantially above the EMS mean, the franc, lira, and Irish pound appreciated in real terms. In other words, the national price levels rose while national currency values remained fixed (or lagged behind). This meant that domestic producers of tradable goods—predominantly manufacturers, as farm prices are supported by European agricultural policies—were under severe cost pressure. Domestic input prices rose much more rapidly than world prices (in domestic currency), so that manufacturers found themselves priced out of world markets. In the past, industrialists had demanded and received devaluations to permit a maintenance of competitiveness, but the EMS reduced or eliminated this possibility. Battles ensued over whether the EMS commitment was more important than the costs to the industrial sector of the real appreciation.

The previous discussion leads to a number of analytical expectations about the role of labor in debates over the EMS. Labor attitudes toward the conscious sacrifice of national monetary policy autonomy are expected to respond to three interrelated factors. First, labor willingness to give up monetary policy in the interest of exchange rate stability should be related to the degree to which it is employed in lines of business for which predictable exchange rates are relatively important. Second, labor views on the desirability of forgoing devaluation should be related to interests on currency depreciation more generally—with labor in tradables production favorable to devaluation and labor in nontradables opposed. Third, at least some portions of the labor movement should evaluate the EMS constraints in the light of the implicit or explicit linkage of the EMS to other EC and international issues.

Labor in the EC, indeed, has become more sensitive to exchange rate fluctuations over the past twenty years. As European economies have become more open on both the current and capital account, more economic agents have developed significant foreign-currency interests. There has been, in other words, a major increase in the proportion of the European economies which is sensitive to exchange-rate fluctuations and can be expected to desire a dampening of these fluctuations—and labor is no exception. Labor in export-oriented and major global firms has a strong incentive to see currency movements reduced, inasmuch as this increases the success of these firms. We expect labor in more internationally oriented sectors to have become more concerned about exchange rate volatility, and more willing to forgo some national policy independence in order to reduce it.

At the same time, labor has divergent interests over the *level* of the exchange rate. This is especially true in traditionally high-inflation countries, in which a fixed exchange rate implies a real appreciation. Workers in tradables sectors such as manufacturing are typically harmed by a real appreciation of the currency, which reduces demand for their products and presumably, thus, tradables employment and wages.[6] Workers in nontradables sectors, such as services, are conversely helped by a real appreciation, as the relative prices of their products increase. This is especially important in France, Ireland, and Italy, as the EMS commitment led to a real appreciation that hurt manufacturing much more than it did services. We anticipate general opposition to the EMS from labor in tradables sectors, and general support from labor in nontradables sectors.

There is little doubt about the importance of the linkage of the EMS to other policies in the EC. In the early 1980s, it was widely believed that countries that were not full members of the EMS would not be full participants in other EC initiatives. The system was launched personally by the French and German prime ministers, and its founding documents explicitly linked monetary stability with broader European integration. In this sense, even those portions of the labor movement that were not enthusiastic about the EMS had to weigh the degree to which their opposition to the EMS outweighed their support for other EC programs.

This linkage is important on a number of dimensions. One of direct interest to labor is the goal of uniform labor standards within the EC. Labor movements in countries with social or labor policies less generous than the EC median have an incentive to promote national subordination to EC policy, and this is unlikely to take place if the country is not fully integrated into the EC. More generally, inasmuch as labor supports European integration as a broad goal, it will be hard pressed to oppose monetary union specifically, even if the EMS appears potentially harmful.

In Europe, then, I expect to see two phenomena. The first is a differentiation of labor on exchange rate policy along the lines discussed above, along with increasing influence of those more favorable to a fixed rate. The second is the linkage of the EMS with other EC issues of interest to labor, and the importance of such linkage to labor's preferences toward European monetary unification itself. These two phenomena can in fact be observed in the two cases that we now examine in detail, that of France and Italy in the early 1980s.

LABOR AND THE EUROPEAN MONETARY SYSTEM IN FRANCE AND ITALY, 1979–1985

Detailed attention to the French and Italian cases is not random, nor is the choice of the 1979–1985 period. On the first count, it is commonly forgotten that the EMS was preceded by a six-year EC experiment with a similar fixed-rate arrangement, the "snake," which was widely regarded as a failure. Five countries were reliable members of the snake, and for them the EMS was simply a continuation of past procedure. Three countries were not snake members but did join and hold to the EMS commitment from the outset—France, Ireland, and Italy. This makes it especially important to understand what changed between the 1970s and the 1980s in these three countries to allow them to bind themselves to fixed exchange rates. It is in fact not coincidental that these were the EMS members with the highest inflation rates: bringing Italy's inflation in line with Germany's was far more of a challenge than bringing Holland's inflation down. And labor was especially important in France and Italy, with their powerful Communist parties. For all these reasons, the role of the labor movement in French and Italian policy toward the EMS is important to a broader understanding of the position of labor toward monetary policy in Europe.

As for the time period in question, expert opinion is roughly agreed that EMS credibility was very low at its creation, but had strengthened substantially by 1985 or so. The turning point most commonly alluded to in this process is the Mitterrand government's decision in March 1983 to remain in the EMS, but other events before 1986 also, as we shall see, contributed. In any case, the early 1980s were certainly years in which French and Italian commitment to the EMS was tested and established, if only provisionally; this makes it a crucial period.

The chronology in the two countries is relatively straightforward. French and Italian inflation rates, compared with those of Germany and the EMS average, are presented in Table 9.1. It can be seen that 1983 was a watershed: before then convergence toward German levels of inflation had been negligible, after then it was rapid. It is instructive to examine the 1981–1985 period in the two countries to see what role was played in these developments by divisions within labor over exchange rates, and by linkages between exchange rate issues and other international themes of interest to labor.

France

François Mitterrand and the Socialist Party (PS) took power in May-June 1981, after five years of mediocre economic performance under President Valéry Giscard d'Estaing and Prime Minister Raymond Barre.[7] In the two years since the EMS had

Table 9.1. Inflation in France, Italy, Germany, and the EMS Annual Average Rates of Consumer Price Increases, 1974–1986

	1974–1978 average	1979	1983	1986
Germany	4.8%	3.9%	3.2%	−0.4%
EMS average	10.9%	9.0%	7.5%	2.2%
France	10.5%	10.7%	9.7%	1.5%
Italy	17.6%	15.1%	14.8%	6.1%

Source: Centro Europa Ricerche, *Lo SME Dieci Anni Dopo* (Rome: Centro Europa Ricerche, 1988), 24.

begun operation, with French inflation still well above German levels, the franc had appreciated about 12 percent against the mark in real terms, putting serious pressure on French manufacturers.[8] As French prices continued to rise and the trade balance to deteriorate, the Mitterrand government negotiated an October 1981 EMS realignment in which the franc and lira were devalued by 3 percent and the mark and Dutch florin were revalued by 5.5 percent. The devaluation proved inadequate in the face of continued French inflation, and in June 1982 another realignment raised the mark and florin by 4.25 percent and lowered the franc by 5.75 percent (the lira was devalued by 2.75 percent).

The second Mitterrand realignment gave rise to serious disputes within the French government, and in French society. Eventually, in March 1983 Mitterrand decided to keep the franc within the EMS and adopt severe austerity measures. For our purposes, it is especially important to evaluate the complex divisions within the Socialist Party, between socialists and communists, and within labor that were central to the debates.

President Mitterrand's government was headed by Prime Minister Pierre Mauroy, and included four ministers from the Communist Party (PCF). Although PCF votes were not essential to a majority, Mitterrand believed Left unity to be both good electoral politics and a demonstration of principle. However, the Communists were less enthusiastic about European integration than the Socialists, and were strong opponents of austerity.

The Socialist-Communist differences were especially important because they implicated the trade unions. The largely pro-Communist *Confédération Générale du Travail* (CGT) was most adamant in its resistance to austerity, even at the expense of French membership in the EC (toward which it had been indifferent or opposed). Inasmuch as economic policies necessary to control inflation affected real wages, as they inevitably must, the CGT and the PCF were recalcitrant at best, obstructionist at worst.[9]

The PS was itself divided in several important factions. Running roughly from Right to Left, the group led by Michel Rocard was economically liberal and strongly pro-European. Mitterrand's faction was more radical than socialist, but more tied to his personality than to any particular policy stance. The group around Pierre Mauroy tended toward standard social democracy—friendly to Rocard's economic liberalism, but committed to traditional socialist goals; Mauroy generally had the support of the regional Marseilles-based federation led by Gaston Deferre. Finally, the CERES *(Centre d'Études, de Recherches, et d'Éducation Socialistes)* faction led by Jean-Pierre Chevènement was the stronghold of militancy, with a nationalistic flavor and economic policy views similar to the Communists.[10] Mitterrand's faction dominated the PS largely by way of tactical alliances with others: at the 1979 Metz Congress, Rocard and Mauroy were in opposition to Mitterrand, who controlled the meeting by way of his alliance with CERES and the Deferre group.

In the labor movement, the Socialists' principal allies were the *Confédération Française Démocratique du Travail* (CFDT) and the *Fédération de l'Éducation Nationale* (FEN). The former was a general labor federation that competed with the CGT; the latter was a teachers' association. There was a Socialist presence in the CGT, but it was a minority of the confederation. A third major federation, *Force Ouvrière* (FO) was not partisan.[11]

There were important socioeconomic differences among these parties and labor unions. The Communist Party was, as elsewhere in Europe, heavily oriented toward blue-collar workers in traditional industries. The Socialist Party was essentially middle class: it was dominated by managers, professionals, and white-collar workers. The PS membership relative to the population at large in 1973, for example, had a heavy overrepresentation of upper managers (10.6% of the party and 6.4% of the labor force), and of teachers (16.7% of the party and 3% of the labor force); workers were seriously underrepresented (18.8% of the PS and 37.4% of the labor force).[12] Of the 169 PS deputies elected in 1981, fully 47 percent were teachers, 22 percent professionals, and 20 percent upper managers and senior civil servants.[13]

The trade unions differed quite a bit as to their composition, as is reflected in Tables 9.2 and 9.3. The distinctions between the CGT and CFDT were particularly interesting. The CGT was especially strong in traditional manufacturing industries. Table 9.2 shows how much heavier was the industrial bent of the CGT than that of the CFDT and FO: while three-fifths of CGT voters were in industry, less than half of CFDT and FO voters were.

The CGT's industrial vocation is indicated by other measures as well. CGT votes in union elections in 1981 were 32 percent of total votes. In such industries as metalworking, pulp and paper, and chemicals, the CGT vote was between 45 and 51 percent of the total; while in finance and services the CGT vote was between 10 and 22 percent of the total.[14] Within the public sector, the CGT dominated the steel, chemical, and auto firms, but had little strength in high-technology and financial firms.[15] Overall, the CGT in 1979 union elections received 50 percent of the votes of industrial workers, 30 percent of the vote among agricultural workers, and 33 percent of the votes of other workers.[16]

As this indicates, the CFDT like the PS tended to be more oriented toward services and high-technology firms than the CGT. Table 9.3 shows some of these differences in several important French firms. While the CGT overwhelmed the CFDT within Renault and led in Michelin, for example, the CFDT dominated such

Table 9.2. France: Sectoral Composition of Votes for Three Major Labor Federations, 1979

	CGT	CFDT	FO	Total[a]
Industry	59.7%	49.1%	45.3%	50.5%
Trade	23.8%	24.1%	26.9%	23.8%
Agriculture	2.6%	5.2%	4.7%	3.5%
Various	9.7%	13.6%	14.7%	11.7%
Management	4.2%	8.0%	8.4%	10.4%
Total	100.0%	100.0%	100.0%	100.0%
Total voting for federation[a] (millions)	3.30	1.80	1.36	7.79

Source: Gérard Adam, *Le Pouvoir Syndical* (Paris: Dunod, 1983), 164.
[a]Total votes for all federations include votes for a number of smaller labor unions. Totals do not add up exactly due to rounding.

Table 9.3. France: CGT and CFDT Strength in Selected Firms, 1979–1981

Firm and date of vote	Percent votes for CGT	Percent votes for CFDT[a]
Renault, 1981	61.2	16.6
Michelin, 1980	46.1	43.8
Banque Nationale de Paris, 1980	25.1	30.0
Assurances Générales de France, 1980	22.4	50.1
IBM-France, 1979	12.4	56.2

Source: Hervé Hamon and Patrick Rotman, *La Deuxième Gauche* (Paris: Ramsay, 1982), 423–27. The elections in question were for enterprise commissions.
[a]In the case of IBM-France, votes for the CFDT include votes for an autonomous union.

financial firms as the Banque National de Paris and the insurance company Assurances Générales de France. The CFDT and an autonomous union swamped the CGT in IBM-France.

The general pattern within the labor movement, then, was that the CFDT was especially concentrated in nontradable (service) sectors and competitive high-technology firms, while the CGT was prominent among tradable producers, especially those most affected by import competition. This division was mirrored to some extent by that between the Socialist and Communist parties. In this context we recall the expected policy differences between import-competing tradables sectors, on the one hand, and internationally oriented firms and nontradables producers, on the other: the former are expected to be favorable to devaluation, the latter indifferent or unfavorable.

These sectoral divisions were exacerbated by the economic trends of the early 1980s. As the franc appreciated in real terms against other EMS currencies, relative prices constantly moved against the tradables sectors and in favor of the nontradables (and cross-border investing) segments of the French economy. The process is clear from the evolution of broad aggregates within the economy. In 1981–1982 the prices of industrial products rose 19.5 percent, while prices of private services rose 28.3 percent and those of public services by 34.8 percent. This (which simply expresses the process of a real appreciation) put serious pressure on tradables producers.[17] Indeed, between 1980 and 1983, employment in tradable sectors declined 7 percent. Meanwhile, employment in construction, trade, and services held steady, while that in energy, transport, telecommunications, and finance rose 5 percent.[18] In this context, it is not surprising that tradables producers were especially interested in further devaluations, while nontradables producers were supportive of maintaining a fixed, and relatively appreciated, exchange rate.

This cleavage was an important component of French debates over the EMS, which were largely couched in terms of austerity and commitment to a fixed exchange rate within the EMS, versus reflation, devaluation, and abandoning the EMS.[19] The Communists and the CGT, along with CERES within the PS, opposed austerity and favored devaluing while leaving the EMS (and perhaps even the EC).

The Rocard and Mauroy factions of the PS, and the CFDT, were pro-European and thus in favor of maintaining EMS commitments, even at the expense of austerity. Mitterrand and his supporters within the PS were in the middle, and they were of course crucial to the ultimate disposition of the issue.[20]

If the general lineup of forces confirms expectations about labor interests toward exchange rates, the French experience also shows the importance of the link between the EMS and other international issues. Throughout the debates, there was little question that opting out of the EMS was likely to call into question France's position in the EC more generally. French commitment to the EMS within Europe, indeed, dated to the very announcement of early plans for the system, which was made jointly by Giscard d'Estaing and German Chancellor Helmut Schmidt. While CERES sometimes hinted that France could leave the EMS without actually leaving the EC, few were under any illusions that breaking with the exchange rate arrangement would fundamentally transform the country's level of involvement in Community affairs. And many opponents of the EMS were in fact willing to see the country leave the EC altogether.

Mitterrand's eventual decision to stay in the EMS and impose austerity measures was strongly influenced by broader European considerations. The days before the March 1983 decision to impose austerity and stay in the EMS saw intense negotiations between the French government and its EMS partners, especially Germany. The Germans indeed agreed to have the Deutsche mark bear much of the adjustment burden in the inevitable realignment that was agreed upon, in which the mark was revalued by 5.5 percent while the franc was devalued by 2.5 percent. The French did commit themselves to significant policy changes, but they had also extracted concessions from the Germans.

Domestic political developments also highlighted aspects of the external link. The economy was in the doldrums during 1982 and 1983, and social conflicts were heating up as well. Most prominent was a series of bitter strikes at Citroën factories, an indication of the difficulties facing tradables producers. On March 6 and 13, 1983, municipal elections were held. The Left as a whole did badly, but the real losers were the Communists.[21] Mitterrand, who was pondering the EMS issue during the two-round elections, read this as an indication that the sort of economic nationalism espoused by the PCF would not succeed in shoring up the Socialists' political base. The municipal elections, in other words, led Mitterrand to conclude that while popular discontent with austerity was widespread, anti-EC sentiment was quite limited. This apparently helped push him toward a decision to keep France inside the EMS.

Italy

The decisions that bound monetary policy to the EMS were less striking, less resolute, and somewhat less public in Italy than in France. Italian policy on this score developed gradually between 1981 and 1986, and there is no single decision equivalent to the March 1983 episode in France. Nonetheless, several important turning points can be identified, and the role of labor in them examined. In most instances we also observe the sorts of divisions within labor familiar from the French case, and a general link between these debates and EC policy more general.

The first major step in reorienting Italian monetary policy was taken in 1981, when the president of the Banca d'Italia indicated that he would no longer be guided by a 1975 commitment to purchase unsold Treasury securities.[22] This shift in policy, known as the "divorce" of the central bank from the Treasury, meant the end of automatic monetization of the budget deficit. Given Italy's chronic deficit spending, central bank monetization was an important inflationary force, and its end signaled a change in monetary policy. The reorientation of monetary policy was strengthened in 1982 by the implementation of a new compulsory reserve system, and strengthened further in 1983 when administrative controls on credit were eliminated. All of these reinforced a restrictive monetary policy that was an essential component of bringing Italian inflation in line with German inflation and allowing the lira to maintain its nominal value.

Almost immediately after the divorce of the central bank from the Treasury, Italian real interest rates shot up from 7.7 percent *below* German levels in 1980 to 1.7 percent *above* German levels in 1983. Overall, real interest rates in Italy went from an average of −1.5 percent between 1977 and 1981 to an average of + 3.8 percent between 1982 and 1986. Meanwhile, the share of the public debt held by the central bank declined from 23.7 percent in 1981 to 16.6 percent in 1984.[23] These policy changes thus served to eliminate one block to fighting Italian inflation, the subordination of central bank policy to the need to finance the country's large fiscal deficit.

However, more restrictive monetary policies were not enough. Italian inflation had a major inertial component, which had been institutionalized in a 1975 agreement between labor and management for an indexation scheme, the *scala mobile*, that compensated workers for virtually all past inflation. Defense of this arrangement had become a rallying cry for labor; destroying it became the goal of those for whom austerity in pursuit of reduced inflation was essential.

Attempts to renegotiate the *scala mobile* to reduce the level of indexation were frustrated through the early 1980s by the strong opposition of the Communist Party (PCI) and the Communist-oriented labor federation CGIL. The Socialists and the Christian Democrats, along with the labor federations associated with them, the CISL and UIL, were willing to reduce indexation. Finally, in February 1984 Socialist Bettino Craxi, newly chosen as prime minister, simply decreed a reduction in the *scala mobile*. The CGIL and the PCI were outraged, and soon began collecting signatures for a national vote on the *scala mobile*.[24]

The campaign leading up to the June 9, 1985 referendum was extremely divisive, and bore some resemblance to the debates that took place in 1982–1983 in France. The undeniable costs of austerity were increasingly counterposed to the high price of being out of step with Italy's partners in the EMS and the EC. In the event, the "no" votes prevailed (with 54.3 percent of the total), and the decree loosening the *scala mobile* stood. This was the second crucial set of policy changes necessary to bring Italian inflation down and make it possible for the country to keep the lira within the ERM.

Divisions within the labor movement over the EMS and EMS-related issues, such as the *scala mobile*, date back to the original debate over Italian entry into the agreement. Bargaining over these issues took place against the backdrop of important political changes in the country. In 1976, the PCI gave its tacit support to the coalition government led by the Christian Democrats (DC). In early 1978 the CGIL announced a significant moderation of its overall strategy.[25]

Nonetheless, both the PCI and the CGIL were ambivalent about Italian entry into the EMS, and opposed to a reduction in wage indexation. In 1978 the Communists voted against the law authorizing Italian accession to the exchange-rate agreement, arguing that a delay of at least six months was advisable to avoid too severe a shock to employment and wages. The Socialists abstained, and the bill passed.[26] As seen above, the PCI and the CGIL similarly fought against the reform of the *scala mobile*.

Some insight into the reason for these divisions is provided by a look at the socioeconomic differences among the major labor federations. It is important to keep in mind that the debate over the EMS took place with Italian inflation much higher than the EC average; it was widely believed that fixing the exchange rate meant in practice a real appreciation of the lira that would put pressure on tradables producers—as indeed happened. In this context, it is not surprising that workers in tradables sectors, especially import-competing industries, were most reluctant to join the EMS, were hardest hit by the real appreciation that ensued, and were most unwilling to forgo wage indexation.

Table 9.4 indicates that the CGIL, dominated by the Communists, was more heavily represented in traditional industries, while the Socialist-oriented CISL and the more independent UIL had larger shares of their memberships in the services. In 1983, for example, 59 percent of the CGIL's membership was in industry and 22 percent in public services. At the same time CISL membership was 46 percent in industry in 1983, with 38 percent in public services. Expressed differently, in 1983 CGIL members were 55 percent of Italy's unionized industrial workers (CISL 29%, UIL 16%), 48 percent of the country's organized workers in private services (CISL 31%, UIL 21%), and 36 percent of union members in public services (CISL 43%, UIL 21%).[27] Although data are not available, impressionistic evidence indicates that the Communist-Socialist social composition mirrored that of their unions, and was therefore similar to that of France. In both instances, the French generalization held for Italy: the Socialists were more representative of those in service and high-technology industries, while the Communists were concentrated in traditional import-competing manufacturing. This, again, helps explain why the PCI was more inclined toward devaluations, with the PSI more favorable to the EMS.

The link between European issues and the EMS was rarely drawn so explicitly

Table 9.4. Italy: Nonagricultural Membership in the CGIL, CISL, and UIL by Sectors, 1983

	CGIL	CISL	UIL
Industry	59.4%	45.6%	44.8%
Services, all	40.6%	54.4%	55.2%
Private	18.4%	16.8%	21.8%
Public	22.2%	37.6%	33.4%
Total	100.0%	100.0%	100.0%

Source: Calculated from Guido Baglioni, Ettore Santi, and Corrado Squarzon, *Le Relazioni Sindicali in Italia: Rapporto 1983–84* (Rome: Edizioni Lavoro, 1985), 196.

in Italy as in France—perhaps because no single decision ever became the focus of popular attention. However, the presence of the link is evident from the beginning of the story. Indeed, when the arrangement was being negotiated in 1978, Prime Minister Giulio Andreotti originally announced that Italy would not participate until domestic economic conditions had improved. Only after substantial pressure was brought to bear on Andreotti by the French and Germans did the government change its position. On the negative side, both Giscard and Schmidt made clear that they would regard Italy's nonadhesion to be a blow to the EMS and to Italy's Europeanist credentials. On the positive side, they permitted the lira a much wider (12%) band of fluctuation and incorporated financial assistance to Italy into the EMS agreement.

Andreotti gradually swung toward entry into the EMS, especially as the implications of nonentry for Italian relations with its EC partners became clear. The issue was also tied up with DC-PCI relations at a time when many of Italy's allies were uneasy about the quasi-membership of the Communists in the government. Extracts from Andreotti's diary entries for the crucial days in December 1978 are instructive. While still undecided he noted in frustration: "If we do not adhere immediately it will be said that the Communists are not 'Europeans' and that the government is their slave." Once Andreotti decided to enter the EMS, he resolved to make clear in his public statements to "distinguish between the EMS and the European commitment more generally *(vocazione europeista)* which remains almost universal among the political forces." And he named as the most important considerations in the decision "the guarantees of Schmidt and Giscard and the need to safeguard our European prestige." [28]

Indeed, the tie between the EMS and other European policy issues served to mitigate the Communists' position. Unlike in France, the PCI and the CGIL were generally Europeanist. Neither was opposed to Italian entry into the EMS, but wanted entry to be delayed until the economy was better able to withstand the exchange-rate shocks. And the PCI was careful not to force the EMS issue into an open test of the government, which might have caused it to fall. The PCI regarded its relations with German Chancellor Schmidt and the German Social Democrats more generally as crucial to its Eurocommunist future, and Schmidt regarded the EMS as a major personal achievement on his part. Indeed, during the Italian parliamentary debate, Schmidt telephoned PCI leader Enrico Berlinguer and asked him not to cause a government crisis over the EMS, a plea to which Berlinguer acceded. [29] In other words, general Communist commitment to the EC and the specific importance of the EMS for European integration softened the PCI-CGIL concern about the exchange rate agreement.

CONCLUSIONS AND IMPLICATIONS

In both France and Italy, divisions within the labor movement were important in debates over entry into the EMS and adoption of domestic economic policies necessary to reduce inflation to EC levels. Unions, parties, and factions more closely associated with traditional industry were most reluctant to forgo devaluation; those in services and high-technology sectors were much more favorable to fixing the exchange rate at what was certain to be a relatively appreciated level.

By the same token, in France and Italy the link between the EMS and other EC commitments was important. Opposition to the EMS and associated economic policies was mitigated for those socioeconomic actors who felt that these sacrifices were worth making in the interest of full national participation in the EC. This linkage operated both in pushing Mitterrand toward the EMS, and in softening PCI and CGIL opposition to it.

One implication of these conclusions is that it is misleading to think of the EMS and resultant policies as necessarily a defeat for labor. The policy choices of the 1980s in France and Italy may have been disastrous for labor in traditional import-competing industries, but the outcome was desired by other portions of the labor movement. And while many portions of the labor movement may have lost on the EMS, some gains may have been made on the EC front. The exact contours of these gains remain to be seen as the future of monetary integration remains unclear, while bargaining over EC social policies continues. Nonetheless, the issue of social and labor policy within the broad EC context might have been moot for those countries that opted out of the EMS if this option had frozen them out of other aspects of European integration.

A related implication of the French and Italian labor experiences of the 1980s is that divisions over economic policies may have changed from an earlier era. Labor's macroeconomic policy preferences appear far from monolithic. If this is the case, it is important for labor movements either to recognize this fact and agree to disagree accordingly, or to attempt to develop unified positions. This problem will certainly persist so long as European nations retain their own currencies, and the run-up to tighter monetary integration can be expected—like the development of the EMS in the early 1980s—to give rise to major debates within European labor.

Financial integration does not eliminate the possibility of labor-oriented economic policies. It does restrict labor's monetary policy options. In this context, exchange-rate issues are likely to be increasingly important in Europe and elsewhere, including to labor. These issues are likely to cut across class lines and thus introduce a set of tensions into labor movements in Europe; they are also likely to be closely linked to broader policy trends in the EC and Europe more generally.

European labor has been, and will be, forced to shift its policy focus somewhat by European financial integration. There is nothing inevitable about this shift leading to inherently less labor-oriented economic policies. A successful labor response, however, requires a serious analysis of the implications for labor of different macroeconomic policies in the context of continentally and globally linked capital markets. It also requires dealing with potentially divisive differences *within* the labor movement on these policy issues, and with the link between these issues and other European concerns.

NOTES

The author acknowledges support from the UCLA Institute of Industrial Relations, the Center for International Business Education and Research, the Social Science Research Council's Program in Foreign Policy Studies, and the German Marshall Fund. He also acknowledges useful suggestions from Paul Ong and Michael Wallerstein.

1. The argument here is elaborated in my "Invested Interests: The Politics of National Economic Policy in a World of Global Finance," *International Organization* 45 (Autumn 1991): 425–51.

2. To be more precise, it is real covered (inflation- and exchange rate-adjusted) interest rates that are constrained to be equal. The insight is that

of the famous Mundell-Fleming approach, which originated with Robert A. Mundell, "The Appropriate Use of Monetary and Fiscal Policy Under Fixed Exchange Rates," *IMF Staff Papers* 9 (March 1962): 70–77; see also his "Capital Mobility and Stabilization Policy Under Fixed and Flexible Exchange Rates," *Canadian Journal of Economics and Political Science* 29 (November 1963): 475–85. The basic model can be found in any good textbook discussion of open-economy macroeconomics; a useful survey is W.M. Corden, *Inflation, Exchange Rates, and the World Economy*, 3rd edition (Chicago: University of Chicago Press, 1986).

3. This of course ignores the potential costs of inflation, and rational-expectations insights on the potential inefficacy of monetary policy generally. The justifications for such blinders are purely empirical: labor has, in the postwar developed world, abhorred unemployment more than inflation, and governments have in fact appeared capable of manipulating nominal variables in ways that have had real effects.

4. As indicated above, this is too simple-minded; workers in a closed economy may well have different interests depending on how monetary policy affects relative prices. Nonetheless, the divergences are far more striking over exchange rates. It should also be noted that the discussion of labor policy preferences toward the exchange rate abstracts from relatively esoteric possibilities, such as about the weight of tradables in labor's consumption basket relative to that of capital.

5. This is because the relative price impact of exchange-rate movements on tradables producers is direct and immediate (it raises the price of imported substitutes), while on nontradables producers it is indirect and slow (it raises the price of all tradables relative to all nontradables).

6. All of this assumes limited mobility of labor between tradables and nontradables production; given the relatively limited inter-sectoral mobility of labor in general, this is probably not too strong an assumption. However, a more nuanced study would have to distinguish among sectors also on the basis of how much labor mobility there is into and out of them.

7. The literature on these years is enormous. Most of the discussion below is drawn from detailed journalistic accounts of the experience, which will be cited as used. More general analyses of the period can be found in Jeffrey Sachs and Charles Wyplosz, "The Economic Consequences of President Mitterrand," *Economic Policy* 2 (April 1986): 262–322; Patrick McCarthy, "France Faces Reality: *Rigueur* and the Germans," in David Calleo and Claudia Morgenstern, eds., *Recasting Europe's Economies* (Lanham, Maryland: University Press of America, 1990), 25–78; David Cameron, "The Franc, the EMS, *Rigueur*, and 'l'Autre Politique': The Regime-Defining Choices of the Mitterrand Presidency" (mimeo, New Haven, 1992); and Julius Friend, *Seven Years in France:*

François Mitterrand and the Unintended Revolution, 1981–1988 (Boulder: Westview Press, 1989). Macroeconomic data are taken, except where noted, from Sachs and Wyplosz. Among the many edited volumes on the experience, the following contain particularly useful discussions of economic policy: John Ambler, ed., *The French Socialist Experiment* (Philadelphia: ISHI, 1985); Philip Cerny and Martin Schain, eds., *Socialism, the State and Public Policy in France* (London: Frances Pinter, 1985); Howard Machin and Vincent Wright, eds., *Economic Policy and Policy-Making Under the Mitterrand Presidency 1981–1984* (New York: St. Martin's Press, 1985); and George Ross, Stanley Hoffmann, and Sylvia Malzacher, eds., *The Mitterrand Experiment* (Cambridge: Polity Press, 1987).

8. Real bilateral exchange rate calculated from Adrian Wood, *Global Trends in Real Exchange Rates, 1960 to 1984*, World Bank Discussion Paper 35 (Washington, D.C.: World Bank, 1988).

9. On the PCF see, for example, Mark Kesselman, "The French Communist Party: Historic Retard, Historic Compromise, Historic Decline—or New Departure?" in *Socialism, the State and Public Policy in France*, 42–59; and Mark Kesselman, "The Economic Analysis and Program of the French Communist Party," in Philip Cerny and Martin Schain, eds., *French Politics and Public Policy* (New York: St. Martin's Press, 1980), 177–90.

10. Two good studies of the arcane complexities of French Socialism are D.S. Bell and Byron Criddle, *The French Socialist Party*, 2nd ed. (Oxford: Clarendon Press, 1988); and David Hanley, *Keeping Left? Ceres and the French Socialist Party* (Manchester: Manchester University Press, 1986).

11. On the French labor movement see Gérard Adam, *Le pouvoir syndical* (Paris: Dunod, 1983); and René Mouriaux, *Syndicalisme et politique* (Paris: Editions Ouvrières, 1985).

12. Patrick Hardouin, "Les caractéristiques sociologiques du Parti Socialiste," *Revue française de science politique* 28 (April 1978): 220–56.

13. Bell and Criddle, 203.

14. Guy Groux and René Mouriaux, *La CGT* (Paris: Economica, 1992), 103.

15. Mouriaux, 201–02.

16. Adam, 164. The elections in question were the "élections prud'homales."

17. Alain Fonteneau and Pierre-Alain Muet, *La gauche face à la crise* (Paris: Presses de la Fondation Nationale des Sciences Politiques, 1985), 319.

18. These are the figures given, and the aggregations (tradable, nontradable, and "sheltered") used, in Sachs and Wyplosz, 275.

19. For accounts of which one can refer to a number of detailed narratives by well-informed journalists: Pierre Favier and Michel Martin-Roland, *La décennie Mitterrand 1. Les ruptures (1981–1984)* (Paris: Seuil, 1990); Philippe Bauchard, *La guerre des deux roses: Du rêve à la réalité,*

1981–1985 (Paris: Bernard Grasset, 1986); Serge July, *Les années Mitterrand* (Paris: Bernard Grasset, 1986); and Catherine Nay, *Les sept Mitterrand ou les métamorphoses d'un septennat* (Paris: Bernard Grasset, 1988).

20. For the purposes of this chapter, the actual transit of the debates, and their outcome, are of secondary importance. I look at the events more fully in "Acquiring Credibility: France and Italy in the European Monetary System, 1979–1985," in Barry Eichengreen and Jeffry Frieden, eds., *The Political Economy of European Monetary Unification* (Boulder: Westview Press, forthcoming).

21. Favier and Martin-Roland, 465–93, and Bauchard, 139–54.

22. The "divorce" is indeed one of the few aspects of Italian economic policy in this period on which there is a substantial literature, among which Guido Tabellini, "Central Bank Reputation and the Monetization of Deficits: The 1981 Italian Monetary Reform," *Economic Inquiry* 25 (April 1987): 185–200; Maria Teresa Salvemini, "The Treasury and the Money Market: The New Responsibilities After the Divorce," *Review of Economic Conditions in Italy* 1 (February 1983): 33–54; Elisabetta Addis, "Banca d'Italia e politica monetaria: la riallocazione del potere fra Stato, Mercato, e Banca centrale," *Stato e mercato* 19 (April 1987): 73–95; and Gerald Epstein and Juliet Schor, "The Divorce of the Banca d'Italia and the Italian Treasury: A Case Study of Central Bank Independence," in Pe-

ter Lange and Marino Regini, eds., *State, Market, and Social Regulation* (Cambridge: Cambridge University Press, 1989), 147–64.

23. Guido Tabellini, "Monetary and Fiscal Policy Coordination with a High Public Debt," in Francesco Giavazzi and Luigi Spaventa, eds., *High Public Debt: The Italian Experience* (Cambridge: Cambridge University Press, 1988), 90–134.

24. On these events, see Peter Lange, "The End of an Era: The Wage Indexation Referendum of 1985," in R. Leonardi and R. Nanetti, eds., *Italian Politics*, Vol. 1 (London: Pinter, 1986), 29–46.

25. On this so-called EUR line, see Peter Lange, George Ross, and Maurizio Vannicelli, *Unions, Change and Crisis: French and Italian Union Strategy and the Political Economy, 1945–1980* (London: Allen and Unwin, 1982), 165–80.

26. For two informed discussions of Italian accession, see Luigi Spaventa, "Italy Joins the EMS: A Political History," Occasional Paper No. 32, Johns Hopkins University Bologna Center, June 1980; and Giulio Andreotti, *Diari 1976–1979: Gli anni della solidarietà* (Milan: Rizzoli, 1981), especially 284–89.

27. Guido Baglioni, Ettore Santi, and Corrado Squarzon, *Le relazioni sindicali in Italia: Rapporto 1983-1984* (Rome: Edizioni Lavoro, 1985), 194–96. Figures exclude retirees.

28. Andreotti, 287–88.

29. Interview, Giorgio Napolitano, Rome, July 21, 1992.

Index

Aerospace industry, labor allocation in, in Toulouse, France, 161–63; in United States, 176–77

AFL-CIO: attitude toward microcorporatism, 23; attitude toward North American Free Trade Agreement, 12, 16–17, 153; and social dumping, 31; and voluntarism, 22

Austria: active union members as share of labor force in, 78, 79f; associational monopoly and concentration of unions in, 80t, 81, 95; centralization of union authority in, 86; impact of economic globalization on labor movements of, 32–33; level of government involvement in wage setting in, 88, 89f; unemployment rates in, European Monetary System and, 9

Automobile industry: Ford-Mazda joint venture, in Michigan, 147n; Japaneseowned factories in United States, 34, 133; and North American Free Trade Agreement, 17. *See also* General Motors; New United Motor Manufacturing Inc., United Automobile Workers

Banca d'Italia, "divorce" from Treasury, 211–12

Bargaining power approach to strike rates, 103, 104–6, 124n; and shifts in labor market and politics, 104–5

Belgium: industrial relations system in, 20; labor compensation costs in, international comparisons, 130–31, 132t; labor compensation costs and productivity in, international comparisons, 13t; union density in, 9, 10t

Benefits. *See* Employee benefits

Bologna, Italy. *See* Emilia-Romagna, Italy

Bretton Woods system, and economic globalization, 4, 5

California, Japanese-owned factories in. *See* Japanese direct investment in United States

Canada: direct investment in United States, and job creation, 132–33; and Free Trade Agreement, 6–7; growth of per capita income in, 184t; labor compensation costs in, international comparisons, 132t; labor

compensation costs and productivity, international comparisons, 13t; and North American Free Trade Agreement, 6–7; union opposition to Free Trade Agreement in, 13

Capital, internationalization of. *See* Economic integration; capital mobility

Capital deepening, as source of labor productivity growth: in Mexican manufacturing industries, 196, 197t; in South Korean manufacturing industries, 192–93t

Capital mobility: cross-border, and national monetary policy, 210–17; and economic globalization, 4; and growth of world trade, 3; labor cost incentives for, 35–53; and labor-based governments, 202–4; and North American Free Trade Agreement, 17. *See also* Social dumping

"Catholic capitalist" societies, France and Italy as, x, 169

Centralization of authority, 96. *See also* Labor unions, in study of status of corporatism; Macrocorporatism

Centre d'Etudes, de Recherches, et d'Education Socialistes. *See* CERES

Centre National d'Etudes Spatiales, 162

CERES, attitudes toward European Monetary System, 210–11

CFDT (France): and aerospace industry in Toulouse, France, 162; attitude toward European Monetary System, 208, 209t, 210, 211; strength in selected firms, 210t

CGB (Germany), 81

CGIL (Italy), attitude toward European Monetary System, 212, 213

CGT (France): and aerospace industry in Toulouse, France, 162; attitude toward devaluation and monetary integration, 153; attitude toward European Monetary System, 208, 209t, 210; opposition to European Community, 14; strength in selected firms, 210t

Chaebol (Korea), 22

Charter of Fundamental Social Rights of Workers. *See* Social Charter